D1537652

In the Kitchen

with

Cleveland's Favorite Chefs

35 Fabulous Meals in About an Hour

Maria Isabella

Foreword by Michael Ruhlman

Black Squirrel Books™

Kent, Ohio

Most of all for my wonderful husband, Joe
—without whose unrelenting encouragement and support this book
would never have even gotten started, let alone finished.

But also just as lovingly for my precious children
and biggest cheerleaders,
Nina, Damien, Julia, Monica, and Andrea

© 2012 by Maria Isabella

All rights reserved
Library of Congress Catalog Number 2012013524
ISBN 978-1-60635-125-3
Manufactured in the United States of America

BLACK SQUIRREL BOOKS™ 🐿™
Frisky, industrious black squirrels are a familiar sight on the Kent State
University campus and the inspiration for Black Squirrel Books™, a trade imprint
of The Kent State University Press
www.KentStateUniversityPress.com

Library of Congress Cataloging-in-Publication Data
Isabella, Maria.
    In the kitchen with Cleveland's favorite chefs : 35 fabulous meals in about an
hour / Maria Isabella ; foreword by Michael Ruhlman.
       p.   cm.
    Includes index.
    ISBN 978-1-60635-125-3 (hbk. : alk. paper) ∞
1. Cooking, American. 2. Cooking—Ohio—Cleveland. 3. Cooks—Ohio—
Cleveland. 4. Cooking, International. I. Title.
TX715.I73 2012
641.59771'32—dc23   2012013524

19 18 17   10 9 8 7

CONTENTS

FOREWORD

Never in this country's history has there been a better time to be a cook or an eater. In fact, we're currently experiencing a food explosion that's exposing us to a decidely broader variety of great food and lots of easily accessible knowledge of exactly what to do with it.

As for those young men and women who decide they want, or more often must, cook for a living (it's too hard a job unless it's simply part of your make-up), there has never been a better time to be a chef. There are simply more opportunities than ever before to cook for your community, whether you're a corporate chef of big business or a small-time chef/restaurateur.

This all-things-food zeitgeist happened in part when we recognized that food as we knew it was really making us sick and hurting our land and water. When you lose something you've always taken for granted (e.g., good, honest food just like the air we breathe), you start to think about it seriously. You start to care. Really care.

Among the many effects of this national movement—and they are multifold—is that chefs no longer need to head to major cities to cook great food for an intelligent, discriminating crowd. What they can do now is move back to their hometowns in smaller cities (such as St. Louis, Kansas City, Norfolk, and Durham), open restaurants, cook what they love best (rather than what they think their customers want), make money, and build businesses. Things have changed. Today, the customer expects deliciousness, not meat and potatoes. At least more and more do.

Cleveland is a fabulous example of this effect—in fact, one of the first—and Maria Isabella's book is proof of the culinary riches this city has in the way of chefs. Thanks to the prominence of Michael Symon on the national media front and chefs like Jonathon Sawyer, Dante Boccuzzi, Ben Bebenroth, and . . . well, frankly everyone in this book, Cleveland's restaurant scene is indeed thriving.

I love Sawyer's audacious culinary imagination, which introduces us to both the old (English peas) and the new (foie gras with clams) as well as the old-new American (devils on horseback with Manjari chocolate and Fresno chile). I love that Boccuzzi left Charlie Palmer's thriving celeb-chef empire to come back to Cleveland with his family and ply his trade here rather than elsewhere. (Better for us, better for his kids!) And I love that Maria has included corporate chefs as well—chefs such as Shawn Cline, Vid Lutz, and James Major—because great cooks don't always cook in great restaurants; they're just as often behind the scenes.

Take a good look at this book. It's packed with talent, like Cleveland itself.

MICHAEL RUHLMAN
Cleveland Heights, Ohio

ACKNOWLEDGMENTS

If it takes a village to raise a child, it almost certainly also takes a village to create a cookbook—at least this particular one. Because if it were not for all the many generous and obliging individuals involved, my idea for this project would have remained just that: simply an idea.

First and foremost, I want to thank my family. You kept me going even when things got crazy, especially during crunch time. Words cannot even begin to describe the appreciation I feel for your endless love, patience, and belief in me.

I want to also enthusiastically thank all the talented chefs who agreed to participate in this book and took time away from their own hectic schedules to allow me into their homes. I loved hearing your fascinating life stories and trying your delicious recipes. You're all my favorite! By the way, so are your hard-working assistants and staff because they really were most helpful.

I cannot overemphasize my appreciation to the unbelievably fantastic A team with whom I had the great honor and pleasure of working at Kent State University Press—director Will Underwood, managing editor Mary Young, acquisitions editor Joyce Harrison (who believed in my concept from the very beginning), design and production manager (and occasional photo shoot assistant) Christine Brooks, marketing manager Susan Cash, and copyeditor extraordinaire Margery Tippie. In addition to these incredible people, I want to extend my appreciation as well to the proposal readers who recognized the value of this book very early on: Charlene Kalo and Gary and Matty Lucarelli.

A special thank-you goes out to the incomparable Michael Ruhlman for writing such an eloquent foreword. Plus, I owe a great deal of gratitude to master sommelier Matthew Citriglia of WineMentor Ltd. for his expert assistance.

Last, but certainly not at all least, I want to thank all the amazing individuals across the U.S. and Canada who volunteered to test and retest each and every recipe in this book. They are: Fitz Anderson, Kelly Anderson, Matt Anderson, Tenoch Ang, Theresa August, Janel Barry, Gail Berzins, Krista Beyer, Lynn Biviano, Jean Bowers, Chris Brooks, Sharon Browarek, Terri Brown, Michelle Bueno, Vicki Bueno, Peggy Cartwright, Edwin Casta, Shawn Christensen, Eric Colby, Angela Costanzo, Julia Costello, T. J. Costello, Andrew Czarzasty, Katie Dever, Laura Fibbi, Maria Frank, Joe Giglio, Kathy Goodwin, Kathy Harris, Joyce Harrison, Luciana Herman, Jo Howell, Joni Howell, Michelle Hyland, Andrea Isabella, Carlinne Isabella, Damien Isabella, Joe Isabella, Monica Isabella, Nina Isabella, Chris Kiel, Diane Konschak, Margaret LaVigne, Marty LaVigne, Pat LaVigne, Marie Lear, Brenda Markin, Kay Mazurik, Donna Nimberger, Michele Normandin, Nancy Notarianni, Shannon Olear, Farrowe Pan, Amy Pascucci, Helen Pastis, Alexis Reid, Michelle Riley, Trish Rooney, Nicole Ross, Barry Smith, Jennifer Riffle Stockdale, Celeste Survoy, Dragi Tijanich, Maddalena Tijanich, Mike Tirpak, Will Underwood, Cindy Verhovitz, Jenn Vojta, Pam Vynalek, Jenny Ward, Amanda Wimsatt, Rhonda Wolfgang, and Mary Young.

I just can't say it enough: "Thank you, everyone!"

INTRODUCTION

It all began one beautiful fall afternoon in a quaint café in upstate New York. I was enjoying a cup of hot chocolate with my oldest daughter, Nina. We were having a wonderful mother-daughter time, talking about our dreams and goals and life ambitions. I confessed to her that I had always wanted to write a cookbook. She probed . . . I pondered . . . and before we both knew it, our lovely outing had turned into a brainstorming session where the seed for this book was planted. And it just kept growing from there.

Cleveland is a great city. A fantastic city! And it just keeps getting better all the time. I was born here . . . I was raised here . . . and there's no other place I'd rather be. The amount of talent here is absolutely amazing—and that includes our culinary superstars.

Without question, Cleveland has finally (and deservedly) been put on the map as a culinary destination. We have so many award-winning chefs making big names for themselves, both locally and nationally. I love eating their delicious dishes. It's a pure treat for me. But in all honesty, it's also just as much a treat for me to cook for my own family and entertain our own friends at home, albeit often with limited time for preparation. Which brings me to the very premise of this book.

"What," I would often wonder to myself, "would my favorite chefs prepare in their own kitchens if they were pressed for time?" This book answers exactly that—meaning now both you and I can take their quick-and-simple, yet absolutely fabulous meals and make them ourselves!

I tried to include a wide variety of chefs who represent the best Cleveland has to offer. They're both male and female. Older and younger. Experienced and up-and-coming. Award-winning and still-to-be-recognized. Classically trained and self-taught. From the East Side, West Side, South Side, and Downtown. Born in Cleveland, elsewhere in Ohio, outside of Ohio, and overseas. They represent restaurant chefs (from small-family to national-chain), chef/owners, corporate chefs, institutional chefs, research chefs, caterers, cooking school instructors, private chefs, ethnic chefs, casual-food chefs, upscale-food chefs, "green" chefs, and even Iron Chefs!

As I got to know them better in researching this book, they never ceased to amaze me. If I had to describe all of them in only three words, I'd say each and every one of them is extremely *hardworking, creative,* and *generous.* Without exception. Their backgrounds and experiences may be different, but their life stories all show extreme

fortitude and vision. The chefs talked openly of their struggles, hardships, and uncertainties over the years. But they also talked of their illuminating moments, successes, and exciting plans for the future. I could clearly hear the passion in their voices—for food, for cooking, and for making people happy.

As time went on, I found them to be exceptionally humble, smart, engaging, and even wickedly funny as well! They are truly some of the most interesting people I've ever met—and I sincerely admire them all greatly.

For this book, I posed the exact same challenge to each featured chef: *If you were suddenly to get a call at home from good friends who wanted to stop by, what would you prepare for them in one hour or less?*

The menus I got back were as varied as the chefs themselves. And that's the beauty of this book. The dishes reflect the personal style and taste of each individual, including a wide range of meat, fish, and vegetarian choices to tempt every palate. Obviously, some meals are more involved than others. Some require ingredients you may already have on hand. Others don't. Still others call for unusual ingredients that may be a bit hard to find. That's why the chefs have tried to include as many substitutions for ingredients as possible, while still keeping the dish true to its intended flavor. That's also why I have included a list of suggested resources for ingredients and equipment at the end of this book to help you locate what you're looking for.

In addition, I have compiled a list at the end of this book of all the individual recipes separated into one of six categories: starters, entrées, sides, desserts, savory fare, and sweet toppings. That way, you can pick and choose whatever dishes you wish to make in order to create your own custom menu. Be sure to look for them under "Mix-and-Match Menu Planner." There's also a very helpful section included on special techniques and processes that I feel will prove to be invaluable, no matter what skill level you're at right now.

There is one other very important point I must make regarding timing. Although every chef in this book can literally make his or her meal in only one hour or less from start to finish (believe me, I watched them do it with my very own eyes), it will probably take us "mere mortals" a bit longer. (Don't forget, they have Ginsu knife skills few of us can match.) That's why my subtitle is "35 Fabulous Meals in *About an Hour.*" Of course, the more often you make a meal, the less time it will take to prepare the next time. So I encourage you to give them all a try—many times over.

There are several other facts you should know, too. In this book:

- The French term *stage* (pronounced "stahzje"), which you will come across in many of the chefs' bios, means a brief time that a cook or chef will work for free in another chef's kitchen in order to learn more about new techniques and cuisines.
- Every meal is for four servings. Granted, some chefs' servings are larger than others. But hey, at least you'll always have enough.
- Make sure you read each recipe all the way through first before starting. Not once or twice, but at least three times. No exaggeration. To paraphrase Julia Child, "First you need to read it, then you need to understand it, and then you need to visualize it."
- Always practice *mise en place*. This French term (pronounced "MEEZ ahn plahs") means "put in place." In cooking terms, it means to have all your ingredients measured and prepped ahead of time. This habit is especially important for meals in a rush.
- Be sure to wash and pat dry all fruits and vegetables well before using.
- If for health reasons you need to decrease salt or eliminate it altogether, please adjust the quantities called for in each recipe accordingly.
- All the wine, beer, and cocktail pairings include at least three choices. The idea is for you to choose only one among the three, not all three—unless, that is, you insist.

As an added bonus, I am pleased to announce that I have created a blog on my website just for you at www.maria-isabella.com.

Note: Although the contents in this book are the most current as of its publication date, there are bound to be some changes by the time you're reading this. That's just the nature of both the chef's profession and the restaurant business. But that's also why I felt a blog would be the perfect vehicle to keep you updated on all the recent developments as they happen—plus offer many other benefits as well.

I invite you to visit this blog often in order to:

- stay up to date with the chefs and their accomplishments
- watch videos showcasing some of the trickier techniques and unusual ingredients listed in this book
- ask any questions you may have about the recipes
- send me feedback about the meals you've prepared from the book (photos are welcome!)
- write to me

I hope you'll enjoy getting to know Cleveland's favorite chefs as much as I did. And I hope you'll turn to the recipes in this book over and over again, both for fast-and-easy family dinners as well as for elegant, last-minute get-togethers—all in good taste.

To many fabulous meals!

Sergio Abramof

Shrimp Santos

Sergio's Picanha Steak

Watercress, Orange, &
Hearts of Palm Salad

Banana-Rum Sundae

Sergio Abramof

Former Chef/Owner, Sergio's in University Circle, Sergio's SARAVÁ

Accolades: Won *Cleveland Magazine*'s Best New Restaurant award; named Best New Restaurant by *Northern Ohio Live*; earned Interior of the Year award from the American Society of Interior Designers; named one of Cleveland's Top 100 Restaurants by the *Plain Dealer*; featured in *Chefs of Cleveland, The Dinah Shore Cookbook, The Joy of Grilling, The Best of the Midwest, Dining in Cleveland,* and *Cleveland Ethnic Eats*; featured in numerous publications and media, including *Gourmet, Food & Wine, Travel Holiday, Money, We, Nation's Restaurant News, ABC News/Money,* the *New York Times,* the *Plain Dealer, Cleveland Scene, Examiner,* WKYC-TV 3, and WCPN.

Although born in Belo Horizonte, Brazil, the late Sergio considered Cleveland home, snow and all. "I will never get used to winters in Cleveland," he admitted. "After all, the tropics are in my blood! But I still love this city."

When he was ten years old, Sergio—who spoke only Portuguese at the time—and his family moved from Brazil to the States so his mother could accept a professorship at Harvard University. Several years later, just as Sergio was about to enter high school, his mother was recruited by Case Western Reserve University and the family moved to Cleveland.

Sergio attended Cleveland Heights High School, where he was elected student council president. After gradu-

Sergio's secret tip for last-minute entertaining? "Keep the preparations simple, make only what you know you'd enjoy eating, and have plenty of drinks available at all times!"

ation, he attended Case Western for a couple of years, focusing on psychology and journalism. When money became tight, he decided to look for a job instead, and he was hired at the then recently opened Giovanni's Restaurant in Beachwood, thus beginning his career in the restaurant business.

During his first few years at Giovanni's, Sergio worked as an apprentice, gaining the invaluable experience that would serve him for the rest of his career. He earned his chef's certification through the American Culinary Foundation and worked his way up to executive chef, remaining at Giovanni's for fourteen years before deciding to try things his own way as an entrepreneur.

In 1995 Sergio opened his flagship restaurant, Sergio's in University Circle, in the heart of Cleveland's academic and cultural crossroads. Ten years later he opened his second restaurant, Sergio's SARAVÁ—a neighborhood gathering place and culinary tribute to the rhythm and flavors of his beloved Brazil.

Not one to sit still, even with two highly successful restaurants to run, Sergio channeled his energy and enthusiasm to establish—and run—Cleveland Independents, a group that supports and promotes local independent restaurants. Sergio's creativity was not limited to the kitchen, however, as he played the surdo in the popular Cleveland-based Brazilian drum band, Samba Joia.

Sadly, Sergio passed away in August 2012.

Shrimp Santos

4 servings

This shrimp dish held a special place in Sergio's heart. As a young boy, he would walk along the beach in Santos (just outside of São Paulo, Brazil) with his father. They would stop at a vendor's stall to get freshly cooked shrimp that had been brought in by the local fishermen that very afternoon. It was simply prepared . . . and incredibly delicious! Shrimp Santos—a variation of that same unforgettable shrimp Sergio ate as a youngster—makes an ideal starter for any special meal.

¼ cup vegetable oil
20 uncooked jumbo shrimp (21/25 count), preferably white Gulf shrimp, peeled but tails left on and deveined
1 cup all-purpose flour
1 tablespoon finely chopped garlic (3 medium-size cloves)
3 tablespoons coarsely chopped fresh Italian parsley
3 tablespoons unsalted butter
Kosher salt and freshly ground black pepper

1. Heat the oil in a large sauté pan over medium-high heat. Pat the shrimp dry with a paper towel and then dust with flour, shaking off any excess. Arrange the shrimp in the sauté pan. Do not overcrowd!

2. Cook the shrimp until golden brown on one side, 1 to 2 minutes. Turn the shrimp, add the garlic, and stir well. Continue to cook until the garlic begins to brown to a medium caramel color. (This step is crucial! Make sure the garlic browns enough. Don't undercook, but also don't let it burn.)

3. Remove from the heat. Add the parsley, butter, and salt and pepper to taste. Stir gently until all the butter is melted and the shrimp are coated with the sauce. Serve at once.

Sergio's Picanha Steak

4 servings

Picanha is a specialized Brazilian cut of beef that is an all-time favorite in the traditional steakhouses—also known as *churrascarias*—so famous in Brazil. Finding its origin with gauchos (or Brazilian cowboys), this particular cut is prized for its unique texture and flavor. Picanha, better known in the U.S. as tri-tip sirloin, is a top sirloin that can sometimes be difficult to find. It is also known as rump cover, rump cap, or triangle steak; your best bet is to ask your butcher to order it. If you simply cannot locate it, substitute either rib-eye steak or strip steak.

4 (8-ounce) picanha (tri-tip sirloin) steaks (can substitute rib-eye or strip steak)
Coarse sea salt

1. Allow the steaks to sit out at room temperature for 15 to 20 minutes before cooking.

2. Preheat the grill (preferably charcoal using natural lump coal) until very hot; coals will be glowing and coated with gray ash.

3. Put the steaks on the grill. Season with salt to taste. When marked on one side, about 2 minutes, flip the steaks and season this side with salt.

4. Remove the steaks from the heat while they are still rare (120° to 125° internal temperature) to medium rare (130° to 135°). Allow to rest in a warm place for 10 to 15 minutes before serving.

WINE PAIRINGS

Germany: Mosel or Rhein—Riesling Kabinett
Italy: Piedmont—Moscato d'Asti
South Africa: Any region—Cabernet Sauvignon or Cabernet blend

Watercress, Orange, & Hearts of Palm Salad

4 servings

This salad is both delicate and refreshing, a result of the interplay of three key elements: peppery watercress, sweet orange, and creamy hearts of palm. It makes a perfect side dish to pair with Sergio's Picanha Steak or to serve as a main first course for a light luncheon. Although available year-round, watercress is most flavorful during its peak season, from May through July. Look for crisp, dark green leaves with no signs of yellowing or wilting.

6 seedless oranges (such as navel)
1 (14-ounce) can hearts of palm, drained and cut into ½-inch bias slices
¼ red onion, sliced very thin
½ cup virgin olive oil
1 teaspoon kosher salt
Freshly ground black pepper
6 bunches watercress (leaves plus 2 to 3 inches stems)

1. Using a sharp knife, cut a small slice off both the top and bottom of each unpeeled orange to expose its juicy interior. It should be able to rest upright on your counter without rolling. Pick up each orange and, beginning at the top, slice away the skin and pith (the white part of the rind) in strips following the natural curve of the orange. Discard the peels. Holding each orange in your hand again, gently slide your knife between the membrane walls toward the center of the fruit to loosen each segment, dropping them as they are loosened into a large salad bowl.

2. Squeeze the remaining orange pulp and membranes over the salad bowl to extract all the residual juice. Add the hearts of palm, onion, oil, salt, and pepper to taste. Mix gently but well and let sit for 10 minutes, allowing the flavors to come together.

3. Add the watercress, toss gently, and serve at once.

Banana-Rum Sundae

4 servings

This dessert is reminiscent of the classic Bananas Foster, only better! Many guests are shocked by just how delicious a simple banana dessert can be when prepared properly.

Generous ⅓ cup packed light brown sugar
3 ounces dark rum
4 ripe bananas, peeled and sliced
4 large scoops high-quality vanilla bean ice cream or vanilla gelato
Sweetened Whipped Cream (recipe follows)
½ cup toasted slivered almonds (see note)

1. Mix the brown sugar and rum together in a large stainless-steel bowl until a light syrup forms and all the brown sugar is dissolved. If all the sugar does not dissolve, add a few teaspoons of warm water.

2. Toss the bananas with the sugar syrup. Allow to rest for 5 to 10 minutes.

3. Put one scoop of ice cream into each dessert bowl and top with the marinated bananas. Garnish with the whipped cream, sprinkle with the toasted almonds, and serve at once.

NOTE: To toast slivered almonds, place in an ungreased heavy skillet over medium heat. Stir or shake often until golden brown, about 1 to 3 minutes.

Sweetened Whipped Cream

1. Whip 1 cup chilled heavy cream, 2 tablespoons sugar, and 1 teaspoon pure vanilla extract in a chilled bowl until firm peaks form.

Michael Annandono

Bagna Càuda

Pan-Seared Black Sea Bass
with Artichoke Puree

Porcini Risotto with
White Truffles

Michael Annandono

Executive Chef/Owner, Michaelangelo's

Accolades: Top Zagat and Gayot ratings; 5-star rating from *Citysearch Guide to Cleveland;* numerous Best awards from *Cleveland Magazine, Cleveland Scene,* and *Northern Ohio Live;* People's Choice and Best Food awards from the Taste of Little Italy competition; featured in numerous publications and media, including *Continental Magazine, Ohio Magazine, Cleveland Magazine, Cleveland Scene,* the *Plain Dealer, Urbanspoon, Metromix,* WKYC-TV 3, and WJW-TV 8.

Born in Euclid, Ohio, but raised in Willowick, Michael was working his first job as a line cook at the Pine Ridge Country Club when he learned how to make a rose out of a tomato. That was the turning point. "It was all history after that!" he says, half serious.

After graduating from Lake Catholic High School, Michael balanced coursework at a local college with kitchen work at several area restaurants. He quickly climbed his way up to sous chef at the elegant Gavi's Italian Restaurant and then pastry chef apprentice at the popular Piccolo Mondo. He even became certified as an Italian wine expert. But something was still missing, and he was determined to find it, even if that meant traveling across the ocean to his ancestral land, Italy.

Michael moved to Acqui Terme in northern Italy at the invitation of

Michael's secret tip for last-minute entertaining? "Be prepared. Have a chest freezer stocked with different meats, fish, and pastas. Keep a pantry stocked with dry goods, pasta, and different rices. And have a diverse vegetable or herb garden. No need to run to the store and pay five dollars for five basil leaves."

Maurizio Parisio, chef/owner of Ristorante Parisio 1933. Under the tutelage of this renowned chef, Michael attended the Italian Culinary Institute, housed in an actual castle in Piedmont, while also working at his mentor's restaurant. During his time abroad, Michael apprenticed with many different European chefs at many different—and interesting—locations. Butcher shops that only handled duck, fowl, and rabbit. Puff pastry shops that only specialized in the labor-intensive *sfogliatella.* A chocolate shop in Nice, France. Professional culinary seminars in Switzerland. And so on and so on. But after three years America eventually beckoned, so he returned to his native Cleveland once again.

The next few years were a whirlwind of activity for Michael. He conceptualized, designed, and worked as executive chef at Circo, Lure Bistro, Osteria, and Gusto. He eventually found a partner investor and, finally, was able to open his very own place: Michaelangelo's in Little Italy.

Regular guest appearances on both TV and radio shows, as well as multiple fund-raising activities now round out his hectic days. As do his two favorite pastimes: skiing and fly-fishing.

Michael and his wife, Stacey, have two young children, Antonio and Giuliana. They reside in Willoughby Hills.

Bagna Càuda
(Warm Dip with Vegetables)

4 servings

A traditional Piedmont New Year's Eve hors d'oeuvres, *bagna càuda* (Italian for "hot bath") is a type of Italian fondue dip made from walnut oil and anchovy. It is served warm, typically in a terra-cotta pot over an open flame, with a variety of fresh vegetables. The beauty of this recipe is that you can experiment with many different combinations of vegetables, depending on what's in season. This recipe includes Michael's favorites, but feel free to improvise.

3 medium-size celery ribs, trimmed and cut into diagonal pieces
1 cup cauliflower florets
Half each red, green, and yellow bell pepper, cored, seeded, and sliced
    lengthwise
1 small fennel bulb, trimmed and sliced lengthwise
1 small head endive, separated into leaves
2 tablespoons unsalted butter
3 tablespoons minced garlic (9 medium-size cloves)
1 cup walnut or olive oil
2 tablespoons anchovy paste
1 teaspoon sea salt
1 teaspoon freshly ground black pepper

1. Arrange the celery, cauliflower, peppers, fennel, and endive on a serving platter. Set aside.

2. Melt the butter in a sauté pan over medium heat. Add the garlic and cook only to soften (not brown) for about 3 minutes.

3. Turn the heat down to low. Add the walnut oil and anchovy paste and cook, stirring occasionally, just until the anchovy paste dissipates or appears dissolved and the mixture is smooth, about 3 minutes. (Warning: Too much heat will cause separation.) Take off the heat and season with the salt and pepper.

4. If a terra-cotta fondue pot is not available, pour the warm mixture into another heatproof container. Serve alongside the vegetables on the platter.

....

WINE PAIRINGS
....

Italy: Piedmont—Barolo or Barbaresco
Italy: Piedmont—Nebbiolo della Langhe
Italy: Veneto—Prosecco di Conegliano or Prosecco di Valdobbiadene

Pan-Seared Black Sea Bass with Artichoke Puree

4 servings

Paired with black sea bass, which is a delicious saltwater fish, this recipe's puree of artichoke hearts, basil, and garlic adds a whole new level of sophistication to an otherwise simple dish. The garnish topping of fried leeks elevates this dish even that much higher, guaranteeing that it will truly impress both your friends and family.

1 cup frozen, canned, or jarred artichoke hearts, thawed if frozen, drained and rinsed if canned or jarred
6 fresh basil leaves
Roasted Garlic (recipe at left), optional
10 to 12 tablespoons extra-virgin olive oil, divided
4 (6-ounce) black sea bass fillets, ½ inch thick, rinsed and patted dry
½ cup all-purpose flour
1 small leek, white part only, well rinsed, trimmed, and cut lengthwise into thin julienne strips
2 tablespoons basil-infused olive oil or other flavored olive oil
24 fresh chive stems for garnish, optional

Roasted Garlic

1. Immerse 5 peeled garlic cloves in 3 to 5 tablespoons olive oil in a small terra-cotta or other heatproof dish.

2. Bake at 350° for 30 minutes.

3. Drain the garlic, saving the oil, and use as directed

NOTE: The saved oil would be ideal on bruschetta.

1. Puree the artichoke hearts, basil leaves, and, if using, the Roasted Garlic in a food processor. Slowly add 3 tablespoons of the oil. If the puree is too thick, slowly add 1 to 2 tablespoons more oil, a little at a time, until the desired consistency is achieved. Set aside.

2. Lightly dredge the fish in the flour, shaking off any excess.

3. Heat 4 tablespoons of the oil in a large sauté pan over medium-high heat. Sauté the fish until golden brown on one side, about 3 minutes. Flip and continue to cook for about another 2 minutes, or until golden brown. Set aside.

4. Heat the remaining oil (3 to 4 tablespoons) in the same pan on medium-high heat, almost to the smoking point. Add the leek strips and fry only until crispy, about 30 seconds. Remove with a slotted spoon and set aside.

5. Immediately drizzle some infused oil on each plate, and top, if desired, with 6 chive stems. Carefully place one fish fillet on top of the oil. Top with a spoonful of artichoke puree and fried leeks to garnish.

Porcini Risotto with White Truffles

4 servings

Plain risotto is good. Mushroom risotto is even better. But mushroom risotto with white truffles? Decadence. Pure decadence. After all, the white truffle, a gastronomical jewel, is world famous for its unique aroma. Imagine an earthy, garlicky scent hinting of tree roots, fall rain, and aged cheese. There's nothing else that can quite compare. And it's only available a couple months out of the year (from September to December), almost exclusively from Alba in Italy's Piedmont region. If you're lucky enough to find one (hence, its optional status in this recipe), be sure to choose one that's firm, well shaped, and free of blemishes. White truffle oil, however, is virtually obligatory for this dish. As a last resort, you can cheat, I suppose, and use extra-virgin olive oil—but you'll probably be sorry.

3½ to 4 cups chicken stock or broth, divided
¼ cup extra-virgin olive oil
2 tablespoons minced garlic (6 medium-size cloves)
¼ cup minced white onion (can substitute yellow onion)
1½ cups Arborio rice
1 cup sliced fresh porcini mushrooms
¾ cup heavy cream
¾ cup freshly grated Parmigiano-Reggiano cheese
1½ tablespoons chopped fresh rosemary
1 tablespoon white truffle oil (can substitute extra-virgin olive oil)
1 medium white truffle (golf ball size), shaved paper thin, optional
Chopped fresh chives for garnish, optional

1. Bring the stock to a simmer in a heavy saucepan. Once simmering, remove from the heat and set aside.

2. Heat the oil in a large, deep skillet over medium heat. Add the garlic and onion. Sauté until translucent. Increase the heat to medium high, add the rice, and cook, stirring constantly, for about 2 to 3 minutes.

3. Reduce the heat to medium and add small amounts of hot stock to the rice at a time, stirring constantly, until all the stock has been added and absorbed and the rice is al dente, about 20 to 25 minutes.

4. Stir in the mushrooms, cream, cheese, rosemary, and truffle oil. If using the optional white truffle, at this point add half of the truffle slices to the rice. Cook for 2 minutes, then remove from the heat.

5. Serve warm, garnished with the remaining truffle slices and chives, if using.

Dave Apthorpe

Vietnamese-Inspired
Poached Shrimp with
Duo Dipping Sauces

Pan-Seared Arctic Char

Rosemary Potato Wedges

Sautéed Kale with Bacon
& Quick Onion Pickle

Toasted Pound Cake
with Seasonal Berries
& Whipped Cream

Dave Apthorpe

General Manager/Executive Chef, Leutner Café at Case Western Reserve University (Bon Appétit Management Company)

Accolades: Received two consecutive Best Chef awards from the Restaurant Reader's Poll of the *Austin Chronicle;* earned a Top 10 Restaurant rating from *Gayot Guide;* Eastern Region winner of the Bon Appétit Management Company's Lisa Haag Leadership Award; featured in numerous publications, including *Food Service Director,* the *Boston Globe,* the *Statesman,* the *San Francisco Chronicle,* the *Austin Chronicle, Austin360, Chowhound, NewsOK, EarthTimes, Bio-Medicine, Buon Forno, Grown Safe, Food Management, Plate & Vine,* the *Sarah Jane English Newsletter, Crain's Cleveland Business,* the *Daily,* and the *Plain Dealer.*

When Dave was young, he would gravitate to TV cooking shows featuring Julia Child and *The Frugal Gourmet.* "Those were pre-cable days," explains Dave, "and much more interesting than watching soaps." But it was enough to kick-start his budding interest in food and cooking.

Growing up in Sheboygan, Wisconsin, Dave and his family would go out to eat every weekend. Those meals were always fascinating to him. But when Dave started to express an interest in the culinary arts, his parents weren't exactly thrilled. "Cooking wasn't a career path that was particularly popular with parents back then as it is today," explains Dave. "The general expectation of most parents in those days was to have their children go to a traditional four-year college."

So, after graduating from Sheboygan South High School, Dave headed to the University of Wisconsin, where he majored in political science. He got a job on the weekends at various eateries around town. "I really enjoyed the energy that came from working in a kitchen," he says.

Three years later, he finally made up his mind to pursue his true passion: cooking. "At that point, my parents were very supportive of my decision," admits Dave. "They knew of my love of restaurants growing up. During that same time, Charlie Trotter was just starting to change the way food and restaurants were viewed. He had managed to graduate from UW with a Poli Sci degree. I figured if he

Dave's secret tip for last-minute entertaining? "Involve your guests in the preparation of the meal—from helping with prep to setting the table. It creates a common goal to inspire conversation, gets things done faster, and demystifies the process while creating a more casual and fun experience."

could do it, so could I. I just skipped the graduating part." So Dave left Wisconsin and headed to Hyde Park, New York, to attend the Culinary Institute of America. He did externships at the historic Harbor House and the landmark White Elephant, both on Nantucket Island.

After Dave graduated—with honors!—he headed to Boston. There he worked at the 5-diamond L'Espalier on Boylston Street and at the award-winning Harvest on Harvard Square. One year later, ready for a new adventure, Dave moved to Texas, joining Austin's innovative restaurant Mirabelle.

Six years later, he moved once more, this time to his new wife's hometown in northeast Ohio. He immediately accepted a position with Bon Appétit Management Company, the exclusive provider of food and dining services to Case Western Reserve University, based on its "commitment to local, sustainable, and from-scratch cooking," says Dave.

Dave started at Case's smaller Fribley Commons dining hall. He was also invited to work alongside some of Wolfgang Puck's architects, who were helping to remodel Case's larger Leutner Commons dining hall. When it finally opened, Dave was asked to become its executive chef and then its general manager.

The difference between a restaurant chef and a university chef? "We're open seven days a week, we change the menu every week, and we serve from 2,000 to 2,800 meals a day to customers who are eighteen to twenty-one years old," explains Dave. "But the biggest difference," he goes on to add, "is cooking different food for the same people rather than the same food for different people."

In his spare time, Dave chops wood to heat his home in the winter and takes care of a half-acre garden in the summer.

Dave and his wife, Katie (also a chef), live on thirty-five sprawling acres in Chagrin Falls, which they share with their German shorthaired pointer, Biz, and cats Angus and Malcolm.

Vietnamese-Inspired Poached Shrimp with Duo Dipping Sauces

4 servings

This is a popular Apthorpe family favorite. "An easy crowd pleaser," says Dave. And with this recipe, your guests can have their choice of two fabulous but drastically different homemade dipping sauces: the sweet and garlicky Nuoc Cham (also good with spring rolls) or the zesty and tangy Traditional Cocktail Sauce. Both choices are clear winners.

1 (4-inch) piece lemongrass
1 lime
1 pound uncooked domestic U.S. shrimp, farmed or wild caught, with shells (EZ Peel shrimp work great for this)
6 garlic cloves, peeled and crushed
2 tablespoons Sriracha or other hot sauce
¼ cup fish sauce (also called nuoc mam)
Nuoc Cham Dipping Sauce (recipe at right)
Traditional Cocktail Sauce (recipe at right)

1. Cut off the lower tip of the lemongrass and peel off the tough outer layers of the stalk. The main stalk (the pale yellow section) is the only part used. Smash with the back of a knife and roughly chop.

2. Squeeze the juice from the lime into a large saucepan. Toss in the squeezed halves, the lemongrass, shrimp, garlic, Sriracha sauce, and fish sauce. Stir to combine.

3. Add just enough cold water to cover everything by 3 inches. Cook over high heat just until the liquid comes to a boil, about 8 minutes. Test doneness by cutting into a shrimp. It should have lost its translucence but should not be rubbery.

4. Remove from the heat and pour out half the water. Add two big handfuls of ice. This will stop the cooking process while allowing the shrimp to absorb the flavor of the poaching liquid.

5. Once the shrimp are cool, peel (leaving the tail intact) and serve with the dipping sauces.

Nuoc Cham Dipping Sauce

1 garlic clove, peeled and minced
Freshly squeezed juice of ½ lime
1½ tablespoons fish sauce (nuoc mam)
1½ tablespoons rice wine vinegar (same as rice vinegar)
1½ teaspoons granulated sugar
⅛ teaspoon chili flakes (or to desired heat)

1. Combine all the ingredients in a small bowl and whisk to mix well and dissolve the sugar.

Traditional Cocktail Sauce

¼ cup ketchup
1 tablespoon prepared horseradish
1½ teaspoons pickle juice or rice wine vinegar (same as rice vinegar)
½ teaspoon Worcestershire sauce
½ teaspoon Sriracha or other hot sauce

1. Combine all the ingredients in a small bowl and stir to mix well.

WINE PAIRINGS

New Zealand: Marlborough—Sauvignon Blanc
USA: California, Santa Lucia Highlands—Pinot Noir
USA: New York—sparkling brut wine

Pan-Seared Arctic Char

4 servings

This is a very simple, elegant, and flavorful entrée that goes well with a variety of side dishes. It's also good to know that wild Arctic char is one of the most nutritious fish products available on the market today!

4 (6-ounce) portions Arctic char fillet, skin on, scaled and boned (can substitute farm-raised ruby trout, wild salmon, walleye, or lake perch)
Salt and freshly ground black pepper
1 teaspoon canola or vegetable oil

1. Check to make sure all scales are removed from the fish. Rinse the fish pieces and pat dry with paper towels. Season both sides with salt and pepper to taste.

2. Preheat either a large, well-seasoned cast-iron skillet or a nonstick sauté pan over medium heat. Add the oil and swirl to coat. Add the fish pieces, skin side down, and cook until the skin is crispy, about 4 minutes.

3. Flip the fish and cook for 2 to 3 more minutes. Transfer to a baking sheet and keep warm until ready to serve.

Rosemary Potato Wedges

4 servings

Crispy on the outside . . . softer on the inside . . . sprinkled with rosemary for color and flavor—these potato wedges are the ultimate easy side dish. Perfect with any meal.

1½ pounds Yukon gold potatoes, unpeeled
Kosher salt
2 tablespoons canola oil
1 tablespoon chopped fresh rosemary
Freshly ground black pepper

1. Cut each potato into 8 wedges. Place in a medium sauce pot and cover with water. Add salt (about 1 teaspoon per cup of water) and bring just to a boil over high heat.

2. Immediately reduce the heat to medium and simmer for 1 minute. Remove from the heat, drain, and set the potatoes aside for 5 minutes.

3. Heat the oil in a cast-iron skillet over medium-high heat. Arrange the potatoes, cut side down, in the pan. Cook until the potatoes release with the gentle pressure of a spatula, about 4 minutes. This means they are ready to turn. If potatoes do not turn easily, let them cook a little more.

4. Turn the potatoes over. Cook until they release again (as in previous step). Toss gently with the rosemary and salt and pepper to taste.

Sautéed Kale with Bacon & Quick Onion Pickle

4 servings

If you're looking to incorporate more dark leafy vegetables into your diet, kale is the perfect choice. Naturally high in vitamins A and C, kale also enjoys powerful antioxidant properties. In this colorful side dish, the kale shares center stage with tasty bacon pieces and tangy onion pickle.

Salt
1 medium-size red onion, cut into ½-inch wedges
2 tablespoons balsamic or sherry vinegar
2 teaspoons granulated sugar
Freshly cracked black pepper
1 large bunch kale, washed, stemmed, and chopped into
    large pieces
2 bacon strips, uncooked, cut into ½-inch pieces
2 tablespoons unsalted butter

1. Fill a large pot mostly full of water. Salt aggressively with about 2 teaspoons per cup. (This will help season the onion and kale while taming their bitterness and keeping the colors vibrant.) Bring to a rolling boil over high heat.

2. Add the onion. Cook until just tender, about 2 minutes.

3. Without draining the liquid, remove the onion with a small strainer and transfer to a bowl. Add the vinegar, sugar, and a few turns of freshly cracked black pepper to the onion. Stir to combine and set aside.

4. Bring the pot of cooking water back to a boil over high heat. Add the chopped kale. Continue to cook over high heat until just tender, about 3 minutes.

5. Drain the kale in a colander. Press out as much water as possible with the back of a large spoon or a bowl that is slightly smaller than the colander. Set aside.

6. Add the bacon to the same pot (without any cooking water) and set over medium to medium-high heat. Stir occasionally, and when the bacon starts to crisp, add the butter, cooked kale, and marinated onions (including the vinegar). Continue to cook over medium to medium-high heat, stirring often.

7. When the kale is heated through, season with black pepper to taste.

Toasted Pound Cake with Seasonal Berries & Whipped Cream

4 servings

When you're hard pressed for time, this light and flavorful dessert is the perfect solution. Toasting the pound cake adds a very nice texture. And you'll detect just a hint of vanilla in the berries. Use whatever berries are at the height of their season, be they raspberries, blackberries, strawberries, blueberries, boysenberries, marionberries, or tayberries. Use all of one kind, or mix and match for the ultimate in flexibility.

2 cups assorted fresh berries, best available, as local as
    possible
Kosher salt
1 tablespoon granulated sugar, plus additional to taste
½ teaspoon pure vanilla extract (can substitute almond
    extract), divided
1 cup heavy cream
Store-bought pound cake, cut into four (1-inch-thick)
    slices
Fresh mint leaves for garnish, optional

1. Preheat the broiler. Place a mixing bowl in the refrigerator to chill.

2. If using strawberries, cut into bite-size pieces if necessary. Place the berries in a second bowl. Add a pinch of salt and sugar to taste. Gently stir in ¼ teaspoon of the vanilla. Set aside to macerate until ready to serve.

3. In the chilled bowl, combine the cream, 2 tablespoons sugar, and the remaining ¼ teaspoon vanilla. Whip until the cream holds soft peaks.

4. Place the pound cake slices on a baking sheet. Toast under the broiler until golden brown, about 3 minutes. Carefully flip and continue to toast until this side is also golden brown, about 2 minutes.

5. When ready to serve, place one slice of pound cake on each dessert plate. Spoon the macerated berries over the slices. Top with the whipped cream and garnish with a mint leaf, if desired.

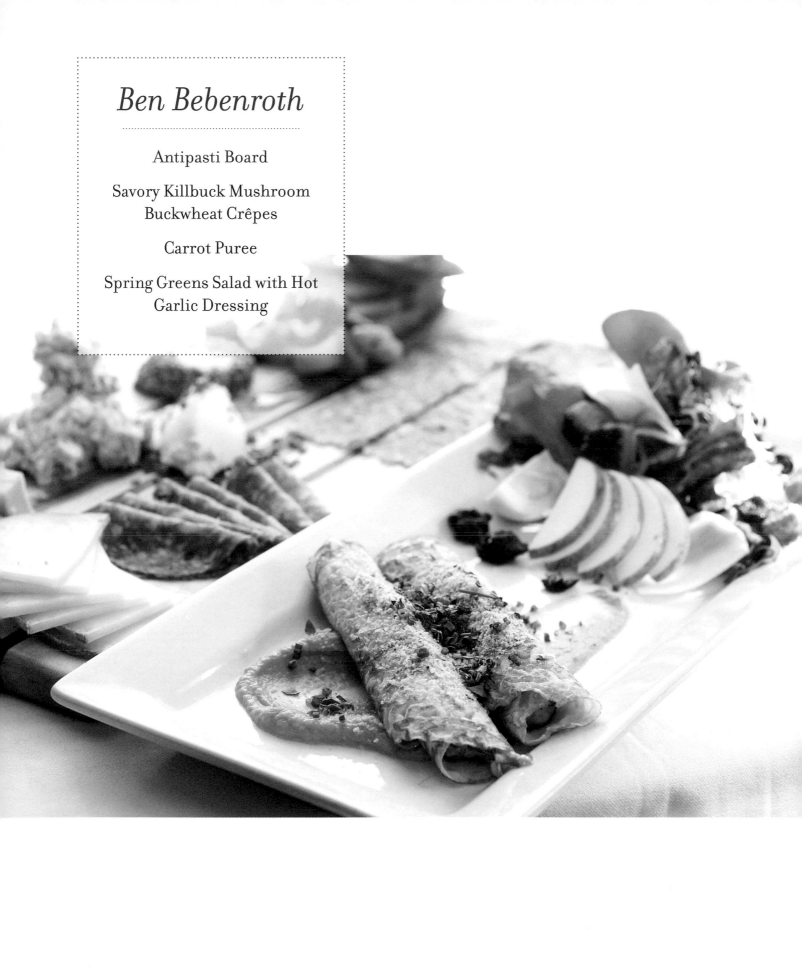

Ben Bebenroth

Antipasti Board

Savory Killbuck Mushroom
Buckwheat Crêpes

Carrot Puree

Spring Greens Salad with Hot
Garlic Dressing

Ben Bebenroth

Chef/Owner, Spice of Life Catering Co., Spice Kitchen+Bar

Accolades: Winner of Johnson & Wales University's national Taste Down Under competition; won the Ten Under 10 award from the Council of Smaller Enterprises; recipient of *Crain's Cleveland Business*'s Forty Under 40 award; numerous national and regional awards for outstanding menu and design, including top award at the Flavors of Northeast Ohio competition; featured in numerous publications and media, including *Continental Magazine, National Culinary Review, Cleveland Magazine, Balanced Living,* and WVIZ-TV.

While Lance Corporal Bebenroth was repairing damaged rotors and engines on helicopters as a Marine Corps flight line mechanic, he probably never envisioned himself one day delicately placing fragile garnishes atop a salad of freshly picked microgreens and shaved fennel. Fast forward ten years, and he's doing exactly that—and loving every minute!

Truth be told, Ben never had any early desires to be a chef as a kid. He grew up in Strongsville, Ohio, and attended Fork Union Military Academy in Charlottesville, Virginia. After graduation, he returned home and for the next few years worked at various restaurants, including Rockne's in Kent. That's where he got a chance to go on the line when one of the pantry cooks didn't show up. "There I was," says Ben, "working with this surly tattooed bunch, swapping jokes and moving fast, when suddenly it hit me. This was the way out of my rut! I saw there was actually a hierarchy with these people who seemed to take a bit of sinister pleasure in the fact that they could do this ungodly hot, greasy, panic-riddled task called cooking and make it look fun. Besides, I've always loved a good challenge!"

But he decided to enlist in the Marines first and got stationed at Camp Pendleton, California, for two years. When he returned home, he immediately enrolled in Cuyahoga Community College's culinary arts program. Ben also had an idea for a small catering business of his own, called Spice of Life, which he started out of his grandparents' basement.

He found work at the Baricelli Inn, Fulton Bar & Grill,

Ben's secret tip for last-minute entertaining? "K.I.S.S. (Keep it simple, stupid!) The best things to eat are worth nothing if you can't sit down for a beer with your guests when they get there."

and Sans Souci, and it was while at Sans Souci that Ben was encouraged to take the placement exam for Johnson & Wales University's accelerated culinary program. He passed, and one intense year later he graduated in the top 10 percent of his class.

But before heading back to Cleveland, Ben first stopped in Australia—a trip that was his prize for winning a national culinary competition. Once home, he resumed building up his catering business. He also taught culinary arts classes at Summit Academy, as well as a "Natural History of Food" series at the Cleveland Museum of Natural History. In addition, he hosted a dinner for Ambassador Peter Baxter at the Australian Embassy in Washington, D.C.—twice!—and emceed the Australian Food and Wine Show in New York City.

Ben eventually accepted a position to open the Foundation Room of the House of Blues entertainment venue. Afterward he joined Parker's New American Bistro, where he learned more about a growing passion of his: sourcing from local farmers.

Then Ben finally made the decision to put all his efforts solely into his catering business. As a result, he is now a premier preferred caterer for many notable venues, including the Cleveland Museum of Art, Cleveland Museum of Natural History, and Holden Arboretum. He has also opened a restaurant called, appropriately enough, Spice Kitchen+Bar.

A unique project Ben runs on the side is a mobile restaurant concept he developed called Plated Landscapes, which offers fine dining in the great outdoors. Another side project is the Cleveland Renegade Lunch Project, which offers the public a complimentary lunch at different surprise locations throughout the city every month.

When not cooking or foraging, Ben likes to indulge in all types of outdoor sports, particularly snowboarding and rock climbing.

Ben and his wife, Jackie, live in Broadview Heights with their two young children, daughter Sydney and son Burke. Their brood also includes a cat, Sally, and two dogs, Riley and Roxy.

Antipasti Board

4 servings

There are antipasti boards . . . and then there's Ben's antipasti board! A rich tapestry of myriad colors, flavors, textures, and choices. Yet it's surprisingly quick and easy to put together. As for the pickled peppers, you can find them at your local farmers' market or any Italian grocer. Ben's own homemade version is a mixture of sweet Cubanelle, Italian bull's horn, and both sweet and hot banana peppers in a cider vinegar–based brine. There's nothing else quite like it.

4 ounces firm creamy white cheese (such as Istara Ossau-Iraty)

4 ounces blue cheese (such as Rogue Smokey Blue Cheese)

4 ounces Mackenzie Creamery chèvre or other goat cheese

4 ounces Gouda (aged 3 years)

2 tablespoons Weber's spicy sweet mustard or other whole-grain mustard

2 to 3 teaspoons black truffle honey (can substitute regular honey)

4 ounces sopressata, thinly sliced

4 ounces Genoa salami, thinly sliced

Jarred pickled peppers

12 pieces crispy breads (such as toasted baguette slices cut on the diagonal, crostini, crackers, and/or matzo)

Sea salt

Chopped fresh chives for garnish

1. Allow the four cheeses to come to room temperature. You can choose to either slice, cube, or leave them whole. You can also form the chèvre into an oval quenelle (see note).

2. Mound the mustard in the center of your serving board or platter. Make a well in the center of the mustard and pour the truffle honey into it.

3. Surround the mustard with groups of the cheeses, cured meats (shingled or folded and fanned), pickled peppers, and bread. Sprinkle the chèvre with sea salt and garnish with chopped chives.

NOTE: To make a quenelle, warm two tablespoons in hot water, leaving them wet to provide some "slip" when transferring the chèvre. Take one tablespoon and scoop out a spoonful of chèvre. Take your second spoon and scoop the chèvre out from the first one in a smooth motion, following the contour of the bottom spoon as much as possible. Continue to alternate from spoon to spoon until you have a smooth result. (Tip: It may help to dip each spoon in hot water again between scoops.)

WINE PAIRINGS

Australia: South Australia—Cabernet-Shiraz blend
USA: California, Sonoma—Chardonnay
USA: Oregon, Willamette Valley—Pinot Noir

Savory Killbuck Mushroom Buckwheat Crêpes

4 servings (2 crêpes per person)

There's nothing that says "elegant brunch or luncheon" like these savory crêpes. Served on an optional bed of silky Carrot Puree (recipe follows), the combination of colors and flavors will transport you to another world. But there's one thing you must keep in mind: the quality of this dish is directly proportional to the quality of the mushrooms you use. Buy local, and you won't be sorry. Tip: After filling, the crêpes can be stored, covered, on the baking sheet in the refrigerator for up to 2 days.

FILLING

1 pound fresh Killbuck Valley oyster shiitake mushrooms (can substitute other shiitake mushrooms or portobellos)
2 tablespoons unsalted butter
2 shallots, minced (can substitute onion)
¼ cup Madeira wine (can substitute Marsala)
½ cup heavy cream
4 to 6 ounces goat cheese
2 ounces arugula
Sea salt and freshly ground black pepper

CRÊPES

1 large egg
½ cup whole milk
3 tablespoons water
½ cup buckwheat flour (can substitute all-purpose flour)
½ teaspoon salt
2 tablespoons unsalted butter, melted, optional

GARNISH

½ cup toasted bread crumbs
2 tablespoons chopped mixed fresh herbs (such as chives, sage, and thyme)

Carrot Puree (recipe on page 19), optional

FILLING:

1. Wipe the mushrooms clean with a dampened paper towel, then remove and discard the stems. Chop the mushroom caps into small, rough-cut pieces.

2. Place the butter in a large sauté pan over medium-high heat and bring to a sizzle. Add the mushrooms. Sauté until browned, about 5 minutes.

3. Add the minced shallots and continue to sauté another 2 minutes, still on medium-high heat. Add the Madeira wine and deglaze the pan by scraping with a wooden spoon or spatula. Reduce until almost dry and there is no more liquid bubbling, about 1 minute.

4. Add the cream and reduce by half, about 2 minutes. Remove from the heat. Add the goat cheese and stir. Briefly fold in the arugula, continuing to stir until it just begins to wilt, about 1 minute. Season with salt and pepper to taste and set aside.

CRÊPES:

1. Place all the ingredients except the butter in a food processor. Pulse until blended.

2. Heat a small nonstick sauté or crêpe pan over medium-high heat. Either spray with Pam or brush with some of the melted butter. Place a small ladleful (about 2 tablespoons) of batter in the center of the pan and quickly roll around to coat.

3. Cook until the edges begin to curl. Bang the pan on a sturdy countertop or an overturned cast-iron skillet to loosen. Slide the crêpe, without flipping or cooking on the other side, onto a plate lined with parchment or waxed paper.

4. Grease the pan again (if needed) and continue to make the rest of the crêpes, placing parchment or waxed paper between each as they are layered on the plate. You should have 8 crêpes.

ASSEMBLY:

1. Preheat the oven to 250°.

2. Place a spoonful of filling across the bottom third of each crêpe. Bring the bottom of the crêpe up to nearly meet the top edge. Pull back down slightly, hugging the filling, and continue to roll securely yet gently. Arrange on a parchment paper–lined baking sheet and place in oven to heat through until ready to serve (no longer than 5 minutes).

3. To serve, mound the Carrot Puree, if using, on each of 4 serving plates. Top each mound of puree with 2 warmed crêpes and sprinkle with bread crumbs and mixed herbs.

NOTE: To make toasted bread crumbs, toast a few slices of bread. Crush or pulse in a food processor.

Carrot Puree

1 pound carrots, peeled and roughly chopped
1½ teaspoons sea salt
Freshly ground black pepper

1. Place the carrots in a deep saucepan. Add enough water to cover and bring to a boil over high heat. Reduce the heat and continue to simmer until the carrots can be easily pierced with a toothpick, about 30 minutes.

2. Drain the carrots, reserving about 2 cups of the cooking water. Place the carrots in a food processor and pulse until smooth, adding some of the cooking water to get the carrots moving if necessary. Add the sea salt and mix. Season with pepper to taste.

Spring Greens Salad with Hot Garlic Dressing

4 servings

If this recipe is doubled, it can certainly be a beautiful meal in itself. The unique salad greens Ben chose to use include arugula, radish sprouts, and mizuna (a delicate Japanese salad green with a piquant, mildly peppery flavor). The garnishes can vary, of course, depending on what you have on hand. But the Jerusalem artichoke (also called sunchoke and, in actuality, the root of a sunflower) lends a wonderful nutty, sweet, and crunchy flavor. Available year-round, it's really at its peak from October to March.

1 pound Jerusalem artichokes (can substitute jícama or 8-ounce can of sliced water chestnuts)
1 teaspoon fresh lemon juice
1 Fuji apple, cored and sliced (can substitute other crisp apple)
1 pound mixed greens
Hot Garlic Dressing (recipe at right)
6 slices smoked bacon, cooked until crispy and each cut into thirds
4 large eggs, hard-boiled, peeled, and quartered or chopped
¼ red onion, thinly sliced
⅓ cup dried cherries
Parmesan Croutons (recipe follows)

1. Peel and thinly slice the Jerusalem artichokes to yield 1 loosely packed cup. Place in a bowl with 1½ quarts of water and the lemon juice. Keep the artichoke slices in this acidulated water for a few minutes. (If substituting jícama, do the same. But if substituting water chestnuts, no need to slice or soak.) Lift out of water with a slotted spoon and place on paper towels to drain. Repeat with the apple slices, using the same bowl of acidulated water.

2. When ready to serve, divide the mixed greens among 4 salad bowls and drizzle with the dressing. Top evenly with the Jerusalem artichokes, apple, bacon, eggs, onion, and dried cherries. Garnish with the croutons.

Parmesan Croutons

6 slices whole-wheat bread
¼ cup olive oil
4 garlic cloves, minced
¼ teaspoon sea salt
¼ cup freshly grated Parmesan cheese

1. Preheat the oven to 350°.

2. Toast the bread in a toaster. Cut into cubes. (Can also use day-old bread, which does not need to be toasted.) Place the cubes in a large bowl.

3. Mix the oil, garlic, and salt in a separate small bowl. Drizzle this mixture over the bread cubes and toss well. Add the Parmesan cheese and coat evenly.

4. Place the bread cubes on a baking sheet and spread out. Bake for 10 minutes, or until golden brown. Remove from the oven and allow to cool.

Hot Garlic Dressing

Makes about ½ cup

1 teaspoon olive oil
4 to 6 garlic cloves, minced
¼ red onion, diced fine
¼ cup cider vinegar
1 tablespoon rice wine vinegar (same as rice vinegar)
½ teaspoon sea salt
8 grinds of a pepper mill
1 teaspoon packed brown sugar
½ teaspoon cornstarch, or as needed
2 tablespoons water, or as needed

1. To make the dressing, place the oil and garlic in a small, cold saucepan. Allow to come up to a sizzle over medium-low heat. There must be no browning of the garlic, just a mild "sweating."

2. Add the onion to the pan and sweat for another 2 minutes. Add the cider vinegar, rice wine vinegar, salt, pepper, and brown sugar. Bring to a boil.

3. Meanwhile, in a small bowl stir the water into the cornstarch and blend into a "slurry" (a thin paste). Add to the pan. Allow to simmer for 3 to 4 minutes, stirring intermittently and being very careful about the viscosity (should achieve the consistency of gravy). Season with more salt, pepper, vinegar, or sugar to taste, if needed. This is also the time to adjust the thickness with either more slurry or more water, if needed. Always bring back to a boil if more slurry or more water is added. Remove from the heat and set aside.

Jonathan Bennett

Roast Chicken

Artichoke–Heirloom
Tomato Gratin

Gingered Apple Tarte Tatin

Jonathan Bennett

Chef/Partner, Moxie the Restaurant, Red the Steakhouse (multiple locations), Rosso Italia (Boca Raton)

Accolades: James Beard award nominee for Rising Star Chef; hosted a James Beard House dinner in New York City; named one of the Best Places to Eat in America by *Gourmet;* named one of the Five Best Steakhouses in the U.S. by *Esquire;* named one of the Ten Best Steakhouses in the U.S. by *Playboy;* won the Silver Plate award from the International Foodservice Manufacturers Association; nominated for an Ivy award by *Restaurant & Institutions;* named Best Restaurant multiple times by numerous publications, including *Food & Wine* and *Cleveland Magazine;* named one of the Top Ten Cleveland Food Rating Restaurants by the *Gayot Guide;* top Zagat ratings; won Best Chef award from *Northern Ohio Live;* won the People's Choice award at the St. John Medical Center's Top Chef competition; featured in numerous publications and media, including *Wine Spectator, Restaurant Hospitality, Basic American Foods,* the *Miami New Times, Ohio Authority, Crain's Cleveland Business, Cleveland Scene, Feast!,* the *Plain Dealer,* WKYC-TV 3, WCPN, and WIOD.

Jonathan's secret tip for last-minute entertaining? "Always keep some frozen puff pastry dough, cheese, and herbs on hand, and you've got an instant appetizer."

When Jonathan was only seven years old, his mother took him to a Japanese steakhouse for the very first time. He was so awestruck by the entire experience that his mom went out the next day and bought him a small, inexpensive electric wok. He set up a makeshift hibachi center next to the kitchen table and, that same evening, pretended to be a Japanese chef preparing stir-fry for his parents and brother. "I made them suffer through my so-called 'flair,'" he recalls with a chuckle.

Yet, in hindsight, that was the precise moment he knew what he wanted to do with his life. It was his first experience of "instant gratification"—and also the moment that would catapult him to eventual culinary fame.

Jonathan didn't grow up around a lot of fancy food and restaurants. In fact, he grew up on a 400-acre farm in Ellerbe, North Carolina (population: 1,000). More specifically, a pig farm. With 2,500 pigs. Which clearly explains his affinity for pork. But we digress.

When Jonathan was only thirteen, he got his first lucky break. A customer at his mom's hair salon, a local chef, offered him a job at his inn. One year later, Jonathan was promoted to line cook. "It was a lot more glamorous than cleaning pig stalls, that's for sure," he laughs.

After graduating from Richmond Senior High School in Rockingham, North Carolina, Jonathan headed straight to the Culinary Institute of America in Hyde Park, New York. He did his externship at the award-winning Clifton Inn in Charlottesville, Virginia.

After graduating from the CIA near the top of his class, Jonathan moved back home to help his ailing father. During that time, he also worked at the historic Pinehurst Inn. After a year, he moved to Hot Springs, Virginia, where he joined The Homestead, a world-famous luxury resort and golf destination. Yet another year later, he moved to Cincinnati to work at Plaza 600.

Then Jonathan did something quite uncharacteristic . . . yet spontaneous and fun. He traveled cross-country with his wife, living out of the back of their pickup truck. For three months, they wandered across the U.S. with no specific plan in mind. They went wherever the wind took them, which was eventually to Cleveland, his wife's hometown.

Jonathan took a job at the 4-diamond Classics restaurant for a year. He was then hired at Moxie the Restaurant as a sous chef. But just four short years later, Jonathan bought into it as a co-owner. Today, several more restaurants (Red the Steakhouse and Rosso Italia) and locations (Miami Beach and Boca Raton) have followed. Jonathan is busier than ever, but never forgets where he came from.

"One of my fondest memories is at Thanksgiving," says Jonathan. "All my aunts and uncles would come down, and we'd all go rabbit hunting. Dinner was cornbread and a pot of beans with ham hocks. It was the best! The absolute best."

In his spare time, Jonathan enjoys woodworking and remodeling his home.

Jonathan lives in Bay Village with his wife, Christine (a pastry chef), and their sons, Alex and Ethan.

Roast Chicken

4 servings

Jonathan half-jokingly suggests that this simple roast chicken recipe, one of his all-time favorites, may very well be the best way to impress a date. "Besides," he says, "roasting a chicken is one of the most essential skills of cooking." Kosher chickens, which are already brined, can be found in better grocery stores and butcher shops. But if you simply cannot find one, try brining your own (see note). It may take more time, but it is definitely worth it.

1 (3- to 4-pound) chicken, preferably kosher or home brined (see note), giblets removed
1 tablespoon olive oil
1 tablespoon kosher salt
1 teaspoon freshly ground black pepper
1 lemon, cut in half
5 fresh thyme sprigs, plus more, chopped, for garnish
1 very large or 2 to 3 medium-size yellow onions, peeled and quartered

1. Preheat the oven to 450°.

2. Rub the chicken with the oil. Season with the salt and pepper inside and out. Stuff the lemon halves and thyme sprigs inside the cavity. Tie the legs together with kitchen twine and tuck the wing tips under.

3. Place the quartered onion pieces in the center of a roasting pan. Rest the chicken right on top of the onion. Place in the oven. After 5 minutes, lower the temperature to 350°. Continue to roast for about 1 hour. Check for doneness by inserting a thermometer between the thigh and the rib cage, being careful not to hit a bone. The temperature should read 160°.

4. Remove from the oven, tent the roasting pan with foil, and let the chicken rest for 10 minutes (during which time it will continue to carry over cooking until it reaches the desired internal temperature of 165°). Remove to a serving platter, carve, and serve immediately, sprinkled with chopped thyme.

NOTE: To brine a chicken, in a container big enough to hold both a 3- to 4-pound chicken and the brine without spilling over, stir together 3 quarts cold water, 1 cup salt, and ¼ cup sugar to dissolve. Remove the giblets from the chicken and slip the bird into the brine. Cover and refrigerate for 4 to 6 hours.

Artichoke–Heirloom Tomato Gratin

4 servings

This easy-to-make side dish involves just cutting up your ingredients, putting them into a heatproof casserole dish, adding flavors, and, after a brief sauté, putting the whole thing in the oven and walking away until it's done. Twenty minutes later, voilà—you've got yourself an impressive, no-fuss showstopper!

4 tablespoons extra-virgin olive oil, divided
2 globe artichokes (can substitute one 9-ounce package frozen artichoke hearts, thawed)
Freshly squeezed juice of 1 lemon
Kosher salt and freshly ground black pepper
3 large tomatoes, preferably a beefsteak heirloom variety
½ cup fresh bread crumbs
¼ cup freshly grated Romano cheese
1 tablespoon chopped fresh thyme
3 sprigs fresh parsley, chopped fine

1. Preheat the oven to 350°.

2. If using fresh artichokes, shave the bottom stems of the artichokes with a vegetable peeler. Using a sharp serrated knife, chop off the top third of each artichoke. Continue to cut away all the tough outer leaves clear down to the pale green/yellow heart. Scrape the fuzzy choke out with a spoon or melon-ball cutter. Slice the remaining stemmed heart into long ¼-inch-thick slices. Sprinkle the lemon juice over the slices to coat.

3. Place 1½ tablespoons of the oil and the artichoke slices (or the thawed frozen artichoke hearts, if using) in a sauteuse or heatproof casserole over medium-high heat. Season with salt and pepper to taste and sauté for about 5 minutes, turning occasionally, or until the artichokes are tender.

4. While the artichokes are cooking, cut the tomatoes into ¼-inch-thick slices. Season with additional salt and pepper, then add to the artichokes and sauté for another 5 minutes.

5. Remove from the heat and sprinkle with the bread crumbs, cheese, thyme, and parsley. Drizzle with the remaining oil.

6. Bake for 20 minutes, or until the top is golden brown. Remove and serve either warm or at room temperature.

Gingered Apple Tarte Tatin

4 servings

Jonathan's been making this tarte tatin for at least sixteen years, and it's still one of his favorite desserts. Although it has a fancy-sounding French name (pronounced "tart tah-*TAN*"), it's basically a very simple upside-down tart in which the apples have first been caramelized. (Note: A firm apple variety is key or else it will turn to mush.) Legend has it that sisters Stéphanie and Caroline Tatin made this dessert quite by accident at their Hotel Tatin in Lamotte-Beuvron, France, back in 1898. But their guests loved it—and a classic was born! Feel free to experiment with other fruit variations as well, including pears, peaches, bananas, or pineapple.

6 local Northern Spy apples (can substitute Granny Smith)
½ cup granulated sugar
¼ cup water
2 tablespoons minced fresh ginger
1 teaspoon fresh lemon juice
¼ teaspoon salt
4 tablespoons (½ stick) unsalted butter
1 sheet frozen puff pastry, thawed but kept chilled
Caramel Sauce (recipe at right), optional

1. Preheat the oven to 450°. Peel, quarter, and core the apples. Toss them in a bowl with the sugar, water, ginger, lemon juice, and salt.

2. Cut the butter into small pieces and scatter over the bottom of a nonstick, ovenproof 10-inch sauté pan. Arrange the apples on their sides in a shingled, overlapping circle, filling in the center as well. Pour in all the remaining liquid. Bring to a simmer over medium heat.

3. Lower the heat to medium low and cook, occasionally giving the pan gentle swirls, for approximately 30 minutes, or until a light-colored caramel has formed around the apples.

4. Cut the puff pastry sheet into a 10-inch circle to fit inside the pan. When the apples are done cooking, take off the heat and place the round sheet over the apples. Carefully tuck the edges of the pastry down between the outer rim of apples and the inside lip of the pan. (Beware: The pan will be hot!)

5. Bake for about 10 minutes, or until the pastry is fully cooked and golden brown. Remove from the oven. Let cool for about 5 minutes.

6. Loosen the edges with a knife. Place a serving plate that is larger than the pan over the pan and carefully flip. Watch out, as the liquid will be very hot! Swirl any leftover caramel over the top. However, if desired, make the Caramel Sauce and drizzle over the top instead. Serve either warm or at room temperature.

Caramel Sauce

½ cup granulated sugar
2 tablespoons water
½ teaspoon salt
⅓ cup heavy cream

1. Combine the sugar and water in a saucepan, stirring to dissolve the sugar. Cook over high heat until amber in color.

2. Remove from the heat. Add the salt and then the cream, slowly and carefully. Whisk gently.

3. Place back on the stove over medium heat. When the sauce returns to a boil, take off the heat. Use immediately.

WINE PAIRINGS

Argentina: Mendoza—Malbec
Italy: Piedmont—Barbera d'Asti
Italy: Veneto—Valpolicella Ripasso

Tim Birkley

BBQ Chicken Pizza

Fried Smoked Mozzarella with
Tomato Chutney

Chicken Cacciatore

Tim Birkley

Executive Chef, Johnny's Bar

Accolades: Won a Distinguished Fine Dining Establishment award from DiRōNA; corecipient of James Beard recognition; top Zagat ratings for America's Best Restaurants, Best Food, Best Service, and Most Popular Restaurant; earned an Award of Excellence from *Wine Spectator* and numerous Silver Spoon awards from *Cleveland Magazine*; top-5 winner of Fox 8's Best Romantic Restaurant award; earned *Cleveland Scene's* Best Power Lunch award; featured in numerous publications and media, including *USA Today*, the *New York Times*, the *Miami Herald*, *Fodor's*, Southwest Airlines' *Travel Guide*, *Currents*, *Cleveland Magazine*, the *Plain Dealer*, *Metromix*, and WKYC-TV 3.

Tim's personal "aha!" moment came when he was only fourteen years old. "My cousin made me try an oyster on the half shell," remembers Tim vividly. "At that very moment, I realized there was a lot more to food than chicken nuggets." And so began his journey to culinary stardom.

Tim was born and raised in North Royalton, Ohio, but spent a lot of time with his aunts and uncles on Cleveland's West Side. "My Italian aunt was an amazing cook," explains Tim, "so I started dabbling in the kitchen from a young age."

During high school, Tim got a weekend job at the upscale Tonight Tonight restaurant in North Royalton. He started as a dishwasher but within six months advanced to line cook. From that point on, there was no turning back! To prove to himself, though, that this was what he really wanted to do for a career and to erase any iota of doubt, right after Tim graduated from North Royalton High School, he tried working for his uncle as a bricklayer. By the end of that long, hot, back-breaking summer, he was

Tim's secret tip for last-minute entertaining? "Hide your expensive booze."

sure. More than anything else, he was determined to follow his true passion for all things food.

That fall, Tim headed to Charleston, South Carolina, to attend the College of Culinary Arts at Johnson & Wales University. While there, he also worked full-time at the now defunct Village Café in Mt. Pleasant and at Kiva Han Café in downtown Charleston.

After graduation, Tim returned to Cleveland and went straight to work at the eclectic Johnny Mango in Ohio City. After nine months he joined the chic Johnny's Downtown as their line cook, staying there for three years. He was then promoted and transferred to Johnny's Bar on Fulton, where he remains today as executive chef. "I really like it here," says Tim enthusiastically. "I just want to keep on cooking and have fun!"

If Tim isn't hard at work in the kitchen, he likes to entertain at home. "I think cooking at home should be enjoyable, not stressful," he says. "The recipes I'm featuring are relatively simple and allow time for the other details of entertaining to be addressed."

And yet, when he's not entertaining, you'll probably find Tim either playing golf (he has an 18 handicap) or riding his treasured Dyna Super Glide Custom Harley motorcycle "anywhere there's pavement." By night, you will most probably run into him at a heavy metal concert.

Tim lives in Cleveland with his girlfriend, Angela, and a houseful of ordinary—plus some not-so-ordinary—pets, including six cats (Goom, Gretyl, Hank, Batters, C. C., and Morris), a chinchilla (Sacha), a horse (Gunner), and last but certainly not least, a red-tailed boa constrictor (Dominus).

BBQ Chicken Pizza

4 servings

Wanting an appetizer that was a little bit fun and different, Tim came up with this winning pizza combination. It starts with a Boboli base, which couldn't be any easier. But then it quickly gets elevated to gourmet status with its tangy BBQ sauce, premium toppings, and cilantro garnish. Be fore-warned—you may very well want to make a double recipe.

2 boneless, skinless chicken thighs
Salt and freshly ground black pepper
5 tablespoons BBQ sauce, preferably Sweet Baby Ray's
1 oven-ready pizza crust, preferably Boboli
4 ounces (or ½ cup, packed) shredded Colby Jack cheese
½ cup julienned red onion
½ cup julienned red pepper
2 tablespoons chopped fresh cilantro

1. Preheat the oven to 375°. Place a rack in the middle of the oven.

2. Season the chicken thighs with salt and pepper to taste. Place in a shallow baking pan and roast in the oven for 20 minutes, or until the chicken reaches an internal tempera-ture of 165°.

3. Remove from the oven and cool the chicken to the touch, about 5 minutes. Meanwhile, raise the oven tem-perature to 450°.

4. Shred the chicken or give it a rough chop. Spread the BBQ sauce over the pizza shell. Top it with the chicken, cheese, onion, and red pepper. Place directly on the middle oven rack and bake for 8 to 10 minutes.

5. Carefully remove the pizza with a long-handled peel or unrimmed cookie sheet. Garnish with the cilantro. Cut into wedges or squares and serve on a platter, family style.

WINE PAIRINGS

France: Burgundy—Beaujolais Villages
Germany: Mosel
USA: Washington State—Riesling
Italy: Piedmont—Moscato d'Asti

Fried Smoked Mozzarella with Tomato Chutney

4 servings

Another great Birkley appetizer, this time a unique twist on traditional fried mozzarella sticks. And because this recipe is so versatile, feel free to change it up a bit. Instead of smoked mozzarella, opt for smoked provolone. Or use any regular semifirm cheese, such as plain mozzarella, provolone, fontina, or young Asiago. "Just don't use any yellow cheeses," Tim warns.

½ cup water
1½ tablespoons red wine vinegar
½ cup plus 2 tablespoons granulated sugar
1 cup diced fresh seeded tomatoes
12 ounces smoked mozzarella, cut into 1½-inch-thick squares (or ½-inch wedges if cheese is round)
1 cup all-purpose flour
3 large eggs, beaten
1 cup seasoned bread crumbs
1 cup olive oil
Salt and freshly ground black pepper, optional
Microgreens for garnish, optional

1. Bring the water, vinegar, and sugar to a boil in a heavy saucepan on medium-high heat. Reduce the heat to medium. Continue to simmer until the liquid begins to thicken, about 20 minutes.

2. Add the tomatoes to the vinegar mixture. Continue to cook on medium heat until thick, about 25 minutes. Take the chutney off the heat. Cool for about 10 minutes. Set aside.

3. Dip the mozzarella in the flour to coat, then into beaten eggs, then bread crumbs, then eggs, then bread crumbs again.

4. Heat the oil in a sauté pan over medium-high heat. Pan-fry the breaded mozzarella for about 1 minute on each side, or until golden brown. (You may need to do this in batches.)

5. Remove the fried cheese from the pan. Place on paper towels to absorb excess oil. If desired, season with salt and pepper to taste. Serve warm, with a spoonful of chutney on top of each slice and garnished, if desired, with micro-greens.

Chicken Cacciatore

4 servings

This classic Italian dish speaks for itself. Using simple, proper techniques, you can easily create an impressive one-pot meal that your guests will think took you all day to prepare. Just be sure to use only fresh herbs, which make all the difference in the world.

8 boneless, skinless chicken thighs
Salt and freshly ground black pepper
All-purpose flour
¼ cup olive oil
1 cup diced Spanish onion
1 cup diced green pepper
½ cup sliced fresh button mushrooms
1 tablespoon minced garlic (3 medium-size cloves)
2 cups canned crushed tomatoes
1 cup chicken stock
¾ cup dry red wine
1 tablespoon chopped fresh basil
1 tablespoon chopped fresh oregano
1 bay leaf
4 cups precooked white rice (instant, boil-in-bag, or
    microwavable pouch)
Fresh basil chiffonade for garnish

1. Season the chicken thighs with salt and pepper to taste. Dust with flour and set aside.

2. Heat the oil in a deep-sided skillet over medium-high heat and add the chicken. Don't overcrowd (you may need to do this in batches). Sear on both sides until golden brown, about 4 to 5 minutes on each side. Using tongs or a slotted spoon, remove the chicken from the skillet and set aside.

3. Add the onion, green pepper, mushrooms, and garlic to the oil in the skillet and reduce the heat to medium low. Sauté until the onion is translucent, about 10 minutes.

4. Return the chicken to the skillet with the vegetables. Add the crushed tomatoes, stock, red wine, basil, oregano, and bay leaf. Increase the heat to medium high and bring to a boil, then reduce the heat back down to a simmer. Continue to simmer for 25 to 30 minutes, or until the chicken reaches an internal temperature of 165°.

5. Meanwhile, prepare the rice according to package directions.

6. Remove the skillet with the chicken and sauce from the heat. Remove the bay leaf. Serve the chicken and sauce on top of the cooked rice, garnished with the basil.

Dante Boccuzzi

Mustard-Crusted Lamb Cutlets
with Garbanzo Beans
& Frisée

Port-Honey–Glazed Pears
with Vanilla Ice Cream

Dante Boccuzzi

Chef/Owner, DANTE Restaurant, Ginko, The D.C. Pasta Company, DBA

Accolades: Two-time James Beard award nominee for Rising Star Chef of the Year; hosted a James Beard House dinner in New York City; earned *Food & Wine*'s Best New Wine List award; scored a 1-star Michelin rating; placed first in a Cervena Plates competition; named a Rising Star by StarChefs; taught classes at the Étoile Culinary Institute in Venice, Italy; featured in numerous publications and media, including *USA Today, Gourmet, Restaurant Hospitality, Zagat Buzz, New York Magazine, Cleveland Magazine,* the *Boston Globe, San Francisco Weekly,* the *St. Petersburg Times,* the *Plain Dealer,* WKYC-TV 3, WEWS-TV 5, and WJW-TV 8.

A local boy at heart, Dante left Cleveland as a relatively naïve and sheltered eighteen-year-old kid. Along the way, he learned a thing or two about cooking . . . traveled across the country and around the world . . . and eventually came right back where he started from—this time as an internationally renowned, award-winning chef with great confidence and élan.

Born and raised in Parma, Ohio, Dante took his first after-school job at a local pizzeria called Stancato's when he was only fourteen. This was his premier glimpse into both the ever-seductive restaurant world and the controlled mayhem of a professional kitchen. "It was truly fun and exciting for me," says Dante. "And since I didn't know what else I wanted to do with my life, I decided to go to culinary school."

After graduating from Cuyahoga Valley Christian Academy in Cuyahoga Falls, he packed his bags and headed to the Culinary Institute of America in upstate New York. While enrolled there, he externed at the tony Pinehurst Country Club in North Carolina. After graduation, he went straight to New York City, where he landed a plum job working alongside revered industry great Charlie Palmer. As chef de partie at Charlie's famed Aureole restaurant, Dante formed a relationship with his mentor that would continue for years to come.

Fast forward two years. After cooking for the likes of Robert De Niro and other celebrity regulars, Dante decided to follow Charlie's sage advice to further his training in Eu-

Dante's secret tip for last-minute entertaining? "Don't panic, work clean, be organized, and rely on things you know. Now is not the time to be experimental."

rope, first at Aquamarina in Sardinia, Italy, and then at the fashionable L'Escargot in London. He eventually returned to Aureole as a pastry assistant, but left again to continue his international training at the famed Les Muscadins in Mougins, France, followed by Gualtiero Marchesi Restaurant at L'Albereta in Northern Italy.

After a brief stint back in Cleveland as a chef consultant to Giovanni's, Dante moved to Washington, D.C., to join the opulent Lespinasse in the Sheraton Carlton Hotel (now the St. Regis). No sooner had he gotten used to living and working in the nation's capital than he got a call from his mentor, Charlie, who at the time was working as a consultant for the brand new Silks restaurant in San Francisco's Mandarin Oriental Hotel. He said he was recommending Dante for the position of chef de cuisine. Was he interested? Absolutely!

Within months, Dante was earning rave reviews at Silks. During his three-year tenure there, he took one more trip overseas to do *stages* in Hong Kong and Taiwan. Yet another recommendation from Charlie landed Dante in Italy again—but this time as executive chef of the chic Armani/Nobu restaurant, housed on the first floor of Giorgio Armani's flagship boutique in Milan. After two years, he returned to Aureole one last time, taking the helm as executive chef for the next five years.

With a growing family and the desire to hang his own shingle, Dante finally returned home to Cleveland. He opened his first eponymous DANTE restaurant in Valley View and eventually relocated it to Tremont. He then opened Ginko, a sushi bar housed in the basement of DANTE, as well as a casual Italian pasta house in Strongsville called The D.C. Pasta Company and an eclectic spot in Akron called DBA (which stands for Dante Boccuzzi Akron).

When not working, Dante loves to indulge in his second passion: music. Specifically, the guitar. His favorite? A Les Paul. He also tries to get in a round of golf every now and then.

Dante lives in Broadview Heights with his Italian-born wife, Monica, and their four children: Francis, Andrea, Julien, and Isabella.

Mustard-Crusted Lamb Cutlets with Garbanzo Beans & Frisée

4 servings (2 cutlets per person)

The three components of this dish require only a few simple steps each. But the result is one entirely sophisticated presentation. Be sure to save yourself some time and trouble by asking your butcher to both remove the chine (backbone) and cut your lamb rack into cutlets. You'll be glad you did.

½ cup olive oil
¼ cup balsamic vinegar
Freshly squeezed juice of 1 lemon
Salt and freshly ground black pepper
1 (15½-ounce) can garbanzo beans (also called chickpeas or ceci), drained
3 tablespoons thinly julienned fresh parsley
3 tablespoons thinly julienned fresh mint
1 (8-chop) rack or loin of lamb, chined (backbone removed) and cut into individual cutlets
¼ cup Dijon mustard
2 cups toasted bread crumbs (see note)
3 tablespoons canola or vegetable oil
2 to 3 cups frisée greens (also called curly endive)
Fresh mint leaves for garnish, optional

1. Mix the oil, vinegar, lemon juice, and salt and pepper to taste in a small bowl. Set this vinaigrette aside.

2. Mix the garbanzo beans, parsley, and mint in a separate bowl. Set aside.

3. Using a butter knife, spread both sides of each cutlet with the mustard. Place the bread crumbs on a plate, then press each cutlet down into the crumbs to coat well on that side. Sprinkle more crumbs over the tops of the cutlets, pressing in to adhere.

4. Heat the oil in a large skillet over medium heat. Panfry the cutlets until they turn golden brown, about 2 minutes on each side. Remove from the skillet and keep warm.

5. Place the frisée greens in a bowl. Drizzle with 3 to 5 tablespoons of the vinaigrette. Mix the remaining vinaigrette with the garbanzo beans.

6. Divide the frisée and place in the center of each serving plate. Lay the cutlets on top of the greens. Spoon the beans around the salad. If desired, garnish with mint leaves. Serve immediately.

NOTE: To make toasted bread crumbs, toast a few slices of bread. Crush or pulse in a food processor.

Port-Honey—Glazed Pears with Vanilla Ice Cream

4 servings

The beauty of this innovative dessert—besides its simplicity and depth of flavors—is its versatility. If Bartlett pears aren't in season (from fall through winter), try substituting fresh figs (in season from spring through fall). The port-honey glaze, which imparts an especially attractive shiny coating, really brings out the flavor of whichever fruit you choose.

2 ripe Bartlett pears, peeled, cored, and cut into wedges (can substitute 4 fresh figs, halved lengthwise)
½ cup honey
½ cup port wine
8 fresh gooseberries, peeled and quartered (can substitute ½ cup whole blueberries)
4 scoops vanilla ice cream

1. Slowly cook the pears and honey in a large sauté pan over medium heat for about 5 minutes, turning the pears while cooking to coat with the honey. Continue cooking until the honey starts to bubble, darkens slightly, and caramelizes in color, about another 2 to 3 minutes.

2. Add the port wine. Reduce the liquid, stirring occasionally, until it reaches a light syrup consistency, about 3 to 4 minutes.

3. Add the gooseberries to the pan and stir just to coat. Take off the heat.

4. Scoop the ice cream into 4 bowls. Spoon the pear mixture (hot from the pan but not boiling) evenly over each. Serve immediately.

WINE PAIRINGS

France: Rhône—Côtes du Rhône
Italy: Piedmont—Nebbiolo della Langhe
USA: California, Sonoma—Zinfandel

Zachary Bruell

Seared Sea Scallops with
Thai Curry Coconut Sauce

Green Bamboo Rice

Sautéed Haricots Verts

Greek Yogurt with Berries
& Honey

Zachary Bruell

Chef/Owner, Parallax, L'Albatros, Chinato, Cowell & Hubbard; Consulting Chef/Restaurateur,
Table 45 at The InterContinental Cleveland

Accolades: Four-time James Beard award nominee for Best Chef: Great Lakes Region; three-time winner of *Esquire* magazine's Best New Restaurants in America award; earned three Santé Awards of Innovation; top accolades from numerous sources, including the *New York Times, USA Today, Food & Wine, Art Culinaire,* and *Nation's Restaurant News;* top Zagat ratings; earned one of Cleveland's Best New Restaurants by *Cleveland Magazine;* featured in numerous publications and media, including *Wine Spectator, Lodging Hospitality, Nation's Restaurant News, America's Cuisine, Wine & Spirits, USA Today,* the *New York Times,* the *Chicago Tribune,* the *Los Angeles Times,* WKYC-TV 3, WEWS-TV 5, and WJW-TV 8.

Zachary (Zack) grew up in Shaker Heights, Ohio, part of a very close-knit family. His mother and father were both good cooks. But as the only son, Zack wasn't really expected to help in the kitchen—which was perfectly fine with him!

After graduating from Shaker Heights High School, Zack entered the University of Pennsylvania, but his Ivy League education was interrrupted by the military draft. After serving, he enrolled at the University of Colorado at Boulder, where he met a guy who would change his life: Michael McCarty. Michael, a fellow student who had studied at Le Cordon Bleu in Paris, was teaching an extension class in French cooking. Zack became interested. Fascinated, in fact. This, he suddenly realized, was the direction he wanted to take in his career.

After finishing his degree in business, Zack worked at different restaurants throughout Colorado and Cleveland. He then attended The Restaurant School in Philadelphia, at that time a leading chef training center.

After graduation, he was invited to stay and teach at the school as an alumnus. He also opened his first restaurant— the 20th Street Café in Philadelphia—with a partner. Just as it was starting to attract national recognition, he got a call from his old friend. "Come work for me," said Michael, who had just opened his own pioneering California nouvelle eatery in Santa Monica. Zack agreed.

Zack's secret tip for last-minute entertaining? "Work with great ingredients and keep it simple."

Two years later, while vacationing back home in Cleveland, Zack was asked to run The Garland, an upscale restaurant at the exclusive Landerhaven Country Club. He agreed, making it part of his two-year plan to move back to California and open his own place. After one year at The Garland, he left and spent a year at Mario's International Spa & Hotel in Aurora. Finally he was ready to achieve his two-year goal—but with a slight modification. The opening of his own restaurant—Z Contemporary Cuisine—ended up being in Shaker Heights, Ohio, not Santa Barbara, California.

Zack began introducing fusion cuisine to Clevelanders with much success. But ten years later something unexpected happened: Zack got burned out. So he closed the restaurant and went into a self-imposed early retirement.

He was thoroughly enjoying his new leisurely lifestyle when he got a call from his old friend Ken Stewart, who owned Ken Stewart's Grille in Akron. He needed help in his kitchen. "No. Absolutely not," replied Zack adamantly. But eventually he relented.

After eight years the bug got to Zack once more. Before he knew it, his new Parallax fusion restaurant in Tremont opened to wild acclaim. Three years later the CEO of the Cleveland Clinic asked him to help rebuild the medical center's existing restaurant. Zack transformed it into Table 45, named for the best seat in the house at Parallax. He consequently opened L'Albatros on the campus of Case Western Reserve University, Chinato on hip East 4th Street, and his latest "jewel" of a restaurant in Cleveland's Theatre District: Cowell & Hubbard (after the famed jewelry store that occupied the same space from 1920 to 1981).

Five restaurants to his name. All hugely successful. And all within the city of Cleveland. We're so glad he's no longer retired.

In his free time, Zack still loves to play golf. (He's a scratch golfer and the club champion at his country club.)

Zack and his family live on Cleveland's East Side. They all continue to be strong supporters of the local community.

Seared Sea Scallops with Thai Curry Coconut Sauce

4 servings

This spicy fusion dish, a favorite at Parallax, merges classic French techniques with traditional Southeast Asian ingredients. The trick is to find the biggest, freshest, highest-quality sea scallops available. The designation "U/10" for the jumbo size recommended here (and the biggest available) denotes that it takes "under 10" of these scallops to make up a pound. Diver sea scallops, which are more ecologically friendly, are hand-picked off a rock by scuba divers from November to April rather than harvested by boat nets dragged across the ocean floor. Be sure to look for scallops labeled "chemical free" or "dry packed." And if bought frozen, only thaw overnight in the refrigerator, never on the counter or in a microwave.

12 jumbo U/10 diver sea scallops (if can only find smaller size, buy more)
Kosher salt and freshly ground black pepper
2 tablespoons olive oil
1 tablespoon unsalted butter
1 cup coconut milk
2 tablespoons fish sauce (also called nuoc mam)
1 teaspoon Thai red curry paste (do not substitute green/ yellow curry paste or curry powder)
½ teaspoon packed brown sugar

1. Pat the scallops completely dry with a paper towel. Season both sides with salt and pepper to taste.

2. Add the oil and butter to a sauté pan over medium-high heat. When the oil mixture gets quite hot and you see the tiniest bit of smoke, add the sea scallops without crowding. If too close together, they will steam instead of sear. If necessary, cook in batches.

3. Sear for about 2 minutes on one side, or until golden brown and caramelized. (Important: Do not touch them until ready to turn or you'll prevent them from forming the nice brown crust you want.) When you think they're ready, take a peek underneath. If you see a nice caramel-colored crust, they're ready to turn.

4. Flip and continue to sear on the other side for about 1 more minute or, again, until golden brown and caramelized. Do not overcook! Their centers should still be slightly translucent (check by viewing them from the side). They should also be quite springy when you press them with your thumb because they will continue to cook after you've taken them off the heat. If they are very firm or stiff, they're overcooked. Remove from the pan and keep warm.

5. In the same pan over medium heat, add the coconut milk, fish sauce, red curry paste, and brown sugar. Whisk only until smooth. Immediately remove from the heat.

6. Pour some sauce onto each plate. If desired to serve, place a mound of Green Bamboo Rice (recipe on page 36) in the center. Frame the rice with three scallops per plate. If serving the Sautéed Haricots Verts (recipe on page 36), use to top the rice. Serve immediately.

Green Bamboo Rice

4 servings

This unique and visually arresting, green-colored Chinese rice is actually short-grain rice infused with chlorophyll extracted from young bamboo leaves—a 1,000-year-old tradition from the Yunnan province of China. The rice has a distinct, lightly sweet, jasmine green tea–like flavor and aroma. It also has a moist and somewhat sticky texture and is nutritionally high in vitamin B. Look for it at Cleveland's West Side Market or a high-end grocery store.

1 cup green bamboo rice, also called jade rice (can
    substitute Japanese short-grain rice)
1 small onion, quartered, optional
1 small knob fresh ginger, unpeeled, optional
1 whole star anise, optional
Kosher salt and freshly ground black pepper

1. Bring 2 cups of water to a boil in a saucepan. Add the rice. Note: Do not rinse the rice first! If desired, also add the onion, ginger, and/or star anise.

2. Bring back to a boil. Stir, cover, reduce the heat to medium low, and simmer for 12 to 15 minutes, or until the water is absorbed. Remove from the heat and let stand, covered, for 10 to 15 minutes.

3. Remove the ginger, star anise, and/or onion, if used, and fluff the rice with a fork. Season with salt and pepper to taste and serve warm.

Sautéed Haricots Verts

4 servings

Fresh. Crisp-tender. Perfectly cooked. And delicious, with just a hint of sweetness. This recipe could not be any simpler. In case you didn't already know, *haricots verts* (pronounced "ah-ree-koh *VEHR*") is just French for green beans. But it is also its own variety, longer and thinner than most American varieties, plus more tender and with a more complex flavor. Also called "French green beans," they are specifically bred for flavorful pods and are stringless. Try growing them in your own garden!

Salt
1 pound fresh haricots verts, washed and ends trimmed
    (can substitute regular green beans)
1 tablespoon olive oil
2 tablespoons unsalted butter
1 shallot, thinly sliced
Freshly ground black pepper
1 tablespoon fresh micro cilantro (can substitute 2
    teaspoons chopped fresh cilantro) for garnish, optional

1. Bring a large pot of salted water to a boil. In the meantime, prepare a large bowl of ice water and set aside.

2. When the water comes to a boil, add the haricots verts. Boil until crisp and tender, about 1 to 2 minutes. Quickly drain and plunge them into the ice water. Drain again and pat dry with a paper towel or dish towel. Set aside.

3. Heat the oil in a large skillet over medium heat. Add the butter and shallot. When the butter has melted, add the haricots verts.

4. Sauté until heated through, stirring often, about 2 to 3 minutes. Season with salt and pepper to taste. Sauté for 1 more minute, then take off the heat and serve either hot or at room temperature, garnished, if desired, with the micro cilantro.

WINE PAIRINGS

Austria: Any region—Grüner Veltliner
France: Alsace—Pinot Gris
New Zealand: Marlborough—Sauvignon Blanc

Greek Yogurt with Berries & Honey

4 servings

In true fusion fashion, this dessert makes the perfect ending to such an innovative meal. It is also the true epitome of minimalism. With the freshest of ingredients and the simplest of preparations, the final result is nothing short of elegant and tasteful—in every sense of the words.

2 cups plain Greek yogurt, chilled
⅓ cup raspberries
⅓ cup blueberries
⅓ cup blackberries
2 tablespoons Greek honey (can substitute good-quality local honey)
4 fresh mint leaves for garnish, optional

1. Place ½ cup of the yogurt into each of four small bowls. Randomly divide and place the berries on and around the yogurt.

2. Drizzle each serving with 1½ teaspoons of the honey. If desired, garnish with a mint leaf. Serve chilled.

Shawn Cline

Sherry-Garlic Shrimp

Creamy Stone-Ground Grits

Wilted Greens

Strawberry Shortcake in a Jar

Shawn Cline

Corporate Executive Chef, Hospitality Restaurants (Blue Point Grille, The Cabin Club, Delmonico's Steakhouse, Rosewood Grill [multiple locations], Salmon Dave's Pacific Grill)

Accolades: Received multiple Awards of Excellence by *Wine Spectator;* rated Extraordinary by Zagat; awarded Best Steak and Best Seafood by *Northern Ohio Live;* won twelve consecutive Cleveland's Best Seafood Restaurant awards as well as Best Fine Dining, Best People Watching, Best Service, and Best Wine List from *Cleveland Magazine;* featured in numerous publications and media, including *Restaurant Hospitality, Cleveland Magazine,* the *Hudson Hub-Times,* the *Plain Dealer,* WKYC-TV 3, and WJW-TV 8.

What does it take to efficiently, effectively, and seamlessly oversee not one, or two, but five super successful, award-winning restaurants—simultaneously? A person just like Shawn. "My job never gets old," says Shawn. "Each location has a different concept. There are always new challenges and new learning experiences. I love every day of it."

Growing up in Canton, Ohio, Shawn spent a lot of time during his childhood at his grandmother's house. Specifically, in her kitchen. Because, with seven children of her own, she was always cooking. And Shawn loved helping her, whether it was gathering fresh tomatoes and scallions from her garden, or picking pears and apples from her trees.

He clearly remembers helping her stir big pots of soup, form salmon patties, bake Texas sheet cakes, and can fruits and vegetables. "It was apparent to me, even at such a young age," reflects Shawn, "that whenever people gathered, for whatever reason, food truly influenced their happiness."

At fifteen Shawn got his first job at a Taco Bell. Showing a lot of natural talent, he was encouraged to apply to the specialized culinary arts program at the Dayton Job Corps Center in

Shawn's secret tip for last-minute entertaining? "Build your pantry! Be adventurous and creative with your meals when time allows. This way, you will, over time, accumulate a plethora of items that can be useful for last-minute meal planning. The more items you have in your pantry and the more creative you continue to be, the better base you will have to successfully create ideas in a pinch and have the necessary products you need on hand. A creative sauce, hot or cold, could easily add the right amount of creativity and originality to an otherwise simple dish."

Dayton, Ohio. After completing the nine-month program and serving an externship at Marriott, he decided to further his training at the Pennsylvania Institute of Culinary Arts (now Le Cordon Bleu Institute of Culinary Arts) in Pittsburgh. At the same time, he also took a job working alongside the fishmongers in the butcher shop at The Duquesne Club, the finest city club in the country.

When Shawn finally returned back home to Canton, he joined the kitchen staff at the private Portage Country Club in Akron, where he remained for nearly a year and a half. He then followed with stints at Grappa's Italian Restaurant in Fairlawn, Opus Twenty One in Warren, Moxie in Beachwood, and Vivo in Cleveland's Old Arcade.

Shawn's defining moment came when he accepted a position as line cook at the chic Blue Point Grille, one of the family of quality restaurants owned and operated by Hospitality Restaurants. He was quickly promoted to kitchen manager, then sous chef, then executive chef. He was eventually offered the plum position of corporate executive chef overseeing all five locations.

"You hold a lot of power in your hands when you're cooking," says Shawn. "The food you prepare is always part of celebrating in some way, shape, or form. And depending on how it turns out, you're either loved or hated!" Unquestionably, Shawn is loved by Cleveland. Really, really loved.

When he's not at one of the five restaurants he supervises, you'll most likely find Shawn with his nose in a textbook (he's working toward finishing a business degree) or watching or attending a sporting event.

Shawn and his wife, Holly, live in University Heights with their two young children, daughter Kaitlyn and son Shawn.

Sherry-Garlic Shrimp

4 servings

This versatile recipe can be used as part of a one-dish meal the way Shawn does here with Creamy Stone-Ground Grits and Wilted Greens (recipes follow), or it could be served by itself with a baguette, tapas-style. It can also be dished up as a quick, simple snack. When in season, you can even substitute soft-shell crab for the shrimp. The possibilities are wide open, but the results are always the same: fantastic!

24 uncooked medium-size (16/20 count) shrimp, preferably black tiger shrimp, peeled and deveined but tail left on
Salt and freshly ground black pepper
2 tablespoons extra-virgin olive oil
1 tablespoon minced garlic (3 medium-size cloves)
2 small-to-medium-size shallots, minced
¼ cup dry white wine
¼ cup sherry vinegar, preferably aged
4 ounces (1 stick) unsalted butter, chilled and cubed
1 vine-ripened tomato, diced
¼ cup chopped fresh parsley
1 tablespoon fresh lime juice
Baguette, sourdough bread, or any kind of crusty bread, sliced on the bias and grilled

1. Dry the shrimp between paper towels. Season lightly with salt and pepper to taste.

2. Heat the oil in a large sauté pan over medium-high heat. Add half the shrimp. Sear for 30 seconds on each side. Remove to a paper towel to drain. Add the other half of the shrimp and sear in the same manner.

3. When the second batch of shrimp has seared, return the first batch to the pan. Add the garlic and shallots. Still over medium-high heat, sauté briefly to release the aroma. Add the wine and vinegar, stirring to deglaze the pan, about 1 minute. Continue to cook over high heat until the liquid is reduced by half, about 2 to 4 minutes.

4. Remove the pan from the heat and whisk in the chilled butter a little at a time to emulsify.

5. Finish by adding the tomato, parsley, and lime juice. Mix well and season with salt and pepper to taste. Serve warm with the grilled bread.

Creamy Stone-Ground Grits

4 servings

This classic, uncomplicated Southern dish is one of Shawn's favorites—and it's actually starting to show up more frequently on menus at upscale restaurants all across the country, not just in the South. Also called hominy grits, it serves as the perfect bed for the Sherry-Garlic Shrimp (recipe at left). But its rich taste and thick, cream consistency also make it perfect for any meal, including breakfast.

4 cups milk, plus additional if needed
1 cup yellow stone-ground grits (can substitute yellow cornmeal)
1 tablespoon unsalted butter, chilled
Salt and freshly ground white pepper

1. Pour the milk into a saucepan and bring to a gentle boil over medium heat. Add the grits in a thin stream to avoid lumping, stirring constantly.

2. Reduce the heat to low. Cook, stirring occasionally, for about 20 to 25 minutes, or until a smooth and creamy porridge-like consistency. If too thick, stir in more milk.

3. Take off the heat, stir in the butter, and season with salt and white pepper to taste. Serve warm.

Wilted Greens

4 servings

Although available year-round, the peak season for escarole (a type of endive that's also called chicory) is from June through October. Be sure to avoid especially thick or tough leaves, which tend to be bitter. A very good source of various vitamins and nutrients, escarole can also be quite sandy, so be sure to wash it well. This recipe is easy, reliable, and delicious.

1 tablespoon extra-virgin olive oil
6 loosely packed cups chopped escarole (can substitute 12 cups baby spinach)
Salt and freshly ground black pepper

1. Heat a large sauté pan over medium-high heat. Add the oil. Immediately add the escarole and stir continuously until the escarole has sufficiently wilted, about 2 to 3 minutes.

2. Season with salt and pepper to taste and serve warm.

Strawberry Shortcake in a Jar

4 servings

This fun jarred dessert—a twist on the traditional strawberry shortcake—is a great take-along for summer picnics! Just prepare up to a day ahead, put the lids on, and store in the refrigerator until ready to pack in your basket. Your guests will enjoy their own individual servings, presented in such a cute and unique way using old-fashioned, eco-friendly Mason canning jars. (Tip: In a real pinch you can go ahead and cheat by picking up a store-bought pound cake instead.)

STRAWBERRIES

1 pint (2 cups) strawberries, stemmed and thickly sliced
¼ to ½ cup granulated sugar, depending on how sweet
    you like it
1 tablespoon Grand Marnier (can substitute orange juice
    for a nonalcoholic version)
Freshly grated zest of ½ orange

POUND CAKE

1 cup all-purpose flour
1 teaspoon baking powder
3 large eggs plus 2 large egg whites, at room temperature
1 tablespoon whole milk, at room temperature
⅔ cup granulated sugar
4 tablespoons (½ stick) unsalted butter, melted and cooled
1 teaspoon pure vanilla extract

WHIPPED CREAM

1 cup heavy cream, chilled
1 tablespoon powdered sugar
1 teaspoon pure vanilla extract

1. Preheat the oven to 350°. Grease a 9 x 5 x 3-inch loaf pan.

2. Combine the strawberries, sugar, Grand Marnier, and orange zest in a bowl. Set aside and let sit for at least 20 to 30 minutes, allowing the strawberries to release some of their own natural juices.

....

WINE PAIRINGS

....

USA: California—sparkling brut rosé
USA: California, Paso Robles—Sauvignon Blanc
USA: Oregon—Pinot Noir Rosé

3. Meanwhile, for the pound cake, sift together the flour and baking powder. Set aside.

4. Combine the whole eggs and milk in a large bowl. Whip on high until frothy, about 3 minutes. Add the sugar and continue to whip on high until thick and pale yellow, about 7 to 8 minutes.

5. Whip the egg whites in a clean bowl with clean beaters until stiff peaks form. Set aside.

6. Gently fold the flour into the egg-sugar mixture. Next, fold in the melted butter and vanilla. Lastly, fold in the whipped egg whites.

7. Pour the batter into the greased loaf pan. Bake for about 30 minutes, or until golden brown. The cake is done when a toothpick inserted into the center comes out clean. Let cool on a rack.

8. While the cake cools, refrigerate a bowl and clean beaters for whipping the cream.

9. Just before serving, combine all the ingredients for the whipped cream in the chilled bowl. Whip until stiff peaks form.

10. For assembly, first cut half of the pound cake into cubes. Reserve the other half for use at another time. (It freezes well if tightly wrapped.)

11. Place half of the pound cake cubes evenly over the bottom of four pint-size glass Mason jars. Add half of the macerated strawberries, then half of the whipped cream. Repeat with the remaining pound cake, strawberries, and whipped cream.

12. Either serve immediately or store in the refrigerator for up to 24 hours, covered with a lid or tightly wrapped.

Ellis Cooley

Pan-Roasted Walleye

Crème Fraîche Beets

Apple, Walnut, & Endive Salad

Individual Chocolate
Lava Cakes

Ellis Cooley

Former Executive Chef, AMP 150 (Cleveland Airport Marriott)

Accolades: Dually honored as both a Top Chef and a Rising Star by *Restaurant Hospitality*; selected by the Almond Board of California and the Culinary Institute of America in Napa Valley to participate in their Almond Innovation Project; designated as one of the Best New Midwest Places to Play, Eat and Stay by *Midwest Living*; named Best New Chef and Best New Restaurant by *Cleveland Scene*; rave reviews in *Cleveland Magazine, Cleveland Scene,* and the *Plain Dealer*; recognized as one of the Top 100 Restaurants by the *Plain Dealer*; listed in the "Best of Cleveland" issue of *Cleveland Magazine*; recognized by *Green Lodging News*; named one of four Top Chefs at the St. John Medical Center's Festival of the Arts; featured on WKYC-TV 3 and WJW-TV 8.

Although Ellis grew up in Atlanta, the world has been his playground. Immediately after graduating from Mount Paran School, he went to work at the nationally acclaimed restaurant Canoe, located in the charming historic Atlanta community of Vinings. But he soon became restless and set his sights on traveling—and cooking—as much as he could.

Ellis's journey first took him to Ft. Lauderdale, where he worked in the kitchen at 3030 Ocean. Then he ventured overseas to Spain with the luxury Hotel Arts Barcelona and the Michelin 3-star restaurant El Celler de Can Roca (also the fourth best restaurant in the world as per *Restaurant*) . . . then to France, Germany, and Austria. While working with star chefs at prime establishments, he was told he had a lot of natural talent—which encouraged him even further. He eventually headed back to the States, this time to New York City.

It was while in New York that Ellis finally started to make his mark. He was asked to open the restaurant at the posh, award-winning Hotel on Rivington on Manhattan's Lower East Side. Next came a plum position at The New York Palace, a spectacular hotel in Midtown. This was followed by a

Ellis's secret tip for last-minute entertaining? "Season your food and taste it before your guests do."

stint in Miami as a consultant for a conglomerate of private condominiums. Then . . . Cleveland came calling.

Because of his background, expertise, and proven success, Ellis was invited to open a newly revamped restaurant at the Marriott Airport Hotel on West 150th Street. The concept for the new restaurant (which was aptly named AMP 150, an acronym for "America's Modern Palate" and a reference to its location) was developed by award-winning chef Dean James Max with an emphasis on farm-to-table cooking, inventive combinations, and small plates.

Ellis was up for the exciting challenge. So he accepted the position and moved to Cleveland. "What better place than Cleveland to work alongside so many up-and-coming chefs and be surrounded by farms, too?" he says.

Ellis got straight to work with a contagious enthusiasm. He was so focused on offering the freshest, highest-quality seasonal ingredients available locally that he decided to plant an onsite garden. With the help of his kitchen staff, Ellis personally helped clear a neglected, quarter-acre plot of land behind the hotel parking lot and sowed a variety of seeds. He suddenly had the freshest vegetables and herbs possible with which to make his fabulous dishes.

Not one to be easily satisfied, Ellis took it even one step further and placed not one or two but *three* beehives on the hotel roof! (Suggestion: Be sure to order a dish at AMP 150 that contains honey. You'll know exactly where it came from.)

Note: Ellis eventually had to make a very hard decision: his love of Cleveland or his young son, Marcus, who lives in Florida. He chose his son and took a position, still with Marriott, in West Palm Beach.

In his time off, Ellis likes visiting exotic places and participating in outdoor activities such as surfing, skateboarding, and organized sports. Believe it or not, he also enjoys going out to eat! It's sometimes nice being on the other side of the kitchen.

Ellis now lives in West Palm Beach, Florida.

Pan-Roasted Walleye

4 servings

Oftentimes less is more—as in this deceptively simplistic pescetarian dish. Four ingredients. Easy preparation. But a flavor so intensely delicious, it's unlike any other. Then again, it helps to live in Cleveland and have access to the freshest walleye available. With spring and fall being the peak seasons for walleye fishing, be sure, if you can, to buy local.

4 (7-ounce) pieces fresh walleye, preferably Lake Erie, deboned
Sea salt and freshly ground black pepper
2 tablespoons extra-virgin olive oil

1. With a sharp knife, score a few short parallel slash marks about 1 inch apart just through the skin of the fish down the middle. (Tip: It helps make cutting easier if you carefully apply some pressure along both long sides of the fish toward the middle to puff it up a bit.)

2. Season both sides of the fish with salt and pepper to taste.

3. Heat the oil in a sauté pan on medium-high heat until it smokes.

4. Add the fish, skin side down, and reduce the heat to medium. Sauté for 3 minutes, or until the skin is crispy.

5. Turn, preferably using a fish spatula, and cook for another 2 minutes. Take off the heat. Let rest at least 1 minute. Serve warm.

Crème Fraîche Beets

4 servings

Even if you're not a fan of beets, this dish is sure to make a convert out of you. The tanginess of the crème fraîche (a soured cream containing about 28 percent butterfat) and the lemon juice balances the earthy sweetness of the beets just perfectly.

Kosher salt
3 large red beets, washed, unpeeled
1 bay leaf
1 cup crème fraîche (see note)
1 teaspoon unsalted butter
1 teaspoon water
Freshly squeezed juice of ½ lemon
1 teaspoon chopped fresh dill

1. In a small pot of salted water, add the beets and bay leaf. Bring to a boil, then turn down the heat and simmer for 15 to 20 minutes, or until the beets are just tender when pierced with a fork.

2. Drain the beets. Peel and quarter them lengthwise, then cut each quarter in half crosswise.

3. Place the cut beets back into the pot along with the crème fraîche, butter, and 1 teaspoon water. Slowly bring to a boil.

4. Once the mixture boils, stir in the lemon juice and dill. Take off the heat and serve immediately.

NOTE: If you can't find or afford store-bought crème fraîche, you can make it yourself, although it does take time. Just add 2 tablespoons of buttermilk to 1 cup of heavy cream (preferably pasteurized versus ultra-pasteurized). Allow to sit out in a warm place, covered, for 12 to 24 hours, or until thick. Stir, cover, and refrigerate (where it will continue to thicken) for up to 10 days.

WINE PAIRINGS

France: Bordeaux—Sauternes or other Botrytis Sémillon/ Sauvignon blend
Germany: Mosel—Riesling Kabinett
USA: Oregon—Pinot Noir

Apple, Walnut, & Endive Salad

4 servings

This is an incredibly versatile salad, just as great for an intimate dinner for two as for a large crowd. And the dressing's secret ingredient? Walnut oil, which lends a rich, nutty flavor. The bonus is that endive is a nutritional powerhouse, loaded with many vitamins and minerals. And be sure to use a crisp apple variety, preferably from a local orchard when in season.

1 head French endive (or Belgian endive)
1 Honey Crisp apple (or other crispy red apple such as Gala, McIntosh, or Braeburn)
½ cup walnuts, toasted and coarsely chopped (see note)
1 tablespoon chopped fresh chives
¼ cup Walnut Vinaigrette (recipe follows)
Sea salt and coarsely ground black pepper

1. Trim the bottom off each endive. Cut in half lengthwise, then cut crosswise into thin strips.

2. Quarter, core, and peel the apples. Cut each quarter into thin lengthwise slices.

3. Immediately toss the endive, apples, and walnuts in a bowl, together with the chives and walnut vinaigrette. Season with salt and pepper to taste.

4. When ready to serve, divide among 4 salad plates.

NOTE: To toast walnuts, preheat the oven to 325°. Spread the walnuts in a single layer on a cookie sheet and bake until golden brown, about 10 to 12 minutes, checking and stirring frequently. Or cook walnuts in a skillet on medium-high heat for 3 to 5 minutes, stirring frequently.

Walnut Vinaigrette

1 tablespoon Dijon mustard
1 tablespoon honey
¼ cup champagne vinegar (can substitute white wine vinegar or any white vinegar)
Scant ⅔ cup walnut oil (can substitute olive oil)

1. Whisk all the ingredients together well. Reserve any remaining vinaigrette for another use.

Individual Chocolate Lava Cakes

4 servings

The beauty of this cake is the surprise in the middle: a warm and lusciously moist center that literally oozes chocolate decadence with every slice. Some call it a molten cake, others a volcano cake. Whatever you call it, it's pure heaven. And the versatility of this particular recipe is that you can make it as four individual-size cakes or eight mini cakes (serving two per person). Then again, you may just want to make a double or triple batch. It's that good.

Melted unsalted butter to grease
Granulated sugar
4 ounces 50% to 66% high-quality dark chocolate, preferably Valrhona, chopped
4 ounces (1 stick) unsalted butter
1 cup powdered sugar
3 large eggs plus 2 yolks
⅓ cup all-purpose flour, sifted
Unsweetened cocoa powder
Chantilly Cream (recipe at left)

1. Preheat the oven to 400°. Brush the interior of four (8-ounce) ovenproof mugs or ramekins (or 8 muffin cups) with the melted butter. Dust with granulated sugar.

2. Melt the chocolate and butter in a saucepan over medium heat, stirring until smooth. Remove from the heat and let cool slightly. (Alternatively, you can microwave until melted.)

3. Combine the powdered sugar, eggs, and egg yolks in a stainless-steel bowl. Stir well just until blended; do not overmix. Add the warm chocolate and stir until smooth. Stir in the flour.

4. Divide the batter evenly among the mugs and bake for about 7 to 8 minutes. Don't overbake! The cakes should still have a wet center.

5. Let cool slightly in the molds, run a knife around the edges, then invert onto serving dishes. Dust each cake lightly with sifted cocoa powder and serve with a dollop of Chantilly Cream.

Chantilly Cream

Makes about 2 cups

1 cup heavy cream, chilled
2 tablespoons superfine sugar
½ teaspoon pure vanilla extract
   (can substitute seeds of ½ vanilla bean)

1. Whisk the cream, sugar, and vanilla in a large chilled bowl until soft peaks form. The cream should hold its shape but still be smooth and satiny in appearance. It should never be grainy, which means it's been overwhipped. (If this happens, just fold in a couple tablespoons of unwhipped cream, which will bring it back to the proper consistency. This won't work, however, if you have overwhipped it to the point where it has completely separated and looks like butter.) If desired, Chantilly cream can be refrigerated, well covered with plastic wrap, for several hours. Before serving, lightly whisk it again to bring it back to its original consistency.

Paul Courtwright

Chunky Guacamole with Feta

Smokin' Chicken Tacos
with Roasted Vegetables
& Cilantro Slaw

Mexican Rice

Mexican Hot Fudge Sundae

Paul Courtwright

Executive Chef, Shoreby Club

Accolades: Featured in numerous publications and media, including *Food & Wine*, the *New York Times*, the *Washington Post*, *Currents*, the *Plain Dealer*, the *Akron Beacon Journal*, *Cvent*, *Cleveland Foodie*, *The330*, *Outside.in*, *Local Wine Events*, and *Cool Cleveland*.

Paul remembers making full-course family dinners when he was only ten years old. Even at that young age, he enjoyed the thrill of it all. The gathering of ingredients . . . the preparation of dishes (albeit simple ones like mac-and-cheese and fried bologna sandwiches) . . . the final presentation on the table . . . and his family's reaction. They loved it! And since both parents worked, they really appreciated their son's newfound interest—and talent. They were also very proud that Paul had found his true passion and calling in life, even if he might not have realized it himself just yet.

Paul grew up in Cleveland but moved to Strongsville, Ohio, when he was thirteen. His first job was at the Pomeroy House as a dishwasher. After graduating from Strongsville High School, he attended Cleveland State University for a year. Then he transferred to Baldwin-Wallace College. After another year, he became adventurous and wanted to try somewhere altogether new, so he transferred to Montana State University. This history major finally returned to Cleveland, where he went back to work at the Pomeroy House in order to hone his natural culinary skills. He quickly worked his way up to lead line cook under the tutelage of the talented chef Chris Olszewski, now a training instructor at Polaris Career Center.

Even though Paul really enjoyed what he was doing, he eventually wanted a break. In fact, after putting in such long hours and such hard work in the kitchen for seven years, he *needed* a break. So he got a new job. A stable, nine-to-five bank job as a data entry clerk.

Paul's secret tip for last-minute entertaining? "Don't panic. Keep it simple. Have a cocktail."

Two years later, he was sitting in his cubicle when all of a sudden it hit him like a ton of bricks. "I suddenly realized," says Paul, "correction, I suddenly *knew* that working behind a desk all day just wasn't for me. I needed to get back into the kitchen and do what I love to do most—cook." Even if that meant long hours and hard work all over again.

Paul decided to join the fine dining services of the exclusive Shoreby Club as a line cook, eventually advancing to sous chef. And then the top position for executive chef became available. "I went for it and applied as a candidate," explains Paul. "I was fortunate enough to have been chosen. Not only do I really love what I do, but I also love where I work."

Admittedly, working in a private club is quite different from working in a restaurant. But how, exactly? For starters, this club/mansion has eight separate dining areas plus a catering division that serves all five hundred of its members. Which means Paul and his staff need to be able to prepare everything from basic waffles and salads to lobster Thermidor and salmon Wellington. They also have to be willing and able to accommodate all special requests, including oxtail soup. The most plates they've had to prepare in a single day? Three hundred!

And then there's the fact that "it's always something different every single day we walk through that door," explains Paul. "It's never, ever boring. It's actually a very strange but wonderful world we live in over here."

In his spare time, Paul, a self-described bookworm, likes to read history and science fiction.

Paul lives in Cleveland's Old Brooklyn neighborhood with his wife, Heather, and their two sons, Kaelib and Aaron.

Chunky Guacamole with Feta

4 servings

Paul says if he could eat only one cuisine, it would be Mexican. Which is why this appetizer is such a favorite of his. It's simple. It's quick. And it's healthy—with a slight twist: feta cheese. Be sure to look for avocados that are relatively free of bruises and yield to pressure when gently squeezed. (Tip: If pressing leaves a dent, the avocado is ready for mashing, which this recipe requires.) If you do end up buying avocados that are hard and unripened, just place them in a brown paper bag with an apple, banana, or citrus fruit, all of which release ethylene. Once the desired stage of ripeness has been achieved, refrigerate and use within 2 to 3 days.

½ red onion, diced
1 jalapeño chile, seeded and diced
1 garlic clove, finely chopped
1 tomato, cored, seeded, and diced
2 tablespoons finely chopped fresh cilantro

3 ripe avocados
Freshly squeezed juice of 1 lime
½ teaspoon salt
3 tablespoons crumbled feta cheese, plus additional for optional garnish
Tortilla chips

1. Mix the onion, jalapeño, garlic, tomato, and cilantro in a small bowl until well combined. Set aside.

2. Cut the avocados in half and pit, then scoop the flesh into a large bowl. Add the lime juice and salt. Mash roughly with a fork or pound with the tip of a whisk until only all the large lumps are gone.

3. Add the onion mix and feta to the mashed avocado. Stir until well combined, then place in a serving bowl. If desired, garnish with additional feta. Serve immediately, with the tortilla chips alongside.

Mexican Rice

4 servings

This version of Mexican rice, a popular staple in many Mexican recipes, is particularly tasty, making good use of the freshest ingredients and a perfect blend of seasonings. Serve it alongside fajitas, tamales, or tacos (as Paul does here), as part of a buffet, or as a healthy lunchtime snack.

1 tablespoon extra-virgin olive oil
1 cup long-grain rice
2 garlic cloves, finely chopped
2 cups chicken stock
¼ cup canned, jarred, or homemade tomato sauce
1 Roma (plum) tomato, cut into 8 wedges
½ Spanish onion, diced
1 jalapeño chile, seeded and diced
1 teaspoon ground cumin

1. Heat the oil in a saucepan over medium heat until it shimmers, 1 to 2 minutes. Add the rice. Cook, stirring occasionally, until the rice browns slightly, 2 to 3 minutes. It's important that you see some browning before continuing!

2. Add the garlic and cook until fragrant, from 15 to 30 seconds only. Add the stock plus the remaining ingredients, stir well, and cover.

3. Reduce the heat to medium low. Cook for 20 to 30 minutes, or until the rice is fluffy and all the liquid is absorbed. Remove from the stove and keep warm until ready to serve.

BEER PAIRINGS

USA: Microbrew—India Pale Ale or other hoppy ale
USA: Microbrew—Pilsner or other pale lager
USA: Microbrew—Vienna or other amber lager

Smokin' Chicken Tacos with Roasted Vegetables & Cilantro Slaw

4 servings (3 tacos per person)

The secret ingredient in this spicy version of chicken tacos? Paul's very own special spice rub. Yes, you can go ahead and use regular paprika instead of the smoked Spanish paprika it calls for, and regular chile powder instead of the chipotle chile powder. But be warned, it just won't have that same intense smoky flavor that Paul loves so much. For a fish variation, feel free to use 1 pound of any white flaky fish (such as tilapia or skin-off striped bass) instead of the chicken.

2 zucchini, quartered lengthwise
1 red bell pepper, cored, seeded, and cut into 1-inch-wide strips
1 yellow onion, cut into thick julienne strips
Extra-virgin olive oil
Spice Rub (recipe at right), divided
4 (4-ounce) boneless, skinless chicken breasts
1 tablespoon vegetable oil
12 (6-inch) soft corn tortillas (can substitute flour tortillas), warmed
Cilantro Slaw (recipe at right)
Sour cream
2 limes, cut into wedges

1. Preheat the oven to 450°.

2. Combine the zucchini, red bell pepper, and onion on a baking sheet. Drizzle with some extra-virgin olive oil and toss to coat.

3. Sprinkle some of the Spice Rub over the vegetables and toss to coat. Roast in the oven for 20 to 30 minutes, or until tender.

4. In the meantime, slice the chicken breasts ½ inch thick, then cut crosswise into ½-inch strips and place in a bowl. Drizzle with more of the extra-virgin olive oil, then toss with enough of the remaining Spice Rub to coat well on all sides.

5. Heat the vegetable oil in a sauté pan over medium-high heat. Add the chicken strips and sauté, tossing occasionally, until cooked through, about 4 to 5 minutes. Take off the heat and remove the chicken strips to a bowl.

6. When the vegetables are done, cut the roasted zucchini into ½-inch pieces, then add all to the chicken in the bowl. Toss to combine.

7. To serve family style, place the chicken and roasted vegetables, along with the tortillas, Cilantro Slaw, sour cream, and lime wedges on the table. Allow your guests to assemble their own tacos. Or assemble the tacos yourself and serve individually plated.

Spice Rub

¼ cup smoked Spanish paprika (can substitute regular paprika)
1 tablespoon salt
2¼ teaspoons chipotle chile powder (can substitute regular chile powder)
1½ teaspoons packed brown sugar
1 teaspoon freshly ground black pepper
2 garlic cloves, finely chopped

1. Combine all the ingredients in a small bowl and stir to mix well.

Cilantro Slaw

4 servings

2 cups shredded green cabbage
½ cup finely chopped fresh cilantro
2 tablespoons fresh lime juice
1½ teaspoons water
1½ teaspoons honey
¼ teaspoon ground cumin
Salt and freshly ground black pepper

1. Combine all the ingredients except the salt and pepper in a glass, stainless-steel, or ceramic bowl and toss to mix well. Season with salt and pepper to taste. Refrigerate until ready to serve.

Mexican Hot Fudge Sundae

4 servings

This version of the iconic ice cream sundae, a favorite dessert at the Courtwright household, has been tweaked until everyone agrees it just can't get any better. With a hint of sweet cinnamon and a touch of spicy chile powder, the uniquely decadent fudge sauce is served warm over cold and creamy dulce de leche ice cream. This flavor of ice cream is readily available today in most supermarkets. Or make your own, like Paul does.

8 ounces bittersweet or semisweet chocolate, chopped
½ cup water
¼ teaspoon ground cinnamon
¼ teaspoon chile powder
¼ teaspoon pure vanilla extract
½ cup evaporated milk
1 tablespoon Kahlúa
12 small scoops dulce de leche ice cream
Sweetened Whipped Cream (recipe at right) for garnish,
    optional
Sliced strawberries for garnish, optional
Spanish peanuts for garnish, optional

1. Combine the chocolate, water, cinnamon, chile powder, and vanilla in a small saucepan over medium heat. Stir until the chocolate is melted and the mixture is smooth. (Do not add any more water than called for.)

2. Remove from the heat and add the evaporated milk and Kahlúa. Stir until blended and smooth.

3. Place 3 scoops of ice cream in each dessert bowl and drizzle with some of the warm chocolate sauce. If desired, top with Sweetened Whipped Cream and sprinkle with sliced strawberries, Spanish peanuts, and more warm chocolate sauce. Serve immediately.

Sweetened Whipped Cream

1. Combine 1 cup chilled heavy cream and 2 tablespoons granulated sugar in a chilled bowl. Whip until stiff peaks form.

John D'Amico

Cream of Butternut Squash
& Roasted Red Pepper Soup

Seared Mediterranean Bronzini
with Verjus Butter Sauce &
Sautéed Fennel

Roast Duck Breast with
Cherry Glace de Viande

Sweet Potato Mousseline

Madeleines

John D'Amico

Chef/Partner, Chez François, Riverfront Café, Touché

Accolades: Named one of the Ten Best International Restaurants by 10Best; multiple winner of OpenTable's national Diner's Choice award; honored with an Award of Unique Distinction by *Wine Enthusiast;* voted the Second Best Waterfront Dining in America by *Power and Motor Yacht;* highest Zagat ratings; recognized as one of the Hot 10 Cleveland Restaurants and Top 10 Cleveland Food Rating Restaurants by *Gayot Guide;* named Best French Restaurant by *Northern Ohio Live;* recognized as an A-List Restaurant by the *Plain Dealer;* featured in numerous publications and media, including *Balanced Living, Crain's Cleveland Business, Cleveland Magazine,* the *Lakewood Observer,* the *Plain Dealer,* the *Toledo Blade,* the *Morning Journal, Chowhound, Hello Cleveland, Travel Muse, Urbanspoon, Midwest Today,* WJW-TV 8, and CBS 11 TV.

John's secret tip for last-minute entertaining? "Always have a good mise en place, which means 'everything in its place.' Make sure you gather all the cooking tools your recipe calls for and have all the ingredients prepped ahead of time. That way you can cook more efficiently and without interruption, which is especially important when you have time constraints."

"Cooking and food have always been a part of my life. In fact, it was actually a *hobby* for my family!" says John, who grew up in a large, extended, multigenerational Italian clan on Cleveland's West Side. "As a result of this 'hobby,' family and friends realized I had a knack for it and suggested I look into becoming a chef, which I did. And that was that."

While attending St. Edward High School, John took his first job as a dishwasher at the now defunct Pagliacci's restaurant, owned by Frank Mars, on the West Side. By the time John left Cleveland for the University of Denver, he had already swiftly moved up to the position of cook.

While in school, he decided to join the Denver Chapter of the American Culinary Federation as an extracurricular activity. John then decided to take it one step further and also enrolled in their apprenticeship culinary arts program through a local country club. Before he knew it, one year later, John left Denver, moved back home, and continued his apprenticeship with the federation's Cleveland chapter at a local country club. Simultaneously, he attended Cuyahoga Community College and graduated with an associate of applied business degree in the culinary arts.

To jump-start his professional culinary career, John joined the University Club of Cleveland as a sous chef-in-charge. He also did *stages* at other clubs, restaurants, and pastry shops so that he could observe and bring those experiences back to his job. Then, always one to keep bettering himself, John decided to seek certification as a chef, too. But in order to do so, he needed to obtain signed verifications of employment from his previous employers. So he went back to Pagliacci's and asked to see Frank. On that fateful day, Frank told him he had just found out a restaurant was suddenly for sale. The restaurant was L'Auberge du Port, a national historic landmark building in Vermilion. "Would you be interested in owning your own restaurant with my help?" asked Frank.

John mulled it over carefully. He finally decided to take up Frank's offer. That was in 1987. Today, decades later, Chez François is still as popular as ever. Not only does it continue to thrive, but it also continues to outdo itself—with John and his business partner (who happens to be Frank's son, Matt) at the helm. They added an adjoining waterfront café called, appropriately enough, Riverfront Café, plus a widely successful wine/martini bar called Touché. They also regularly host sold-out signature dinners and wine dinners.

The restaurant is indeed a family affair for John. His wife answers the phones and takes reservations. And his children work in the kitchen. "It's the only way I get to spend time with them!" says the busy chef.

In order to "regroup," John shuts down the restaurant every January and February—almost unheard of in the business. During those two months, he does any necessary remodeling to the restaurant, hires and trains new staff for the upcoming spring season, travels, visits the kitchens of other restaurants, and spends time with his family. In fact, a lot of quality time is spent fishing, camping, having fun, and just plain relaxing.

John and his wife, Heidi, live in Sheffield Village with their four grown children, John, Zachary, Samantha, and Maggie.

Cream of Butternut Squash & Roasted Red Pepper Soup

4 servings

This puree of butternut squash is so incredibly easy to make, yet the result is so impressive, you'll have your guests convinced you slaved over it all day. The secret ingredient here is the roasted red pepper, which lends an added layer of complexity and a depth of sweetness. If you have the time, roast your own pepper for the best taste (see note). Otherwise, just buy it jarred. (Tip: Double the recipe and serve the soup with crusty bread for a simple and satisfying stand-alone meal.)

1 large (about 2 pounds) butternut squash
2 tablespoons unsalted butter
1 small onion, diced
1 tablespoon chopped garlic (3 medium-size cloves)
1 tablespoon chopped shallot
2 cups heavy cream
1 large roasted red bell pepper, jarred or homemade (see note)
Sea salt and freshly ground white pepper
Crème fraîche or sour cream for garnish, optional
4 scallions (green onions), sliced, for garnish, optional

1. Using a sharp serrated knife, cut away the thick skin of the butternut squash until you reach its deeper orange color. Cut lengthwise in half and remove the seeds, then chop coarsely into small chunks. Set aside.

2. Heat the butter in a 4-quart saucepot over medium heat. Add the onion, garlic, and shallot and sauté until translucent. Remove with a slotted spoon and set aside.

3. Wipe the saucepot clean, then pour in 2 cups of water and bring to a boil over high heat. Add the squash and simmer for about 10 minutes, or until the squash is tender when pierced with a fork.

4. Without draining the water, mash the squash in the pot with a potato masher. Add the cream, roasted red pepper, onion mixture, and salt and pepper to taste. Stir together. Pour a small batch at a time into a blender. Puree for a creamy consistency, 30 to 60 seconds.

5. Divide the soup among 4 warm bowls. If desired for richness, garnish with a spoonful of crème fraîche and sprinkle with the scallions.

NOTE: To roast, rub a large red bell pepper with olive oil. Place the pepper over a flame on your grill, directly over a lit burner on your stovetop, or under a broiler and turn often until the outside is blackened, 3 to 4 minutes. Once it's blackened, remove to a small bowl and cover with plastic wrap for 5 minutes. Remove the skin and seeds.

Seared Mediterranean Bronzini with Verjus Butter Sauce & Sautéed Fennel

4 servings

While bronzini (also known as Mediterranean sea bass and extremely popular in Italian, Spanish, and Greek cuisines) may not be the easiest fish to find, it certainly is worth the search for its sweet-flavored, semifirm white meat. Try your better grocery or seafood stores. This delectable version is served over braised fennel, topped with a light verjus butter sauce, and garnished with delicate, fried fennel fronds. As an FYI, verjus is a mildly acidic juice usually made from unripe grapes. Its slightly sour taste is used to heighten the flavor of many wonderful dishes, including this one.

4 (3-ounce) skin-on portions bronzini fillet (can substitute barramundi or perch)
1 large fennel bulb with fronds
6 to 8 tablespoons olive oil, divided
Sea salt and freshly ground black pepper
½ cup white verjus (can substitute white grape juice)
4 ounces (1 stick) unsalted butter
2 tablespoons chopped fresh parsley

1. Using a sharp knife, score just the skin (not the flesh) of each bronzini piece three times with a small "x." This will keep the fish from curling while cooking. Set aside.

2. Separate the fronds from the fennel and set aside; this will be your garnish. Slice the fennel paper thin, ideally on a mandolin if you have one.

3. Heat 2 tablespoons of the oil in a sauté pan over medium heat and sauté the fennel until transparent. Remove from the pan and set aside.

4. Wipe the pan clean. Season the bronzini pieces on the skin side only with salt and pepper to taste. Heat 2 tablespoons of the oil in the same pan on medium-high heat just until it starts to steam. Add the fish, skin side down.

5. Sear on the skin side only until the fish pieces are almost white or opaque, about 3 minutes. Do not flip. If you need more oil, add up to 2 tablespoons.

6. Remove the fish from the pan. Deglaze the pan with the verjus, scraping with a spoon or spatula to dislodge the fond (the flavorful brown bits stuck to the bottom of the pan). Add the butter and chopped parsley. Keep cooking just until the butter is melted. Take off the heat and remove to a small bowl.

7. Wipe the pan clean. Heat the remaining 2 tablespoons oil in the same pan on medium-high heat. Add the fennel fronds (just the frilly tips). Lightly fry until crispy.

8. To assemble, divide the sautéed fennel among 4 serving plates. Top carefully with a portion of bronzini fillet, skin side up. Drizzle with the verjus butter sauce and garnish with the fried fennel fronds.

Roast Duck Breast with Cherry Glace de Viande

4 servings

Duck breast, which is known for its dark, succulent meat, is generally available fresh from late spring through early winter. But you can also find it frozen year-round in your grocery store. This particular version features a lightly peppered breast served over a bed of sweet potato mousseline and finished with a Frangelico and cherry *glace de viande* (French for "meat glaze"). One bite and you'll swear you're in heaven.

2 (8-ounce) duck breasts, thawed if frozen
1 teaspoon coarsely ground black pepper
Pinch of sea salt
½ cup olive oil
1 cup chicken or veal stock, divided
1 teaspoon cornstarch
1 cup dried cherries
2 ounces (¼ cup) Frangelico
Sweet Potato Mousseline (recipe at right)

1. Preheat the oven to 350°.

2. Lightly season the duck breasts with the pepper and salt. Heat the oil in a sauté pan over medium-high heat and sear the duck breasts, skin side down, for about 3 to 4 minutes, or until golden brown.

3. Remove the duck breasts from the pan and transfer to a baking dish, skin side up; set the pan with the drippings aside. Bake the duck breasts for 10 minutes, then remove from the oven and let rest for 5 minutes.

4. Meanwhile, stir ½ cup of the stock into the cornstarch in a bowl until smooth. Set aside.

5. To the duck drippings in the sauté pan, add the cherries, Frangelico, and remaining ½ cup stock. Bring to a boil and cook, stirring occasionally, for 2 minutes. Slowly add the cornstarch mixture, stirring constantly. Continue to stir until reduced by half, about 2 minutes.

6. Slice the duck meat, then assemble the dish by placing a mound of Sweet Potato Mousseline on each serving plate. Top with a sliced duck breast, then drizzle with the cherry sauce. Serve immediately.

Sweet Potato Mousseline

4 servings

1 pound sweet potatoes
4 tablespoons (½ stick) unsalted butter, at room temperature
Sea salt and freshly ground black pepper

1. Peel the sweet potatoes and cut into small chunks. Bring 2 cups of water to a boil in a saucepan. Add the sweet potatoes and cook for 10 minutes. Drain.

2. With your mixer on high speed, whip the sweet potatoes and butter until a light and delicate texture has been achieved. Season with salt and pepper to taste, then set aside and keep warm, covered.

WINE PAIRINGS

Australia: South Australia—Semillon blend or Chardonnay
France: Rhône—Gigondas
Spain: Rias Baixas—Albariño

Madeleines

4 servings (5 cookies per person)

How to best describe these delicacies lauded by Proust in his literary masterwork, *Remembrance of Things Past?* Some may say they are small, buttery, feather-light sponge cakes resembling elongated scallop shells that have a moist interior and an exquisitely crisp exterior. But even this elaborate description does them little justice, really. Serve fresh and warm, straight out of the oven, and you'll quickly see why absolutely no words seem quite adequate enough.

1 cup all-purpose flour
½ cup granulated sugar
Pinch of salt
2 large eggs
Freshly grated zest of ½ lemon
¼ cup clarified butter (see note)
Powdered sugar for dusting

1. Preheat the oven to 350°. Thoroughly grease a madeleine pan with a vegetable spray such as Pam.

2. Combine the flour, sugar, and salt in a bowl. Stir in the eggs to mix thoroughly, then the lemon zest. Stir the clarified butter into the mixture until smooth.

3. Scoop about 2 tablespoons of the batter into each greased indentation of the madeleine pan. Bake for about 10 to 12 minutes, or until the edges are golden brown.

4. Unmold immediately and dust the ridged side lightly with powdered sugar. Best served warm.

NOTE: To clarify butter, melt 4 ounces (1 stick) unsalted butter slowly in a pan over low heat. Do not stir! Also, do not cook too much longer after it has all melted; you don't want it to burn. Let it sit for a bit to separate. With a tablespoon, skim off and discard the white foam that rose to the top. Then either slowly pour the butter out, being careful to leave the remaining solids at the bottom of your pan, or strain the butter through a fine sieve or cheesecloth-lined strainer. (Any unused clarified butter can be refrigerated, covered, almost indefinitely.)

Matt Del Regno

Trio of Steak, Chicken, &
Veggie Skewers

Maytag Spinach Pasta Salad

Blackberry Buckle

Matt Del Regno

Executive Chef, Levy Restaurants at Cleveland Browns Stadium

Accolades: Handpicked by Wolfgang Puck as one of only several nationwide Five Star Sensation chefs to join him for a University Hospitals Seidman Cancer Center fundraiser; headed over forty significant events or grand openings across the country; chef coordinator/contributor for both Super Bowl XL in Detroit and Super Bowl XLIII in Tampa; three-time host chef for the Taste of the NFL; two-time Levy Legend award winner; featured in numerous publications and media, including the *Chicago Tribune,* the *Chicago Sun-Times,* the *Pioneer Press, Nation's Restaurant News, 60035, Ravinia Magazine,* the *Plain Dealer,* NBC5's *Morning Show,* WKYC-TV 3, WJW-TV 8, and WXRT.

Self-described as being "high maintenance" when he was young, Matt needed to keep busy to stay out of trouble. So his mom would have him help her bake. Together, they would make lots of cookies (peanut blossoms and cream wafers) and tons of breads (zucchini and carrot). As a result, "I wasn't exactly a slim kid," laughs Matt. "But I knew what I liked. And I liked spending time in the kitchen."

At only fifteen, Matt got his first job with Novotny Catering, a family-owned business in Avon Lake, Ohio, where he grew up. "Seeing the ins and outs of food service and hospitality got me hooked," he recalls. "Plus, I loved the free meals!" But it wasn't until his junior year at Avon Lake High School that he realized his future might very well be in restaurants. "I remember thinking about other careers and not being able to imagine not being in a kitchen," he confesses.

So, after graduating from high school, Matt headed straight to the Pennsylvania Institute of Culinary Arts (now Le Cordon Bleu Institute of Culinary Arts) in Pittsburgh. He did his externship at, of all places, Disneyland Paris! It was supposed to only be for five weeks, but in order to extend his stay, he applied for—and was granted—a separate apprenticeship with them, which turned into five glorious months in France.

Matt's secret tip for last-minute entertaining? "Always have a bottle of champagne chilled. And don't be afraid to use it!"

Back in the U.S. with a new culinary degree in hand, Matt went to work for Interstate Hotels at the Marriott in Pittsburgh. Less than a year later, he returned to Ohio, accepting a position in Cleveland with Levy Restaurants at Jacobs Field (now Progressive Field), in their Terrace Club. After five seasons there, he spent the next several seasons at different Levy-run venues, including the Qwest Center in Omaha, Nebraska; the Green Bay Packers' Lambeau Field in Wisconsin; and Ravinia Music Festival in Chicago (summer home of the Chicago Symphony Orchestra), where he cooked nightly for the likes of Aretha Franklin, Tony Bennett, and hundreds of other performers.

It was at Ravinia that Matt spent three years helping to develop a huge, brand-new, state-of-the-art restaurant complex. But just six months after this magnificent complex opened, he got a call from one of his most trusted longtime friends who had just taken a position at the Cleveland Browns Stadium. She called to tell Matt that the executive chef there had resigned right before opening season. Was he interested in the job?

"It was one of the most difficult decisions I have ever had to make," says Matt, considering he had just opened such a mammoth project so dear to his heart. "But Cleveland is my home, and I couldn't pass up the opportunity to bring my family back to its roots." So when Levy offered him the position, Matt jumped at the chance. His duties are now both diverse and exciting: running eight mini restaurants, overseeing the chef's tables and club action stations, supervising game-day catering for 145 suites, and managing all private catering events. Go Browns!

When not working, Matt can be found tinkering on a 1974 Volkswagen Beetle he's trying to restore and which he hopes to have ready by the time his daughter is ready to drive—five years from now.

Matt and his wife, Melisa, live in Avon Lake with their four young children, Sophia, Louis, Amelia, and Oliver. Their mutts, Monkey and Rooney, are part of the clan, too.

Trio of Steak, Chicken, & Veggie Skewers

4 servings

A Del Regno family summertime favorite, this colorful and flavorful dish has something for everyone: meat, poultry, and vegetables. If preparing during the winter, feel free to use your oven broiler or indoor grill pan. Helpful tip: When buying the skirt steak, be sure to ask your butcher to trim the fat in order to save yourself the grief!

1 pound skirt steak, fat trimmed (can substitute any grilling steak but not pre-diced stew meat)
4 large boneless, skinless chicken thighs (can substitute chicken breast)
1 red bell pepper, cored, seeded, and cut into 2-inch pieces
1 small Vidalia onion, cut into wedges
8 ounces medium-size fresh cremini mushrooms
8 green patty pan squash (can substitute 8 thick slices of green zucchini)
8 yellow sunburst squash (can substitute 8 thick slices of yellow crookneck squash)
3 cups Honey Mustard Vinaigrette (recipe at right)
Kosher salt and freshly cracked black pepper

1. Soak 12 wooden bamboo skewers, totally submerged under water, for at least 10 minutes before grilling. Preheat the grill (preferably hardwood charcoal) to medium-high heat, or to 450° if using a propane or natural gas grill.

2. Slicing against the grain, cut the skirt steak into 4-inch pieces, then into 2-inch cubes.

3. Remove the excess fat from the chicken thighs. Cut them into 2-inch cubes.

4. Place all the vegetables in one large zippered plastic bag, then put the steak and chicken each into their own bag. Pour 1 cup of the Honey Mustard Vinaigrette into each bag and seal. Work around with your hands to ensure proper coating, then let rest for 10 to 15 minutes on your countertop.

5. Remove the marinated vegetables from the bag and thread onto four of the presoaked wooden skewers, alternating vegetables. Place the skewers on a plate.

6. Thread all the steak pieces onto four more skewers. Place them on another plate.

7. Thread the chicken pieces onto the remaining four skewers. Place them on a third plate. (This separation eliminates cross contamination.)

8. Place all the skewers on the preheated grill, turning often to prevent burning. As you turn the skewers, season liberally with salt and pepper to taste.

9. Once the vegetables and steak are charred, take off the grill and set aside.

10. Continue to cook the chicken through, moving to a cooler part of the grill if necessary to prevent them from burning. Before removing from the grill, slit a few chicken pieces open to check for doneness. If any pink remains, place back on the grill, checking frequently. Do not overcook.

11. Serve each person three skewers (one steak, one chicken, and one vegetable), arranging them, if desired, alongside a bed of Maytag Spinach Pasta Salad (recipe on page 61).

Honey Mustard Vinaigrette

Yields 4 cups

This very versatile vinaigrette actually serves a triple purpose in Matt's meal. Of the 4 cups the recipe makes, 3 cups are used as the marinade for the skewers, ½ cup is used as the dressing for the salad, and the last ½ cup is saved as a salad dressing for lunch or dinner tomorrow!

½ cup Dijon mustard, preferably Grey Poupon
6 tablespoons champagne vinegar (can substitute rice wine vinegar, same as rice vinegar)
6 tablespoons red wine vinegar
¼ cup honey
1 tablespoon dried oregano
1 teaspoon minced garlic (1 medium-size clove)
2 cups extra-virgin olive oil
½ cup crumbled Maytag blue cheese
1 teaspoon kosher salt
½ teaspoon freshly ground black pepper

1. Combine the Dijon mustard, champagne vinegar, red wine vinegar, honey, oregano, and garlic in a blender or food processor and process until thoroughly blended. With the motor still running, slowly and carefully add the oil to emulsify.

2. Turn off the motor. Gently stir the blue cheese into the mixture with a wooden spoon or spatula until incorporated, then season with the salt and pepper. Taste and adjust the seasonings to your liking.

Maytag Spinach Pasta Salad

4 servings

This is not your ordinary spinach salad. The surprise is the pasta, in the delightful shape of *campanelle* (Italian for "little bells"). This delicate but sturdy shape adds a touch of elegance and charm to the salad. Its hollow center also serves to capture the Honey Mustard Vinaigrette and give a tangy burst of Maytag blue cheese flavor with every bite.

Kosher salt
10 slices bacon
½ cup campanelle pasta
4 ounces baby spinach
1 small head radicchio, torn
½ pint grape tomatoes, halved
½ small red onion, julienned
½ cup Honey Mustard Vinaigrette (recipe on page 60)
½ cup gently crumbled Maytag blue cheese for garnish

1. Preheat the oven to 350°. Bring a small pot of well-salted water to a boil.

2. Place the bacon on a cookie sheet. Bake in the oven until crisp, about 20 to 25 minutes. If using a thicker cut of bacon, flip once the top looks done and continue cooking until crisp.

3. While the bacon cooks, add the pasta to the boiling water. Cook according to package directions until al dente, then drain in a strainer or colander and rinse under cold running water until cool. Drain again well, then set aside in a salad bowl.

4. When the bacon is done, remove from the oven and place on paper towels to blot. When cool enough to handle, dice into ½-inch pieces.

5. Add the bacon, spinach, radicchio, tomatoes, and onion to the pasta in the salad bowl. Add the vinaigrette and toss well.

6. Divide the salad evenly among 4 salad plates or bowls. Garnish with the blue cheese to serve.

Blackberry Buckle

4 servings

This is a particularly satisfying comfort dessert. With its dense, firm filling, it's not at all too sweet. Its aromatic scent, puffy appearance, and beautiful golden color offer plenty of smell and eye appeal, too. Feel free to use any berry that's in season. And don't forget, a scoop of vanilla bean ice cream makes the perfect topping.

2 cups all-purpose flour
2 teaspoons baking powder
½ teaspoon ground cinnamon
½ teaspoon salt
8 ounces (2 sticks) unsalted butter, at room temperature
1½ cups granulated sugar
6 large eggs
1 pint blackberries
Vanilla bean ice cream, optional

1. Preheat the oven to 375°. Grease a 2-quart casserole dish or four 10-ounce ramekins.

2. Sift together the flour, baking powder, cinnamon, and salt. Set aside.

3. In a large bowl, beat the butter and sugar together until light and fluffy. Add the eggs, one at a time, and beat until well combined. Then add the flour mixture, a third at a time, beating well after each addition until smooth and consistent.

4. Pour the batter into the casserole dish or ramekins, then press the blackberries into the batter by hand. Bake for 45 to 60 minutes, depending on the size of the baking container, or until golden brown. To test for doneness, insert a toothpick into the center. It should come out clean.

5. Remove the buckle from the oven and allow to rest for 10 minutes. If desired, top with vanilla bean ice cream when ready to serve.

WINE PAIRINGS

USA: California—Red Meritage or Cabernet blend
USA: California, Napa or Sonoma—Zinfandel
USA: Washington State—Riesling

Brandt Evans

Farmers' Market Soup

Grilled Sirloin with
Maple-Chipotle Glaze

Banana Dulce de Leche
Flatbread

Brandt Evans

Chef/Owner, Blue Canyon Kitchen & Tavern (multiple locations), Pura Vida by Brandt

Accolades: Awarded multiple 5-diamond designations by AAA; appearance on the Food Network's *Cooking Live with Sara Moulton* show; won title of Grand Champion at the Taste of the NFL competition; named Best Chef and Best Restaurant by *Northern Ohio Live;* awarded Best Local Chef, Best Restaurant, Best New Restaurant, Best Place to be Seen, and Best Service by *Cleveland Magazine;* won *Akron Life & Leisure's* Best Chef award; named one of the Top 5 Restaurants on the Akron-Canton Hot List by FOX 8 News; regular contributor to *Better Homes & Gardens, Plate,* and *Texas Monthly Living;* featured in numerous publications and media, including *Restaurant Business,* the *Plain Dealer,* WKYC-TV 3, and WJW-TV 8.

It all started because of a dance. Brandt, only fifteen at the time, was a popular football player who wanted to go to homecoming. He asked his father for money. But his dad told him he'd have to earn the money himself. So Brandt got a dishwashing job at The Inn at Turners Mill in Hudson, Ohio. "That's the first time I ever saw gourmet ingredients," he admits. "Candy beets and watermelon radishes! Spaghetti squash! And yellow fin tuna, which didn't come from a can! I instantly fell in love with food and never turned back."

Brandt grew up in Hudson, the "baby" of the family, with two older brothers. His father expected the boys to help around the yard. But Brandt hated yard work, so he'd pretend he had to help his mother in the kitchen. "For us, food was at the center of everything we did," says Brandt, "whether celebrating or mourning. My mom taught me all about how to love food. So did my nana."

After graduating from Hudson High School, Brandt attended the University of Akron. His plan was to become a family and drug counselor. But his true passion kept

Brandt's secret tip for last-minute entertaining? "Hire me. I would love to come over and cook for you! But if that's not an option, try to get as much prep done ahead of time so you can spend time with your guests. Don't forget to season your food. And don't try new items out for the first time. Go with what you know."

nagging—until he finally relented and left to attend the Culinary Institute of America in upstate New York.

While a student at the CIA, Brandt did an externship at the fabled Four Seasons Hotel in Philadelphia under master French chef Jean-Marie La-Croix. After graduation, he left for the Big Apple and joined Charlie Palmer's late-night eatery, Alva, near Gramercy Park.

Brandt was there for a year and a half when he got a call from an old mentor, Tom Ward. "I was literally in Alva's kitchen when Tom phoned," says Brandt. "He asked me to come back to Cleveland and head his new restaurant, called Ward's Inn." Brandt accepted.

Brandt served as the executive chef of this Moreland Hills restaurant for three years. Then he started getting antsy. "I was thinking of moving to Atlanta, where my brother was living at the time," explains Brandt, "when I suddenly got another call, this time from Bob Voelker. He wanted me to open Kosta's in Tremont, Ohio. So I stayed there for almost four years as its executive chef. It was fun."

Brandt and Bob went on to become business partners, opening several restaurants together, including their flagship Blue Canyon in Twinsburg, Ohio, as well as related restaurants in Montana and Texas.

Brandt's newest venture, Pura Vida (loosely meaning "the good life"), is located in the old May Company building on Cleveland's Public Square. He's excited to be right next door to the new Tri-C Hospitality Center, which will be sharing many synergies and resources with him.

In his spare time, you'll most likely find Brandt doing one of two things: either studying (he's working toward his master's degree in business) or playing Latin percussion.

Brandt lives in Hudson with his wife, Kristen, and daughter, Madison. Their yellow Lab, Sunny, thinks he's part of the family, too.

Farmers' Market Soup

4 servings

This is what Brandt likes to call "Old World modern soup." Comforting. Delicious. And powerfully healthy. With the gaining popularity of farmers' markets throughout the country, it's easy to find any number of other greens you can substitute for the ones listed below. Just remember: the darker the green, the healthier. And for a modern twist, you may want to add any of the following ingredients to the soup at the very end to just heat through: sautéed or grilled shrimp; leftover roasted chicken, chopped up or shredded; or cooked rice or lentils.

6 cups chicken stock
5 ounces spinach leaves, stemmed and chiffonaded
5 ounces Swiss chard greens, tightly chiffonaded
5 ounces fresh sorrel leaves, chiffonaded (can substitute equal spinach plus 1 tablespoon lemon juice)
2 cups loosely packed fresh chervil (can substitute fresh basil)
1 cup loosely packed celery leaves
1 sweet white onion, diced (can substitute yellow onion)
1 garlic clove, minced
4 large egg yolks
Salt and freshly ground black pepper
Toasted bread cubes (see note) for garnish
Extra-virgin olive oil for drizzling

1. Heat the stock in a 4-quart saucepot over high heat. When the stock comes to a boil, add the spinach, Swiss chard, sorrel, chervil, celery leaves, onion, and garlic. Reduce the heat to medium low and simmer slowly for about 15 minutes.

2. Whisk the egg yolks in a small bowl. Season with salt and pepper to taste. When the soup is done simmering, slowly pour a ladleful (about ½ cup) of the hot liquid into the bowl with the egg mixture, stirring well. Slowly add this egg mixture back to the pot of soup, stirring well.

3. Remove the pot from the stove and ladle the soup into 4 warmed bowls. Right before serving, scatter the toasted bread cubes over the soup and drizzle with oil.

NOTE: To toast bread cubes, preheat the oven to 300°. Stack 4 slices of white bread on top of each other. Using a serrated knife, cut into large cubes; removing the crust is optional. Arrange the cubes in a single layer on a baking sheet and bake for 10 to 15 minutes, shaking once or twice, until lightly browned and crisp. Let cool.

WINE PAIRINGS

France: Champagne—sparkling brut
France: Languedoc—Coteaux du Languedoc Rouge or other red Languedoc
Germany or Canada or Ohio: Trockenbeerenauslese or Eiswein (ice wine)

Grilled Sirloin with Maple-Chipotle Glaze

4 servings

This glazed steak is a classic study in yin and yang. Sweet *and* spicy. Once you've taken one bite, you'll see what makes it the perfect combination. As a bonus, Brandt explains in this recipe just how to achieve those picture-perfect diamond grill marks, guaranteed to impress your guests each and every time.

1 cup maple syrup (preferably from Ohio, but definitely not pancake syrup)
1 chipotle pepper in adobo sauce (canned), chopped
1 teaspoon chopped garlic (1 medium-size clove)
4 (8-ounce) USDA prime sirloin steaks
Salt and freshly ground black pepper
Cilantro sprigs for garnish, optional
Chipotle peppers for garnish, optional

1. Mix the maple syrup, chipotles, and garlic together in a bowl. Reserve a few tablespoons in another small bowl to use later as a glaze.

2. Place the steaks in a pan. Pour the maple syrup mixture (less the reserve) over the steaks. Cover the pan with plastic wrap. Let sit in your refrigerator for at least 30 minutes, but the longer, the better—ideally up to 24 hours.

3. Preheat the grill to high heat for about 5 to 10 minutes. Make sure your grates are clean and well oiled.

4. Remove the steaks from the marinade. Season both sides of each steak with salt and pepper to taste.

5. Now picture a clock. Pick one edge of a steak to use as a guide. Place that edge at two o'clock on the hot grill, repeating the process for all the steaks. Cook for 3 to 4 minutes. Now take that same edge and place it at ten o'clock on your grill, again repeating for all the steaks. Cook for an additional 3 to 4 minutes. Repeat this process in exactly the same way on the other side of the steaks. Use a thermometer to check the internal temperature for the level of doneness you prefer: rare 120°, medium rare 126°, medium 135°, medium well 145°, or well 160°.

6. Remove the steaks from the grill. Brush a little of the reserved glaze on top of each and serve warm, garnished if desired with cilantro and a chipotle pepper (which will make the dish very spicy!).

Banana Dulce de Leche Flatbread

4 servings

This easy-yet-delicious dessert is a popular choice on the menu at Blue Canyon. It's sweet, smooth, and crunchy, all at the same time. For a different variation, in place of the cream mixture, you might want to try Nutella (a chocolate hazelnut spread) instead. Experiment with the ice cream flavor, too! A very versatile recipe. And a keeper.

2 (8-ounce) packages cream cheese, softened at room temperature
2 tablespoons granulated sugar
1 teaspoon pure vanilla extract
½ teaspoon ground cinnamon
2 (12-inch) flour tortillas
2 medium-size bananas, peeled and sliced on the diagonal
½ cup Dulce de Leche, store-bought or homemade (recipe at right; can substitute ¼ cup caramel sauce)
1 tablespoon salted sunflower seeds
Vanilla bean ice cream

1. Preheat the oven to 375°. Line a baking sheet with a Silpat (nonstick baking mat) or parchment paper.

2. Combine the cream cheese, sugar, vanilla, and cinnamon in a bowl and beat with an electric mixer until well blended, about 2 minutes.

3. Lay the tortillas out flat in a baking pan large enough to hold both or in two separate pans. Spread each with half the cream cheese mixture, up to about ¾ inch of the edge, then arrange the sliced bananas evenly on top. Drizzle with the Dulce de Leche and sprinkle each tortilla with half the sunflower seeds.

4. Place the baking pans in the oven and bake for 15 to 20 minutes, or until the filling bubbles and the edges become deep golden brown.

5. Cut each flatbread into triangular serving pieces, like a pizza. Serve warm with a scoop of ice cream on the side, if desired.

Dulce de Leche

Makes about 1½ cups

Dulce de leche (pronounced "DOOL-say day LAY-chay") loosely translates to "milk candy." You can easily find it in the ethnic section of your local grocery store, gourmet specialty shops, and Latin markets. However, you can also just as easily make it yourself. Once you do, you'll never go back to buying it again.

1 (14-ounce) can sweetened condensed milk (not evaporated milk), label removed

1. Place the unopened can of sweetened condensed milk in a deep, large pot. Add enough water to completely cover the can (by at least 3 to 4 inches) and bring to a boil. Continue to boil steadily for 2 to 3 hours, depending on how thick you like it. *Warning! Make absolutely sure the can is sufficiently covered with plenty of water and totally submerged at all times—or it will explode! Check frequently and continue to add more water regularly.*

2. Carefully remove the can with tongs and place on a wire rack to cool before opening. Any unused sauce can be refrigerated for up to 2 weeks.

Matt Fish

Goat Cheese–Stuffed
Piquillo Peppers

Firecracker Chicken
Grilled Cheese Sandwich

Hand-Cut French Fries

Matt Fish

Chef/Owner, Melt Bar & Grilled (multiple locations)

Accolades: Named one of the Best Sandwiches in America by *Esquire;* voted one of America's Top 10 Best New Sandwiches by *Huffington Post;* listed as one of the Best Sports Bars by *ESPN the Magazine;* featured on the Food Network's *Diners, Drive-ins and Dives* and *The Best Thing I Ever Ate* shows plus the Travel Channel's *Man v. Food* show; featured on the NBC *Today Show;* four-time consecutive winner of *Cleveland Magazine's* Best Sandwich award; numerous other Best awards by *Cleveland Magazine;* recognized by *Crain's Cleveland Business* as one of Cleveland's Most Memorable Restaurants of the Past 30 Years; numerous Best awards by *Northern Ohio Live;* featured in numerous publications and media, including *Travel + Leisure, USA Today, Restaurant Hospitality, Nation's Restaurant News,* the *Plain Dealer,* WKYC-TV 3, WEWS-TV 5, and WJW-TV 8.

Matt's secret tip for last-minute entertaining? "Always have plenty of beer, wine, and alcohol on hand at all times. This applies even when not entertaining!"

Although he grew up in suburban Parma, Ohio, Matt spent his summers at his grandparents' two hundred–acre farm in North Ridgeville, helping to plant soybeans and sweet corn. He also helped raise cows and chickens, butchering them as well. That's how his natural, hands-on approach and love of fresh food began.

But it would take years for that love to transform into the culinary career he enjoys today. Matt needed to follow his first dream first: music. He formed a band while in high school called Whatever. They signed to a label and cut a few records. They even toured Europe. Twice. In the meantime, Matt graduated from Lutheran High School West and started attending Cuyahoga Community College with the hope of becoming a grade school teacher. But as fate would have it, he started dating a girl who worked at a place called Rocky's Pizzeria.

While visiting his then-girlfriend at work, Matt would end up helping in the kitchen for fun. Suddenly he got hooked. "I loved it so much that I would go there just to help with the food prep," says Matt. "I quit my grocery job and started working there the next week!"

Matt worked at Rocky's, first as a cook, then as a kitchen manager. He also switched majors, graduating with a degree in culinary arts and restaurant management. He eventually took a job as head chef at Marco Polo's in Brecksville. In the meantime, he was still playing in the band.

After that band broke up, Matt joined another band, the Chargers Street Gang. They also signed to a label, cut a few records, and toured. Meanwhile, Matt took a job at Fat Fish Blue and then Johnny Mango, both in Cleveland. It was while at Johnny Mango that Matt began to seriously think about fulfilling a dream he always had: to own his own bar.

Matt was only two months away from opening his dream bar when he suddenly realized it needed a name. He came up with "Melt." Here's why. When Matt would come home late at night from his restaurant jobs, he would make himself a grilled cheese sandwich. Then he started making them at work. When word got around, he would make them for the staff, too. In time, his sandwiches became more and more elaborate. So he decided to center his bar menu around gourmet grilled cheese sandwiches.

However, shortly after opening, something very strange happened. Instead of Melt becoming known as a bar with a fantastic beer selection that also happened to serve some tasty grilled sandwiches, it became known as a restaurant with fantastic grilled sandwiches that also happened to serve some tasty beers.

The restaurant enjoyed instant success—as well as a cult-like following. Case in point: Melt's unusual, now-famous tattoo promotion. A few years ago, Matt announced a 25 percent lifetime discount to anyone who came in sporting a Melt logo tattoo. Two days later, a guy named Jay Reed walked in with one. To date, over four hundred people and counting—have joined the Melt Tattoo Family!

The success of the original restaurant in Lakewood prompted Matt to open a few more locations. And he plans to open even more.

Matt lives in Lakewood with his girlfriend and their 140-pound English mastiff, Doris.

Goat Cheese–Stuffed Piquillo Peppers

4 servings

This is one of Matt's go-to appetizers whenever company comes over. The piquillo pepper is a variety of chile traditionally grown in northern Spain, in the town of Lodosa. Its name means "little beak" in Spanish. Another, more common name is Peppadew pepper or piquanté pepper, resembling a cross between a cherry tomato and a very small red pepper. Look for it fresh in either the antipasto section of the deli department or the olive bar/marinated section of better grocery stores, or in jars or cans in the pickle aisle of most supermarkets.

8 ounces goat cheese, softened
½ cup chopped fresh chives
¼ cup fresh basil leaves, thinly sliced
⅛ teaspoon red pepper flakes
Freshly grated zest and juice of 1 lemon, reserved separately
20 to 25 fresh or 1 (16-ounce) jar or can of sweet piquillo peppers (can substitute Peppadew peppers, piquanté peppers, or any kind of pickled peppers), drained
2 tablespoons agave syrup (can substitute honey)
Kosher salt and freshly ground black pepper

1. Combine the goat cheese, chives, basil, red pepper flakes, lemon zest, and lemon juice in a bowl. Mix well.

2. Using a small spoon or a piping bag, stuff the peppers with the goat cheese mixture. Place them on a serving dish. Drizzle with the agave syrup and season with salt and pepper to taste.

Hand-Cut French Fries

4 servings

You've never had home fries quite like these! They're double-fried to produce a crisp, golden brown exterior and a moist, delicious interior. A perfect accompaniment to any casual meal.

2 tablespoons kosher salt
2 tablespoons freshly ground black pepper
6 to 8 large Russet Burbank (Idaho) potatoes, unpeeled
2 quarts canola oil

1. Mix the salt and pepper together in a small bowl. Set aside.

2. Thoroughly wash each potato and dry very well. Cut each potato in half lengthwise. Cut each half one more time lengthwise. You should be left with 4 equal potato slices. Cut each slice into long fries that are as thick or thin as you desire.

3. Place the oil in a tall sauce pot with at least 4 inches between the top oil line and the top of the pot. Using a candy or fry thermometer, heat the oil to 300° on medium-high heat.

4. Slowly place a quarter of the potatoes in the oil. Fry for about 5 minutes. The potatoes should be about 40 percent cooked (still firm but with a slight bend to them). The color should also be a dirty white. Using a slotted spoon or a wire skimmer, remove the potatoes from the oil to paper towels to drain. Repeat with the rest of the potatoes.

5. Set the blanched potatoes aside until ready to refry. At that time, reheat the oil, bringing it up to a temperature of 350°, still over medium-high heat. Add a quarter of the blanched potatoes to the oil. Fry until deep golden brown in color, at the same time making sure they are crisp and not undercooked. Again remove the potatoes to paper towels to drain, and while still warm, transfer to a large bowl and toss with some of the salt/pepper mixture.

6. Repeat the frying and draining with the rest of the potatoes, adding them as they are drained to the bowl with the other potatoes and tossing with additional salt and pepper to taste. Serve immediately.

BEER PAIRINGS

Mexico: Any brewery—Vienna or dark ale with a lime
USA: Microbrew—India Pale Ale or other hoppy ale
USA: Microbrew—Belgian-style dark ale
USA: Microbrew—pilsner or other pale lager

Firecracker Chicken Grilled Cheese Sandwich

4 servings

This dish is actually served at Melt as a specialty menu item every year, but only during the month of July. The special Diablo Spice Rub recipe is Matt's own. This is, in fact, the secret ingredient that gives the chicken its extra kick. Together with the tartness of the pepper Jack cheese, it complements the sweetness of the pineapple and the creaminess of the avocado so well. So very, very well. And for a spicy vegetarian version, just substitute fried firm tofu for the chicken.

2 cups Diablo Spice Rub (recipe at right; can substitute store-bought premixed blackening seasoning rub)
4 (6-ounce) boneless chicken breasts
1 small fresh pineapple
Vegetable oil
2 ripe but firm Hass avocados
1 (3-pound) loaf good-quality fresh artisan Italian bread
Unsalted butter or margarine, softened, not melted
16 (1-ounce) slices of pepper Jack cheese

1. Preheat the oven to 350°. Preheat the grill (gas or charcoal) to medium-high heat. Set a large seasoned cast-iron skillet over medium-high heat on the stove to preheat.

2. Place the Diablo Spice Rub in a shallow pan. Dredge the chicken in it, making sure each piece is completely but lightly coated.

3. Place the chicken in the hot cast-iron skillet, and with the heat still on medium high, "blacken" on each side for 3 minutes. Remove the skillet from the heat and place in the oven until the chicken is completely cooked through, to an internal temperature of 165°, 10 to 15 minutes. (The chicken will begin to take on a reddish color from the rub, so taking the internal temperature to ensure doneness is suggested.) Carefully remove the hot skillet from the oven, then, using tongs, remove the chicken to a plate and set aside. Keep the oven heated at 350°.

4. Clean and core the pineapple so that the exterior brown skin and hard core are completely removed. Cut the pineapple in half lengthwise. Lay each half flat on the cutting board and from each cut four to six ½-inch slices.

5. Wipe down the grates of the grill with the oil. Add the pineapple slices and grill on each side for 1 to 2 minutes. You should achieve deep grill marks and a slight char to the pineapple flesh. Remove from the heat and set aside in a covered dish.

6. Cut each avocado in half. Remove the pits and discard. Delicately placing a spoon between the flesh and the skin, attempt to scoop the entire half out in one piece. Place the halves on a cutting board, flat side down, and cut each into thin slices.

7. Cut the loaf of bread into 8 slices, each approximately 1-inch thick. Spread enough of the butter on each side of each slice of bread so that a nice thin layer completely covers the entire surface of the bread.

8. Heat a sauté pan or griddle on medium heat. When hot, place the bread in the pan and toast each side to a deep golden brown. It is crucial that the bread be toasted evenly.

9. Place all the toasted bread slices on a baking sheet. Place 2 slices of pepper Jack cheese on each bread slice. Place 2 to 3 grilled pineapple slices on each of 4 slices, and place the blackened chicken on the other 4 slices.

10. Either bake at 350° for 3 to 5 minutes until the cheese is melted, or place the slices on the grill, away from direct heat, until the cheese is melted. Remove from the heat source.

11. Arrange the avocado slices evenly over the chicken. Close the sandwiches, inverting the bread slices with the pineapple over those with the avocado and chicken, and cut in half. Serve immediately.

Diablo Spice Rub

Makes about 3 cups

½ cup chipotle chile powder
½ cup ancho chile powder
½ cup pasilla negro chile powder
½ cup ground red (cayenne) pepper
½ cup regular chile powder
¼ cup kosher salt
2 tablespoons ground cumin
2 tablespoons freshly ground black pepper

1. Combine all the ingredients in a large bowl. Blend with a wire whisk. (You only need 2 cups for the Firecracker Chicken Grilled Cheese Sandwich recipe. Reserve the rest for a future use.)

Carmella Fragassi

Herb- & Feta-Stuffed Scampi

Sautéed Veal Scaloppine with
Lemon Sauce & Artichokes

Italian Orange Salad

Cavatelli with Pancetta,
Tomatoes, & Hot Pepper

Sautéed Brussels Sprouts
with Garlic

Carmella Fragassi

Chef/Owner, La Campagna

Accolades: A finalist for the Gallo Family Vineyard Gold Medal Award in the Top Artisanal Food Products category three years in a row; won first-place Taste of Italy award; featured in *Cleveland Ethnic Eats;* featured in numerous publications and media, including *Feast!,* the *Plain Dealer, Metromix, Urbanspoon, Yelp,* and PBS TV.

Carmella has always loved to cook. And she has always had fun cooking. But it took years for Carmella to get to the point she's at now, being able to share her passion for cooking family-favorite recipes with others. Her life path had to take quite an interesting direction first.

Carmella grew up in Sheffield Lake, Ohio, part of a large extended Italian family. "Eating in my home was family art," says Carmella. "It was practiced for and by the whole family to celebrate not just the most important meal of the day but more than likely the most important *event* of the day."

Carmella would watch—and help—her mother, father, grandparents, aunts, and uncles prepare traditional meals using the freshest ingredients from their garden. They would also can fruits and vegetables during the harvest. "We were all creating a rich family life while at the same time maintaining a link between the generations in this sharing of a common joy," she says.

After graduating from Brookside High School in Sheffield Lake, she joined the Lorain County Administrator as an assistant clerk and personal secretary. She quickly worked her way up to executive secretary of two drug enforcement groups. After completing a couple intense government training programs, she became an undercover drug enforcement agent and crime scene photographer. During her seventeen-year tenure in law enforcement, she also obtained a degree in psychology from Heidelberg College, became a certified officer

Carmella's secret tip for last-minute entertaining? "Always keep your pantry well stocked with garlic, olive oil, pasta, canned tuna, cannellini and garbanzo beans, home-canned tomatoes and fruit, wine, coffee, and espresso. Salami, cheese, and milk are always good to have on hand, too."

training instructor, and taught at a number of private police academies throughout the Cleveland area.

After Carmella retired, she began to seriously consider a dream she had always had: to own her own small Italian restaurant. More of a trattoria, if you will. Just like the ones she would visit in Italy. Finally, she found a site in Westlake and did just that. The restaurant was enjoying quiet success when, only two years later, a raging fire in an adjacent business caused so much damage to her property that she had to shut it down.

Carmella was devastated. She decided to regroup and started freelancing as an investigator for a law firm. But five years later, she actively sought another restaurant site in Westlake. She soon reopened her business, at first providing only catering service and gift baskets. "But repeated requests by my customers to offer on-site dining again led to my current, intimate, seven-table restaurant concept, where I provide a strictly 'personal chef' style of service," explains Carmella. "Every single dish is made to order using only the freshest produce of the day."

Although she's not exactly taking it easy postretirement, Carmella is truly having the time of her life. Besides running the restaurant, she also teaches classes at Laurel Run Cooking School in Vermilion. And she organizes culinary tours to Italy. In fact, during her last trip, she was invited to become the exclusive distributor in the U.S. for a line of fine olive oils and wines.

"When you appreciate good food and like to cook, you always find joy in making a masterpiece," says Carmella.

In her free time, Carmella likes to read, sew, and relax at the family's rustic cabin in scenic Cook Forest, Pennsylvania.

Carmella shares a home in Sheffield Lake with Leanarda, her mother and the loving matriarch of the family.

Herb- & Feta-Stuffed Scampi

4 servings

A gastronomic delicacy, *scampi* is actually the Italian name for the tail por-tion of lobsterettes, most notably the Dublin Bay prawn. Serve as an elegant appetizer before any meal, or as a main course, if you'd like. No one will mind either way! Carmella likes to use the versatile stuffing mixture to fill other types of fish and chicken as well. A helpful side note: Use whatever greens you have on hand for the bed.

2 ounces feta cheese, preferably Lake Erie Creamery, crumbled
2 ounces mascarpone cheese (can substitute cream cheese, softened)
1½ teaspoons finely chopped fresh Italian parsley
1½ teaspoons finely chopped chives (can substitute green onion)
½ teaspoon minced garlic (½ medium-size clove)
Kosher salt and freshly ground black pepper (to taste)
8 uncooked scampi, peeled and deveined (can substitute jumbo shrimp)
4 cups spinach leaves, rinsed thoroughly and drained
½ head red cabbage, cored and shredded
Balsamic vinegar for drizzling
Chopped fresh chives for garnish

1. Preheat the oven to 450°.

2. Combine the feta, mascarpone, parsley, chives, garlic, and salt and pepper to taste in a small bowl. (Depending on how salty your feta is, you may want to omit the salt altogether.) Using your hands, mix thoroughly.

3. Make a cut ½-inch deep along the back of each scampi to "butterfly." Spread open. Place the filling equally onto each scampi.

4. Place the scampi on a baking sheet, cheese side up, and bake until the scampi are pink, about 5 to 6 minutes. Remove from the oven.

5. Place the spinach and cabbage on each serving plate to create a bed of greens. Arrange the cooked scampi on the greens, cheese side up. Drizzle with the balsamic vinegar and garnish with the chives to serve.

WINE PAIRINGS

Italy: Piedmont, Roero—Arneis
Italy: Tuscany—Sangiovese or "Super Tuscan" blend
Italy: Veneto—Pinot Grigio, Sauvignon Blanc, or blend
USA: California, Lodi—Pinot Noir or Sangiovese

Sautéed Veal Scaloppine with Lemon Sauce & Artichokes

4 servings

Scaloppine is the Italian term for scallops (thin, boneless slices) of meat. This version is at once delicate, flavorful, and tangy—assisted in part by the addition of marinated long-stemmed artichokes, which can easily be found jarred or canned in most grocery stores.

2 tablespoons olive oil
4 tablespoons (½ stick) unsalted butter
½ cup all-purpose flour
1 pound veal for scaloppine, sliced thin and pounded flat (can substitute chicken or pork cutlets)
2 tablespoons dry white wine or white vermouth
2 tablespoons heavy cream
2 tablespoons fresh lemon juice, plus additional for serving, optional
1 teaspoon minced garlic (1 medium-size clove)
Salt and freshly ground black pepper
8 marinated long-stemmed artichokes (can substitute good-quality jarred or canned marinated artichoke hearts, drained)
½ lemon, thinly sliced, for garnish
1 tablespoon finely chopped fresh parsley for garnish

1. Heat the oil and 2 tablespoons of the butter in a large skillet over medium-high heat. It should be quite hot. Thinly sliced veal must cook quickly or it will become leathery.

2. Spread the flour in a shallow dish or on waxed paper. Dip both sides of the scaloppine in the flour. Shake off the excess. Working in batches, place the scaloppine, no more than will fit comfortably without touching, into the skillet. If the oil is hot enough, the meat should sizzle.

3. Cook the scaloppine until they are lightly browned on one side, about 3 to 4 minutes. Turn and brown the other side, about another 3 to 4 minutes. Return all the batches to the skillet and add the wine, cream, lemon juice, garlic, and salt and pepper to taste. Simmer for 4 to 5 minutes.

4. Cut the artichokes in half lengthwise (skip if using only hearts). Add to the skillet until only warmed through, about 2 to 3 minutes.

5. Using a slotted spatula, transfer the scaloppine and artichokes to a warm platter and pour the sauce from the skillet over. Drizzle with a squeeze of lemon juice, if desired, and garnish with the lemon slices and parsley. Serve immediately, family style.

Italian Orange Salad

4 servings

This traditional southern Italian salad is a refreshing end to a hearty meal. For a beautiful holiday version, add thin slices of crunchy raw fennel (a licorice-flavored member of the parsley family) to the layers of oranges. *Delizioso!*

Extra-virgin olive oil
Sea salt and freshly ground black pepper
3 navel oranges
1 teaspoon minced garlic (1 medium-size clove)
Finely chopped fresh Italian parsley for garnish
1 scallion (green onion), chopped, for garnish, optional

1. Lightly drizzle each serving plate with some of the oil and salt and pepper to taste. Set aside.

2. Peel the oranges, removing both rind and white pith. Using a very sharp serrated knife, cut the oranges crosswise into ¼-inch-thick slices (or a little thicker if you prefer).

3. Place about 3 sliced oranges on each prepared plate. Sprinkle with some of the minced garlic and salt and pepper to taste. Drizzle with some oil. Garnish with some of the parsley and, if desired, the scallion to serve.

Cavatelli with Pancetta, Tomatoes, & Hot Pepper

4 servings

Although served as a side dish in Carmella's elegant meal, this could also be prepared as an easy weeknight meal in itself. Just add a salad and some crusty bread, and you're golden! Cavatelli—a type of pasta that's short and narrow with a rolled edge—is typically available frozen. As for pancetta (also called Italian bacon), it is usually sold rolled and can be found at Italian import stores as well as some grocery stores, most likely in the deli department.

Salt
3 tablespoons olive oil
2 tablespoons unsalted butter
1 medium-size yellow onion, finely chopped
1 (¼-inch-thick) slice rolled pancetta, cut into 1 x ½-inch strips (can substitute 4-ounce package cubed pancetta)
1½ cups canned chopped or diced (not pureed) Italian tomatoes
½ small dried hot red pepper, seeded and finely chopped (can substitute a pinch of red pepper flakes)
1 pound frozen cavatelli
3 to 4 tablespoons freshly grated Romano cheese, plus additional for optional garnish

1. Bring 4 quarts of salted water to a boil in a large pot.

2. In the meantime, heat the oil and butter in a saucepan over medium heat. Add the onion and sauté until pale gold, about 5 minutes. Add the pancetta and sauté for about 1 more minute.

3. Add the tomatoes, hot red pepper, and ½ teaspoon salt. Bring to a simmer and cook, uncovered, over medium heat. The sauce is done when the tomatoes and the cooking fats separate, about 15 minutes. Take off the heat, taste for salt, and set aside.

4. Drop the cavatelli into the boiling salted water. Cook according to package directions until al dente.

5. Drain the pasta and transfer to a bowl. Add the sauce and mix. Add 3 tablespoons cheese and mix again. Taste for salt and spiciness. If you like it somewhat sharper, add a little more cheese, but not so much as to overwhelm the other flavors. If desired, garnish with extra grated cheese.

Sautéed Brussels Sprouts with Garlic

4 servings

Brussels sprouts, high in vitamins A and C, are actually a member of the cabbage family. The smaller they are, the more tender. Look for bright green color and compact heads during their peak season, which runs from late August through March.

2 to 3 cups Brussels sprouts (about 1 pound)
¼ cup olive oil
2 teaspoons finely chopped garlic (2 medium-size cloves)
1 tablespoon chopped fresh thyme
Salt and freshly ground black pepper
Pancetta or bacon, cooked and crumbled, for garnish, optional

1. Cut off the stems of the Brussels sprouts. Pull off any bruised outer leaves. Cut each Brussels sprout lengthwise in half with a sharp knife.

2. Heat the oil in a skillet. Add the Brussels sprouts and garlic. Sauté for about 5 to 10 minutes, or until the sprouts are slightly tender.

3. Remove from the heat and toss with the thyme and salt and pepper to taste. Transfer to a serving bowl and garnish, if desired, with crumbled pancetta.

Heather Haviland

Shipwreck Casserole

Buttermilk Herb Biscuits

Seasonal Fruit Salad with
Honey Poppy Seed Dressing

Mango Berry Lassi

Heather Haviland

Chef/Owner, Lucky's Café, Sweet Mosaic

Accolades: Featured on both the Food Network's *Diners, Drive-ins and Dives* and *The Best Thing I Ever Ate!* shows; James Beard honorable mention for signature 40-Layer Cashew Crêpe Torte; named One of the Best Places to Have Brunch in America by *GQ*; featured panelist at the Cleveland's Emerging Chefs presentation sponsored by The City Club of Cleveland; featured in numerous publications and media, including *Food & Wine*, the *New York Times*, *Modern Bride*, *Taste!*, *Northern Ohio Live*, *Cleveland Magazine*, *Cleveland Scene*, the *Plain Dealer*, *Chowhound*, *Cool Cleveland*, and WKYC-TV 3.

Although Heather makes a mean macaroni and cheese, she's really a pastry chef at heart. "I was working as a line cook at an Italian place near D.C. when their pastry chef up and quit," recalls Heather. "So they had me fill in 'temporarily.'"

As she goes on to explain, a few days later the owner walked in and handed her a family recipe for tiramisù. He wanted her to make it for that evening's dessert menu. When she got home from work late that night, she found a voice message waiting for her. "Your tiramisù brought back such warm memories of my grandmother!" her boss said, choking up. The next day, there was a chef's jacket hanging in her locker with her name emblazoned across it and "Pastry Chef" embroidered underneath. "From that moment on," she says, "I just knew baking was what I wanted to do."

Heather grew up in Lakewood, Ohio. As a young girl, she would help her mom with her catering business. After graduating from Lakewood High School, Heather left for Kent State University, where she studied political science and anatomy of peaceful change. But then an opportunity to volunteer in a third world country changed her focus, as did her subsequent decision to move to Maryland and help her grandmother, who was ill at the time.

Heather's secret tip for last-minute entertaining? "Start with great ingredients and continue with the best of intentions. You need to be patient with yourself. People will enjoy the effort."

Eventually, Heather left Maryland to roam the U.S. in search of amazing culinary opportunities, equipped with nothing more than sheer ambition and a gutsy spirit. She found several such opportunities in Chicago, Seattle, and eventually upstate New York, where she co-owned The Peterson House and worked as a weekend personal chef to the ultrarich and famous (who shall remain nameless).

But home beckoned her. So she ultimately decided to sell her partnership and make her way back to Cleveland and family again. This time, with years of professional experience under her belt, she joined several highly respected establishments, including Seballos Pastries, Fire Food & Drink, and Parker's New American Bistro, before opening her own place, Sweet Mosaic (a special event bakery).

After a couple more years, Heather chose to take over Lucky's Café in Tremont from its original owner. She began offering just a few brunch items at first, all prepared on two tiny propane burners, since the place had no kitchen to speak of—no small feat for a suddenly booming business! Two years later, she remodeled the postage stamp–sized kitchen. Then, in a self-professed moment of weakness, Heather went on to open yet another café, the (now closed) Vine & Bean Café—this time on the other side of town near Shaker Square.

"I've always wanted to bring people together through my food," says Heather. Everyone would agree she's done precisely that.

When not working, Heather likes to "doodle" with colored pencils and craft beautiful beaded jewelry.

Heather lives in Cleveland's Old Brooklyn neighborhood with her husband, Andrew (also a chef), and their two fat cats, Bella and Sammy.

Shipwreck Casserole

4 servings

This was the first dish Heather ever made at Lucky's—and it's still one of her most popular menu items! In fact, it's perfect as a last-minute meal, especially for breakfast or brunch, because it's so versatile and forgiving. Leave out the ham for a vegetarian version. Use any other cheese you wish (except blue). And grab any vegetables that are in season—or none at all. But please note, unless the vegetable you use can be properly cooked in a skillet (like sweet peas and corn), it will need to be precooked. One example: asparagus, which you would need to blanch first before adding it to the skillet.

4 medium-size Russet potatoes, unpeeled
Kosher salt
½ small red onion
½ red bell pepper, cored and seeded
½ green bell pepper, cored and seeded
½ small zucchini
6 medium-size fresh mushrooms, trimmed and wiped
    clean with a dampened paper towel
11 large farm-fresh eggs
Vegetable oil
Freshly ground black pepper
4 to 8 ounces Black Forest deli ham slices, cut into small
    strips, optional
8 ounces sharp cheddar cheese, grated
Chopped scallion (green onion) for garnish
Hot sauce for serving, optional

1. Scrub the potatoes, pat dry, and cut into 1- to 1½-inch cubes. Place in a medium-size saucepan, cover with cold water, and add 5 tablespoons of salt (should taste like ocean water). Place on high heat. Watching closely, cook only until the potatoes are tender but not mushy. This should not take long (about 10 to 15 minutes); to test, pierce with a fork. When done, drain and set the potato cubes aside on a baking sheet, spreading out to cool.

2. Slice the onion, red pepper, green pepper, and zucchini into ½-inch-wide strips. Cut the mushrooms into ½-inch pieces. Set aside.

3. Whisk the eggs in a bowl with 1 teaspoon salt and ⅛ teaspoon pepper until smooth. Set aside.

4. Place a large sauté pan over medium-high heat and heat until hot. Add enough oil to just cover the bottom of the pan. When the oil is hot, add the cooled potatoes. Sprinkle with salt and pepper to taste. Sauté, stirring occasionally, until most sides are golden brown, about 10 to 15 minutes.

5. While the potatoes cook, preheat the oven to 400°. Grease a 13 x 9-inch baking pan.

6. Remove the potatoes from the sauté pan and return to their baking sheet. In the same sauté pan, still over medium-high heat, add more oil to cover the bottom of the pan and heat until hot. Add the sliced onion, red pepper, green pepper, zucchini, and mushrooms. Sprinkle with salt and pepper to taste, then continue to cook, stirring frequently, until the vegetables are about halfway cooked, approximately 3 minutes.

7. Add the potatoes and, if desired, the ham. After the potatoes are heated through and the ham starts to get a little color, about 5 minutes, add the egg mixture. Using a heatproof rubber spatula, stir frequently so the eggs don't get any color but cook through, about 1 to 2 minutes.

8. Remove the sauté pan from the heat and carefully transfer the egg mixture to the greased baking pan. Sprinkle with the grated cheese and bake until the cheese melts and turns lightly golden brown, approximately 8 to 10 minutes. Serve warm, garnished with the chopped scallion and, if desired, alongside the hot sauce.

COCKTAIL PAIRINGS

Bellini
Blood Orange Mimosa
Bloody Mary

Buttermilk Herb Biscuits

4 servings (2 to 3 biscuits per person)

The secret to the success of this recipe is to not overmix the dough. Repeat, do *not* overmix the dough! It should be both wet and dry with patches of flour. Ideally, the biscuits should be baked as close to eating time as possible. Right out of the oven, they are truly a bit of heaven on earth. Utterly flaky and impossibly amazing. Nirvana, really.

3½ cups all-purpose flour, plus additional for shaping the biscuits
2¾ tablespoons baking powder
1 tablespoon granulated sugar
2 teaspoons kosher salt
6 ounces (1½ sticks) unsalted butter, cut into ½-inch cubes and chilled
1 teaspoon chopped fresh dill
1 teaspoon chopped fresh parsley
1⅔ cups buttermilk, plus additional for brushing
Unsalted butter, honey, and/or jam for serving, optional

1. Preheat the oven to 400°. Line a baking sheet with a Silpat (nonstick baking mat) or parchment paper.

2. Sift together the flour, baking powder, sugar, and salt into the bowl of a stand mixer. Add the butter, dill, and parsley. Using the paddle attachment of a stand mixer, turn on low speed and mix until the butter is the size of peas.

3. While the motor is still running, slowly add the buttermilk. Mix just until the dough starts to come together. There should be both wet and dry patches.

4. Remove the dough from the bowl and place on a lightly floured surface. Knead the dough a couple times until it is more consistent but not perfect. You want it to be irregular, with visible patches of flour. Press the dough with your hand or a floured rolling pin until it is about 1 inch thick.

5. Using a 3-inch biscuit cutter, cut the dough into rounds. In between cuts, dip the cutter into flour so that the dough does not stick to the cutter. (You can gently press any scraps together to form the last couple of biscuits.) Do not overhandle; perfection is overrated.

6. Place the biscuits 2 inches apart on the lined baking sheet. (They can now sit for up to 20 minutes before baking.) When ready to bake, brush the tops with a little additional buttermilk.

7. Bake until the biscuits are risen and golden brown, about 20 to 25 minutes. Serve warm.

Seasonal Fruit Salad with Honey Poppy Seed Dressing

4 servings

Although the fabulous selection of fruit Heather lists below is optimal, feel free to mix and match whatever fruit you have on hand—or whatever is in season. You just can't go wrong because, quite frankly, it's the dressing that's actually the magic ingredient of this salad. Creamy, satiny, and simply delectable! You'll taste a hint of sweetness highlighted by the mild, nutty flavor of the poppy seeds, which add just the right amount of texture and eye appeal.

¼ fresh pineapple, peeled and cubed
1 ripe mango, peeled, pitted, and cubed
½ Granny Smith apple, cored, cubed, and tossed in a little lemon juice (can substitute any tart apple)
1 ripe papaya, peeled, seeded, and cubed
1 banana, peeled, cubed, and tossed in a little lemon juice
1 kiwi, peeled and cubed
1 nectarine, cubed
12 strawberries, sliced
½ cup blueberries
Honey Poppy Seed Dressing (recipe follows)
Fresh mint leaves for garnish, optional

1. Divide all the prepared fruits among 4 dessert bowls. When ready to serve, pour the dressing evenly over the fruit and stir to combine. If desired, garnish with a few mint leaves.

Honey Poppy Seed Dressing

Makes about 1 cup

⅔ cup honey, preferably local
2 tablespoons Hellmann's real mayonnaise, not Miracle Whip salad dressing
2 teaspoons fresh lemon juice
1 tablespoon poppy seeds

1. Whisk together the honey, mayonnaise, lemon juice, and poppy seeds to blend well. Keep refrigerated until ready to use.

Mango Berry Lassi

4 servings

A lassi is a popular Indian beverage that can most easily be described as a smoothie concocted with mango and yogurt. This unique beverage is best served chilled. But one caveat: Make sure your mangoes are ripe or you won't get the desired sweetness. How to tell if a mango is ripe? You'll be able to indent it slightly with your thumb. Also, with the stem end up, smell it. A ripe mango will have a sweet, fruity aroma. A few brown speckles are also a normal indication of ripeness, but avoid any that have brown marks and feel mushy.

2 cups whole-milk yogurt
6 ripe mangoes, peeled, pitted, and chopped
1 cup assorted fresh berries (strawberries, raspberries, blueberries)
½ cup honey, preferably local
4 teaspoons fresh lime juice
½ teaspoon ground mace (can substitute allspice)
Pinch of salt

1. Puree the yogurt and mangoes together in a blender until smooth. Pour into another container, preferably one with a lip for pouring, and set aside.

2. To the same blender container add the berries, honey, lime juice, mace, and salt. Puree until smooth, then add to the mango mixture and stir until well combined.

3. Pour into 4 tall glasses and refrigerate, covered with plastic wrap, until ready to serve. (Best served chilled.)

Randal Johnson

Tuscan White Bean Dip

Creamy Garlic Bread Soup

Shrimp & Root Vegetable
Risotto

Randal Johnson

Chef/Owner, Molinari's

Accolades: Received an Award of Excellence from *Wine Spectator;* voted one of the Top 1,000 Italian Restaurants in the U.S. by Zagat; regularly featured in numerous publications and media, including *Cleveland Magazine, Cleveland Scene,* the *Plain Dealer,* the *News-Herald,* the *Tri-County Business Journal,* and WJW-TV 8.

Randal considers his mother extremely gifted in the kitchen. "I was her willing guinea pig for most of my life," he laughs. They would sit together, glued to the TV, watching Julia Child and Graham Kerr, who were all the rage at that time. "Those chefs had a profound effect on my mother and, ultimately, on me, too," he says. The irony is, Randal would end up appearing on TV as a celebrity chef himself years later!

Randal was born and raised in Euclid, Ohio. When he was only seventeen, he got his first job as a dishwasher at The Flame in Euclid. After he graduated from Euclid High School, he headed to Oxford, Ohio, to attend Miami University.

He did well in college, but his heart was elsewhere. After two and a half years, he finally admitted to himself that what he really wanted to go into was wine making—a major Miami evidently didn't offer. The only school that did offer such a program at that time was in California—and Randal couldn't afford to go that far. He decided to go to culinary school instead.

But first, Randal needed to work in a food-related position for a year before he could even apply to the Culinary Institute of America. So, he went back to The Flame and worked there as a cook for the next twelve months. After fulfilling his prerequisite, he immediately headed to Hyde Park, New York, to attend the legendary CIA.

After graduation, Randal took a number of restaurant management positions at various places and in some pretty exotic locations, too, including Club Cleo on the Caribbean island of Saint Martin; The Ground Floor in Beachwood and The Restaurant in Moreland Hills, both in Ohio; San Juan Inn on San Juan Island in Washington

Randal's secret tip for last-minute entertaining? "Always have a well-stocked pantry and know what you can do with various ingredients in a pinch."

State; and Cuisines in Cleveland.

"I was finding it really difficult to hire good, qualified chefs," recalls Randal, "so I started to turn my skills to the kitchen instead." He subsequently accepted a position as the executive chef of the exclusive Shaker Heights Country Club. But after five years, Randal was ready to leave the restaurant business. He was tired of the long hours, the nights, and the weekends. Yet somehow, some way, he still wanted to stay involved in food and wine, both of which remained his passion.

That's when Randal decided to open Molinari's, which, in Italian, means "the miller," or the person who grinds wheat into flour. He turned the small storefront into an Italian-themed market offering prepared gourmet foods (including homemade breads and pasta), specialty food items, and over seven hundred different fine wines. He also conducted cooking classes, which the local foodies enjoyed immensely. They kept prodding Randal to open a dining room, but he would hear nothing of it. Until one day . . .

A young architect suggested designing a small restaurant in the middle of the food store, and a friend of the architect offered to build the space. Randal started warming up to the idea. It would be small—only twenty-six seats—and quite manageable. Hmm, maybe not such a bad idea after all.

A few months later, the restaurant became a reality, and over the years Randal has expanded it even further. First to accommodate sixteen more seats and a bar. Then to accommodate fifty more seats by annexing the space next door. And, most recently, to accommodate a stone pizza oven. "I'm enjoying life right now," says Randal. In other words, he's living *la dolce vita!*

When not working, you'll more than likely find Randal fly-fishing, another passion of his. In fact, he's so into it that he also designs his own flies.

Randal lives in Concord with his wife, Fran. They have two grown children: son Kyle, a chef in Seattle, and daughter Dana.

Tuscan White Bean Dip

4 servings

This healthy and economical appetizer is quick and easy enough to throw together at the last minute as a party hors d'oeuvre. You'll enjoy the simplicity of it—and your guests will enjoy the deliciousness of it!

1 (15-ounce) can cannellini beans, drained and rinsed
¼ cup extra-virgin olive oil
1½ teaspoons finely minced fresh rosemary
1½ teaspoons minced garlic (1½ medium-size cloves)
1 teaspoon freshly ground black pepper
½ teaspoon salt
¼ cup pitted kalamata olives
Flatbread, crostini, crackers, or bagel chips for serving

1. Combine the beans, oil, rosemary, garlic, pepper, and salt in a food processor. Puree for about 1 minute or until creamy and smooth. Add the olives and pulse three times for 5 seconds each time.

2. Chill until ready to serve with your choice of breads.

WINE PAIRINGS

Italy: Piedmont—Barbera d'Asti
Italy: Piedmont—Dolcetto d'Alba
Italy: Umbria—Orvieto

Creamy Garlic Bread Soup

4 servings

This rustic soup definitely falls under the category of delicious comfort food. Rich, creamy, and mellow, it's sure to satisfy even the pickiest eaters. And if you don't have any day-old bread on hand, just lightly toast fresh bread instead.

2 tablespoons unsalted butter
2 tablespoons minced garlic (6 medium-size cloves)
2 tablespoons all-purpose flour
2 cups chicken stock
2 cups milk
1½ cups cubed, day-old hearty homestyle crusty bread
1 (14.5-ounce) can diced tomatoes, drained
2 tablespoons chopped fresh chives
Salt and freshly ground black pepper
4 tablespoons freshly grated Romano cheese for garnish

1. Melt the butter in a heavy saucepan over medium heat. Add the garlic and sauté for 1 minute. Add the flour and stir to form a paste. Cook for 1 minute.

2. Add the stock and milk and bring to a boil, stirring constantly. Reduce the heat to medium low and cook for 5 minutes.

3. Place the bread in a blender. Slowly add only enough soup to the blender container to fit comfortably without the threat of spilling over during processing. Cover and puree carefully for about 2 minutes, or until smooth. Pour into a bowl and set aside while you puree any remaining soup.

4. Return all the soup to the saucepan. Add the tomatoes, chives, and salt and pepper to taste. Stir over medium heat until well blended and heated through, then serve in warmed soup bowls, garnishing each serving with a tablespoon of grated cheese.

Shrimp & Root Vegetable Risotto

4 servings

Be forewarned: This recipe yields very hearty portions! But then again, risotto is always even more delicious the next day. In fact, it may be one of the best reheated dishes there is. And if you've never worked with rutabagas or turnips before, just be sure to look for ones that are smooth, firm, and heavy for their size. Wash, trim, and peel these root vegetables carefully before dicing. (Hint: This dish can be prepared ahead of time through step 6 and then completed when you're just about ready to serve.)

5 to 6 cups chicken stock, divided
3 tablespoons extra-virgin olive oil
1 cup finely minced sweet onion
2 cups Arborio rice
1 cup dry white wine
1 cup diced carrot
1 cup diced rutabaga (can substitute parsnip or butternut squash)
1 cup diced turnip
2 pounds uncooked jumbo (16/20 count) shrimp, peeled and deveined
3 tablespoons unsalted butter
3 tablespoons minced fresh chives or parsley
Salt and freshly ground black pepper
Freshly grated Parmigiano-Reggiano cheese for garnish, optional

1. Heat the stock in a saucepan to simmering. Keep simmering on low while moving on to the next step.

2. Pour the oil into a large, deep skillet over medium heat. Add the onion and sauté for 2 minutes, or until soft.

3. Add the rice and sauté, stirring constantly, for 2 minutes. Add the wine, stir, and cook for 2 minutes more.

4. Add 1 cup of the hot stock to the rice mixture. Stir constantly until absorbed, about 3 to 4 minutes.

5. Add the carrot, rutabaga, turnip, and another cup of the hot stock. Stir until absorbed, 3 to 4 minutes, then add another cup of the stock. Stir until absorbed again, about another 3 to 4 minutes. Then add another cup of the stock. Stir until absorbed, about 3 to 4 minutes.

6. If not yet ready to serve, take the skillet with the risotto off the heat and set aside. Turn off the heat under the saucepan with the remaining stock.

7. When ready to serve, reheat the stock and add 1 cup to the risotto along with the shrimp. (If necessary, add remaining cup of stock for moistness.) Stir to mix. Cover, bring to a boil over medium heat, and cook for 2 minutes or until the shrimp turn pink and the risotto is creamy. Take off the heat and let rest, covered, for 3 minutes.

8. Add the butter and chives and season with salt and pepper to taste. Stir well. Serve warm and garnished, if desired, with grated cheese.

Pete Joyce

Heirloom Tomatoes
with Gorgonzola

Grilled Wild Alaskan Salmon

Salad with Heirloom Tomato
Vinaigrette

Peaches with Peppered
Ice Cream

Pete Joyce

Former Executive Chef/Partner, Bistro on Lincoln Park

Accolades: Won first-place award for Best Neighborhood Gem from OpenTable; finalist for *Cleveland Magazine's* Best Local Chef and Best New Restaurant awards; guest chef at a Cleveland Museum of Natural History special event; featured in numerous publications, including *Wine Savant, Hospitality Restaurant, Houston Restaurant Guide, Cleveland Magazine, Cleveland Scene,* the *Plain Dealer,* the *Sun News, NileGuide, Examiner, SpotCleveland, Metromix,* and *Cleveland Foodie.*

Pete always enjoyed cooking. In fact, his parents noticed how, even from a very young age, he liked to cook. But the real moment—that luminous "aha!" moment—when he finally realized he could turn this "hobby" into a career was when he decided to attend culinary school. That was the point when he truly committed himself to becoming a professional chef.

Pete grew up in a small town—tiny, really—called Pine Hill in the Catskill Mountains of upstate New York. Population: 210. He started working in kitchens when he was only fourteen and had the privilege of learning from one of the best: chef Dan Smith. Dan was both a mentor and a friend to Pete throughout his high school years and into college as well. In fact, it was Dan who inspired and encouraged Pete to move forward in the culinary field. After graduating from high school, Pete enrolled in the highly respected culinary program at Johnson & Wales in Providence, Rhode Island.

After receiving his associate's degree in occupational

Pete's secret tip for last-minute entertaining? "Whenever you cook something at home, usually make a little extra of things that will freeze well, such as sauces, breads, and desserts. That way, when you do have unexpected guests, you can pull them out and save yourself some time."

food science, Pete decided to continue his schooling and went right back to Johnson & Wales, this time for a bachelor's degree in hospitality management. While still a student, Pete gained invaluable experience in the corporate kitchens of J.P. Morgan on Wall Street in Manhattan.

Armed with two degrees, Pete headed to Cape Cod, where he joined the Old Jailhouse Tavern in Orleans, Massachusetts. From there, he moved to Las Vegas, where he worked at a seafood restaurant called Kiefers. He eventually moved back to the Adirondacks in New York's north country in order to open and run his own restaurant, The Fire Tower.

Five years later, Pete was drawn to Cleveland. He heard about an opening at Hospitality Restaurants and walked in off the street to apply. He was hired on the spot. As he points out, "It was the best decision I ever made." Pete first worked at their upscale Blue Point Grille, and then later at their sister restaurant, Salmon Dave's. After a brief switch to Pier W, he returned to Blue Point Grille as executive chef for a subsequent five-year run.

Finally, when the right opportunity presented itself, Pete felt he was ready to make the leap to owning his own restaurant again. He bought the former Sage restaurant space in Tremont, renamed it Bistro on Lincoln Park, and has been making his distinctive mark on the Cleveland culinary scene ever since.

Pete and his wife, Megan, live in Bay Village with their two dogs, Rusty and Shadow.

Heirloom Tomatoes with Gorgonzola

4 servings

This refreshingly light and simple side dish makes the best use of tomatoes that are grown locally and are in season. That's not to say you can only prepare this dish in the summer. But be forewarned: No matter what season it is, look for the juiciest tomatoes you can find that feel heavy for their size. And make sure they are fully ripe . . . or you'll be sorely disappointed. Heirloom tomatoes, in particular, have a magnificent, full flavor that's unmatched by common red varieties. Buy them in different colors for an even more impressive presentation.

2 heirloom or locally grown tomatoes in season
1 medium-size sweet onion
4 ounces Gorgonzola cheese
Balsamic vinegar, preferably high-quality aged, for
   drizzling
Extra-virgin olive oil for drizzling
Sea salt and freshly ground black pepper

1. Slice the tomatoes and onion. Alternating tomato and onion slices, arrange in an overlapping pattern on a platter.

2. Crumble the cheese over the entire platter of tomatoes and onions and drizzle with the vinegar and oil. Season with salt and pepper to taste.

Grilled Wild Alaskan Salmon

4 servings

From the icy waters of Alaska, wild salmon boasts a full, robust flavor. It also offers the superb health benefits of omega-3 fatty acids. Simply prepared and sublimely delicious, grilled salmon is a classic. For this menu, it's served atop the Salad with Heirloom Tomato Vinaigrette (recipe on page 88)—a combination that's sure to become a family favorite.

4 (6-ounce) portions wild Alaskan salmon fillet

1. Preheat the grill (gas or charcoal) to medium-high heat. (Tip: It's best to cover your grill rack with aluminum foil first.) Lightly oil the grill rack or foil.

2. When ready to cook, turn the grill to low. Place the fillets skin side down on the rack or foil and grill for a total of about 10 minutes, or until opaque, turning only once during cooking.

3. Serve, if desired, on top of the Salad with Heirloom Tomato Vinaigrette (recipe on page 88).

NOTE: Keep the grill hot to prepare the Peaches with Peppered Ice Cream (recipe on page 88).

WINE PAIRINGS

Austria: Wachau—Grüner Veltliner Federspiel
USA: California—Moscato
USA: California, Carneros—Pinot Noir

Salad with Heirloom Tomato Vinaigrette

4 servings

The sweetness of corn . . . the saltiness of feta cheese . . . the range in taste and texture of young field greens (from sweet and tender, to bitter and crisp, to peppery and pungent). Each by itself is a treat. But all together? Let's just say it's truly a flavorful, fragrant, and delightful explosion in your mouth! Add the tomato vinaigrette and you'll never make a plain salad again.

2 ears sweet corn, preferably heirloom, shucked
4 ounces goat's milk feta cheese, preferably locally made
2 cups young field greens or mesclun greens
Heirloom Tomato Vinaigrette (recipe at right)

1. Boil a pot of water for the corn. Add the corn and cook for 3 minutes. Drain, and when cool enough to handle, cut the kernels (in chunks, if you like) from the cobs. Scoop into a bowl and place in the refrigerator to cool off.

2. Drain the feta cheese and reserve the brine liquid. Roughly crumble the cheese.

3. Place the greens in a salad bowl. Add the cheese, 1 teaspoon of the brine, and the corn. Toss gently.

4. If serving with the Grilled Wild Alaskan Salmon (recipe on page 87), spoon some of the heirloom tomato vinaigrette onto each of 4 serving plates, then place the salad over the dressing, dividing evenly. Lightly drizzle the remaining vinaigrette over the salad and top with the grilled salmon. (If serving the salad by itself, toss with enough of the vinaigrette to coat nicely, reserving any remaining dressing to use within a day or so.)

Heirloom Tomato Vinaigrette

Makes about 2 cups

1 large heirloom tomato, chopped
¼ cup sherry vinegar
1 teaspoon Dijon mustard
1 shallot, peeled
2 garlic cloves
1 cup olive oil
Sea salt and freshly ground black pepper

1. Place the tomato, vinegar, mustard, shallot, and garlic in a blender or food processor. Puree to a smooth consistency. With the motor still running, slowly stream in the oil until nicely emulsified. Season with salt and pepper to taste.

Peaches with Peppered Ice Cream

4 servings

This combination may very well be the biggest surprise of this book. *Ice cream with vinegar and pepper?!* Rest assured, it is absolutely, unequivocally, and utterly delicious. You've just got to taste it to believe it. And be sure to try and find the specific local type of peach Pete recommends below, available from late July to end of August. Otherwise, feel free to substitute any other variety in season.

4 fresh, ripe peaches, preferably Ohio Red Heaven, unpeeled
Olive oil
1 pint vanilla ice cream
Balsamic vinegar, preferably high-quality aged
Freshly ground black pepper

1. Preheat the grill (gas or charcoal) to medium-high heat.

2. Cut the peaches either in half (pitted) or in thick slices. Brush a little oil on all the cut sides.

3. Grill the peaches, cut side down, for 2 minutes. Remove from the grill.

4. Scoop the ice cream into 4 individual dessert bowls. Divide the peaches evenly among the bowls, then drizzle with balsamic vinegar to taste. Season with pepper to taste and serve.

Marlin Kaplan

Bruschetta with Fresh
Tomato Topping

Gourmet Mushroom
Trio Risotto

Mascarpone Quenelles
with Strawberries &
Balsamic Reduction

Marlin Kaplan

Former Chef/Owner, Luxe Kitchen & Lounge, Dragonfly

Accolades: Named one of theTop 100 Chefs to Watch by *Esquire;* multiple awards as one of the Best Restaurants in America by *Gourmet;* participant in the James Beard Celebrity Chef Tour; recognized by *Wine Spectator, Midwest Living,* and *Northern Ohio Live;* won Best New Restaurant award by *Cleveland Magazine;* past president of Cleveland Independents; featured in numerous publications and media, including *Nation's Restaurant News, Restaurant Hospitality, Wine Savant, CBS MoneyWatch, Continental Magazine, Frommer's, Gayot Guide, Cleveland Magazine, Cleveland Scene,* the *Plain Dealer, CDKitchen, Metromix, Cleveland Foodie,* WKYC-TV 3, WJW-TV 8, and WCPN 90.3.

During the course of one week back in the '80s, Marlin went from being a thirty-five-year-old hotshot Madison Avenue advertising exec with a graduate degree in English literature from New York University, wearing Armani suits and living the high life, to talking his way into a job as an *under*-sous chef. On a whim. By choice.

Marlin's secret tip for last-minute entertaining? "Have a chef as your best friend."

To this day, he still marvels that the chef he approached gave him a chance that fateful afternoon. Marlin literally had forty-eight hours to prove himself. So even though he was clueless in the kitchen, he watched, he mimicked, and he worked like crazy. In other words, he was driven to succeed in this new arena and was forcing himself to learn fast. It was a crash course from "the school of hard knocks," as he likes to call it. The chef ended up hiring him after the two-day trial period . . . and Marlin's been in the restaurant business ever since. Quite happily and quite successfully, we might add.

After continuing to learn the ropes at a series of restaurants throughout New York City (his hometown), Marlin worked his way up to chef position with the popular Italian restaurant Sfuzzi in Manhattan. When asked to move to Cleveland as the executive chef of Sfuzzi's then newest restaurant in Tower City, Marlin didn't even hesitate. But after finally having proved himself as a serious chef, Marlin did something he never dreamed of—or had ever planned to do. He opened his own restaurant.

The casual-but-sophisticated Marlin—his eponymous bistro—immediately earned rave reviews. Shortly afterward, this ambitious chef quickly followed with two more eateries: Pig Heaven (an upscale barbecue house) and Lira (a northern Italian venue). For a variety of reasons, they all eventually closed, making way for Marlin's next signature endeavor: One Walnut, the epitome of fine opulent dining in Cleveland's financial district. In fact, in those days, this was the place where anyone who was anyone went to eat and be seen. Marlin ran this posh, award-winning eatery for over a decade before eventually opening his smash hit in the up-and-coming Gordon Square Arts District (Luxe Kitchen & Lounge), as well as the newly rebranded Dragonfly in Ohio City. He truly is having the time of his life.

When he's not playing golf or climbing one of the highest mountains in the world (as he did in 1997 on Africa's Mount Kilimanjaro), Marlin can be seen on TV hosting lively, informative cooking shows.

Marlin lives in Cleveland's Ohio City neighborhood.

Bruschetta with Fresh Tomato Topping

4 servings

This sensational starter—particularly delicious in late summer using ripe tomatoes straight from the garden—is an easy-to-make appetizer for any party or impromptu get-together. The steps are few, and the cooking method is quite straightforward. In fact, the only step of any complexity at all (and it's not even that hard once you get the hang of it) is the chiffonading of the basil. Simply pile the leaves on top of each other, roll them into a tight bundle, and slice them into delicate green ribbons. Voilà! That's all there is to it.

1 loaf crusty French baguette, sliced into ¼-inch-thick slices
6 tablespoons extra-virgin olive oil, divided
4 Roma (plum) tomatoes, seeded and diced
6 fresh basil leaves, chiffonaded
Salt and freshly ground black pepper
Pecorino Romano cheese, shaved, for garnish

1. Preheat the oven to 350°.

2. Arrange the baguette slices in a single layer on a cookie sheet. Brush evenly with 3 tablespoons of the oil. Bake until golden brown, about 6 to 8 minutes. Remove from the oven and allow to cool.

3. Mix the tomatoes with the remaining 3 tablespoons oil in a bowl. Add the basil and mix. Season with salt and pepper to taste.

4. Place a spoonful of tomato mixture on each toasted baguette slice. Garnish with the cheese to serve.

WINE PAIRINGS

Italy: Piedmont—Barolo
Spain: Any region—Cava
USA: California—Late Harvest Riesling or Sauvignon Blanc/Sémillon blend

Gourmet Mushroom Trio Risotto

4 servings

Although risotto needs constant, careful attention and patience (above all, patience), it isn't hard to prepare—and the results are oh so worth it! This version is particularly creamy and hearty, using three different types of mushrooms. Mix and match your own variations if you'd like. (Just be sure to wipe gently first with a dampened paper towel, then remove and discard the stems.) But when it comes to the rice, use only Arborio, a plump, short-grain Italian rice named after the town of, appropriately enough, Arborio. Because it undergoes less milling than ordinary long-grain rice, it retains more of its natural starch content, thus yielding an extra creamy texture when cooked.

5 cups chicken broth, divided
5 tablespoons olive oil, divided
8 ounces fresh portobello mushrooms, wiped clean and
    sliced
8 ounces fresh cremini mushrooms, wiped clean and
    sliced
8 ounces fresh shiitake mushrooms, wiped clean, stems
    removed and discarded, caps sliced
Sea salt
2 shallots, finely diced (can substitute 1 small onion)
1½ cups Arborio rice
½ cup dry white wine
4 tablespoons (½ stick) unsalted butter
1 tablespoon finely chopped fresh parsley
1 tablespoon finely chopped fresh chives
1 tablespoon finely chopped fresh cilantro
⅓ cup freshly grated Parmesan cheese
Freshly ground black pepper
Portobello Garnish (recipe at right), optional

1. Heat the broth in a saucepan over low heat. Remove from the heat and keep warm.

2. Heat 3 tablespoons of the oil over medium-high heat in a large, deep skillet. Stir in the portobello, cremini, and shiitake mushrooms. Cook, stirring frequently, until soft and mushrooms have released their juices, about 3 minutes. Season with salt to taste. Pour the mushrooms and their liquid in a bowl. Set aside.

3. In the same skillet, over medium heat, heat the remaining 2 tablespoons oil. Stir in the shallots and cook for 1 minute. Season with salt to taste, then add the rice and stir to coat. Continue to cook, stirring, for about 2 minutes.

4. Pour in the wine, stirring constantly until the wine is fully absorbed. Add ½ cup of the warm broth to the rice. Stir until the liquid is nearly absorbed. Continue adding warm broth, ½ cup at a time, stirring continuously, until all the liquid is absorbed and the rice is al dente, about 15 to 20 minutes in total. Remember, you're cooking the rice, not boiling it.

5. Remove the skillet from the heat. Stir in the mushrooms and their liquid, then the butter, parsley, chives, cilantro, and cheese. Season with pepper to taste and serve immediately, topping each serving, if desired, with a whole Portobello Garnish.

Portobello Garnish

4 teaspoons extra-virgin olive oil
4 large fresh portobello mushrooms, stemmed and wiped
    clean

1. Heat the oil in a medium-size sauté pan over medium heat. Add the mushrooms and sauté until tender and lightly browned, 3 to 4 minutes on each side.

Mascarpone Quenelles with Strawberries & Balsamic Reduction

4 servings (2 quenelles per person)

Whoever said elegant desserts have to be fussy? This sophisticated dessert uses simple ingredients, yet is still a showstopper. We've broken the recipe down by steps, which are easy to understand and even easier to execute. And if you're wondering what a quenelle is, the term refers to a shape that is much like a rugby ball (or oval football). Chefs are using it for everything from mashed potatoes to ice cream nowadays. If you've never made one before, just follow the simple instructions below. It takes a little practice but is actually quite easy once you get the hang of it.

1 cup high-quality balsamic vinegar
Granulated sugar
4 ounces mascarpone cheese
1 vanilla bean, split, seeds scraped out and pod discarded
1 cup heavy cream, chilled
8 strawberries, stemmed and left whole
Fresh mint leaves for garnish

BALSAMIC REDUCTION:

1. Bring the balsamic vinegar to a boil in a small nonreactive saucepan over high heat. Once boiling, reduce the heat to medium. If desired, add ½ teaspoon sugar at this point. Simmer the vinegar, uncovered, until reduced by 75 percent. Remove from the heat and allow to cool.

QUENELLES:

1. Combine the mascarpone, vanilla seeds, and a pinch of sugar in a bowl, stirring gently to mix well. In another bowl that's been chilled, whip the cream until stiff peaks form. Gently fold the whipped cream into the mascarpone mixture.

2. To make the quenelles, warm two tablespoons in hot water, leaving them wet to provide some "slip" when transferring the mascarpone mixture. Take one tablespoon and scoop out a spoonful of the mascarpone mixture. Take your second spoon and scoop the mixture out from the first one in a smooth motion, following the contour of the bottom spoon as much as possible. Continue to alternate from spoon to spoon until you have a smooth result. (Note: It may help to dip each spoon in hot water again between scoops.) Place each finished quenelle on a plate in the refrigerator, covered.

3. Continue with the rest of the mascarpone mixture until you've made a total of eight quenelles. Keep refrigerated until ready to assemble the dessert.

TO ASSEMBLE:

1. Place two strawberries on each of 4 small dessert plates. Place a quenelle next to each berry. Drizzle with the balsamic reduction, garnish with the mint, and serve immediately.

John Kolar

Lobster Quesadillas
with Mango Salsa

Seared Ahi Tuna with
Mediterranean Pasta

Mock Baklava Napoleon

John Kolar

Chef/Owner, Thyme²

Accolades: Named one of the 20 Best New Restaurants in America by *Esquire*; mentioned in *Bon Appétit*; named Best New Restaurant by *Cleveland Magazine*; featured in numerous publications and media, including *Continental Magazine*, the *Los Angeles Times*, the *Cincinnati Post*, *Northern Ohio Live*, *Cleveland Magazine*, *Cleveland Scene*, the *Plain Dealer*, the *Akron Beacon Journal*, the *Medina Gazette*, *Chowhound*, *HelloCleveland*, *Cleveland Foodie*, and WKYC-TV 3.

It took a while for John to decide he wanted to cook for a living. In fact, it took about a dozen years. But hey, better late than never is the way John figures it. And we couldn't agree more.

Having grown up in Hinkley, Ohio, John graduated from Highland High School and went to college for a couple years. "But," he says with a laugh, "I really didn't know what I wanted to be when I grew up." So he left school and fell back on the job he had had since he was fourteen years old at his family's popular K&K Portage Meats store on Cleveland's West Side.

John continued to work there for the next eleven years, when suddenly he began to seriously consider a career as a chef. He spoke to several noted Cleveland-area chefs in order to seek their advice. The only one who gave him any true encouragement was Doug Katz. "He was literally the only one who didn't tell me I was crazy for wanting to go into this profession," remembers John.

In fact, Doug offered John a part-time job as a prep cook on the night shift at Moxie, his restaurant at the time. "The very first night I worked at Moxie, I was hooked," says John. "I was working the pantry, peeling carrots and making salads, but I couldn't keep my eyes off

John's secret tip for last-minute entertaining? "If you want to select items that are going to give you a bang for your buck, fondue is great. Different dips and salsas work great, too."

the hot line. I knew right then and there that cooking was what I really wanted to do 'when I grew up.'"

John went home and drew up an eight-year plan. His goal was to own his own restaurant by the age of forty. So, in line with the first part of his plan, he packed his bags and headed off to Hyde Park, New York, to attend the famed Culinary Institute of America. He also worked at various places while in school, among them the 5-star French restaurant, Equus, at the luxurious Castle on the Hudson in Tarrytown.

After graduation, a friend introduced John to world-class chef Jean-Georges Vongerichten, who offered him a position at his 3-star restaurant, Vong, located on midtown Manhattan's East Side. Under the tutelage of this culinary great, John learned all there was to learn about Thai-inspired French cuisine for the next two and a half years. But when his mother-in-law suddenly became ill, John left this post to return to Cleveland.

His old friend, Doug, once again offered him a position, this time at his Fire Food & Drink restaurant. John worked there briefly before being offered the plum role of executive chef with the then brand-new Three Birds restaurant in Lakewood.

After several years at the helm of this award-winning eatery, John left to finally open his own place, Thyme the Restaurant—a mere three months after his fortieth birthday. His plan had indeed come to fruition! Several years later John relocated his original restaurant to new space on Medina Square and renamed it Thyme² for its dual restaurant concept: one level for fine dining and the other for casual dining. Brilliant.

During his spare time, John likes to experiment with photography and get in a game of golf every now and then.

John and his wife, Kathy, reside in Medina with their two young sons, Logan and Christian.

Lobster Quesadillas with Mango Salsa

4 servings

This upscale take on a Mexican classic gets the royal treatment, not only because of its sweet, delicate lobster meat filling, but also because of the rich, buttery French Brie you'll find oozing out with every bite. The tropical mango salsa also adds just the right amount of extra zing and burst of freshness. You can find canned or frozen lobster meat in the seafood department of your grocery store or at a fish store. Then again, the beauty of this recipe is that you can also substitute so many other options, including crabmeat, shrimp (halved), chicken, or tofu, for the lobster meat. Or just leave meat out altogether for a light vegetarian version. Look for the chili paste in the Asian section of your grocery store.

MANGO SALSA

1 ripe mango, peeled, pitted, and diced small
¼ red onion, peeled and diced small
½ cucumber, peeled, seeded, and diced small
½ red bell pepper, cored, seeded, and diced small
1 tablespoon chopped fresh cilantro
2 teaspoons chili paste

GARNISH

1 cup crème fraîche
1 tablespoon chopped fresh tarragon (can substitute 1½ teaspoons dried tarragon)

QUESADILLAS

8 (6-inch) flour tortillas
8 ounces Brie cheese, edible rind trimmed off if desired, thinly sliced into ½-inch pieces
¼ red onion, thinly sliced
8 ounces roasted red peppers, canned or jarred, drained and julienned
12 ounces lobster meat, fresh cooked, canned, or frozen (and thawed), coarsely chopped
Vegetable or canola oil

1. To make the mango salsa, combine the mango, onion, cucumber, red pepper, cilantro, and chili paste in a bowl. Mix well, then set aside.

2. To make the garnish, combine the crème fraîche and tarragon in a second bowl and whisk together until thickened, about 15 seconds. Do not overwhisk! Keep chilled until needed.

3. To make the quesadillas, lay 4 of the tortillas on a flat surface. Divide half of the Brie pieces among the tortillas, arranging them evenly over each surface. Continue to top each tortilla with the evenly divided onion, roasted red peppers, lobster meat, and remaining half of the Brie pieces, in that order. Cover with the remaining tortillas and press down with firm pressure.

4. Set a dry skillet on medium-high heat. Add 2 tablespoons of the oil and heat until it shimmers. Place one quesadilla gently in the skillet, and when it turns golden brown on one side, about 3 minutes, flip gently with a spatula and continue to cook until the other side is also golden brown. Remove from the skillet. Repeat with the remaining 3 quesadillas, adding oil as necessary.

5. Cut each quesadilla into quarters. Top with the mango salsa, garnish with the crème fraîche, and serve warm.

WINE PAIRINGS

Germany: Mosel—Riesling QbA
USA: California—Chardonnay
USA: Oregon—Pinot Noir

Seared Ahi Tuna with Mediterranean Pasta

4 servings

This dish is a true symphony of complementary flavors. In fact, the seductive combination of spicy crusted ahi tuna (also known as yellowfin or bigeye, and characterized by a delicate flavor, enticing color, and meaty texture), salty capers, and sweet, juicy tomatoes—infused with the buttery richness of beurre blanc—will have everyone begging for more. Just don't be daunted by the number of steps in this deceptively easy recipe. Each step is truly quite simple and quick.

TUNA SPICE

2 tablespoons pink peppercorns
4 tablespoons coriander seeds
2 pieces star anise
1 tablespoon Szechuan peppercorns

BEURRE BLANC

½ cup cider vinegar
¼ cup dry white wine
¼ cup fresh lemon juice
1 medium-size shallot, thinly sliced
1 teaspoon black peppercorns
2 sprigs fresh thyme
1 bay leaf
2 tablespoons heavy cream
8 ounces (2 sticks) unsalted butter, chilled, cubed

PASTA

2 tablespoons extra-virgin olive oil
1 cup cherry or grape tomatoes, halved
½ cup kalamata olives, halved
¼ cup capers, drained
1½ teaspoons minced shallot
½ teaspoon minced garlic
½ pound angel hair pasta
¼ cup seasoned bread crumbs

TUNA

4 (4-ounce) ahi tuna steaks, each about 3 x 1 x 1 inches (see note)
1 teaspoon kosher salt
Vegetable or canola oil

1. To make the tuna spice, toast all the ingredients in a dry heavy skillet over moderate heat, stirring, until very fragrant and smoking, about 3 to 5 minutes. Be careful not to let the spices burn! Remove from the skillet and grind to a powder in a blender or electric coffee/spice grinder. Sift through a fine sieve, discarding the hulls. Set aside.

2. To make the beurre blanc, combine the vinegar, wine, lemon juice, shallot, peppercorns, thyme, and bay leaf in a saucepan on medium to medium-high heat. Stir to mix, then let reduce until almost dry, about 5 to 7 minutes. Stir in the cream and reduce again, about 1 to 2 minutes. Turn heat down to low. Add the butter a little at a time, whisking continuously between additions. Once all the butter has been incorporated, strain and reserve in a warm place.

3. To make the pasta, heat the oil in a large sauté pan over medium heat. Add the tomatoes, olives, capers, shallot, and garlic. Heat through, but do not let the garlic color! Turn off the heat and set aside.

4. Cook the pasta according to package directions until al dente. Drain. Add the cooked pasta to the pan with the tomato mixture. Stir well. Reheat over low heat. When warmed through, take off the heat and set the pan aside.

5. Season all sides of the tuna steaks with the salt, then dredge in the tuna spice.

6. Heat a second sauté pan over medium-high heat. Add a thin layer of oil and heat until it smokes. Add the tuna steaks and sear for about 20 seconds per side (or a little longer if you like your tuna more well done). Remove from the pan and cut each steak crosswise into 6 even slices.

7. Divide the pasta among 4 bowls or rimmed plates and drizzle with the buerre blanc. Sprinkle with the bread crumbs, then top each bowl with 6 tuna slices and serve warm.

NOTE: Have your fishmonger cut each tuna steak of the appropriate weight into the required 3 x 1 x 1-inch piece.

Mock Baklava Napoleon

4 servings

An impressive finale to an impressive meal, this unusual twist on two magnificent classic desserts—Greek baklava and French napoleon—is an ingenious interpretation. Purely ingenious. Phyllo (the Greek word for "leaf"; also spelled *fillo* or *filo*) can be found fresh at ethnic import stores or in the freezer section of your grocery store right next to the puff pastry. In fact, the world's largest producer of phyllo dough—Athens Foods—is located right here in Cleveland!

4 (14 x 9-inch) sheets phyllo dough (if frozen, thaw first)
4 tablespoons (½ stick) butter, melted, divided
3 tablespoons granulated sugar, divided
½ cup finely ground walnuts (can substitute almonds; see note)

FILLING

1 cup mascarpone cheese
¾ cup traditional ricotta cheese
½ cup dried cherries, chopped to size of mini chocolate chips
¼ cup mini chocolate chips
1 tablespoon powdered sugar

Honey for drizzling

1. Preheat the oven to 350°. Line a baking sheet with parchment or waxed paper. (You can also use a 13 x 9 x 1-inch pan, but you will need to fold the leaves to make them fit.)

2. Place one phyllo leaf on the parchment paper. (Cover the remaining leaves with a damp towel to keep them moist because they dry very quickly.) Brush the entire surface of the phyllo with some melted butter, about 1 tablespoon. Sprinkle about ¾ tablespoon of the sugar evenly over the entire surface. Repeat the process of stacking, brushing, and sprinkling two more times. Place one last phyllo leaf on top. (Your stack should now consist of a total of 4 phyllo leaves).

3. Brush the top layer with the remaining butter and sprinkle with the remaining sugar. Spread the walnuts evenly over the entire surface.

4. Score the top layer into the shapes and size of your choice (John chose triangles). The shapes should be about 3 inches long, and there should be at least 12. Then cut all the way through all the layers; however, do not separate the shapes.

5. Cover the top layer with another sheet of parchment paper. Press and bear down firmly by rolling with a small rolling pin, wine bottle, or can of vegetables so that the layers stick together. Place another baking sheet on top of the layers. (This will prevent the phyllo from curling up.)

6. Bake in the oven for about 20 minutes, or until the top layer of phyllo is light golden brown. Remove the top baking sheet. Let cool slightly.

7. Mix all the ingredients for the filling together in a bowl.

8. On each dessert plate, place one individual phyllo crisp. Carefully spoon some filling in the middle. Repeat until the layers reach your desired height, at least 3 layers per serving, with a phyllo crisp being the top layer. Drizzle honey over each napoleon.

NOTE: To finely grind shelled walnuts yourself, use a food processor, clean coffee grinder, nut mill, or blender. Pulse the nuts in small batches, continuously scraping down the sides of the container, until the desired consistency is reached. Don't overgrind or the nuts will turn to butter. (It helps to freeze the nuts before grinding.)

Nolan Konkoski

Bacon, Brie, & Peach Toasts

Crab-Topped Arctic Char
with Wilted Watercress &
Tabasco Butter

Bourbon-Glazed Bananas
with Butter Pecan Ice Cream
& Vanilla Wafers

Nolan Konkoski

Chef/Owner, SOHO Kitchen & Bar

Accolades: Named one of Top 10 Best Restaurants by *Food & Wine;* received Hot 10 List award from *Bon Appétit;* won two *Cleveland Scene* Best New Restaurant awards; host chef instructor at Solari; featured in numerous publications and media, including *Northern Ohio Live, Cleveland Magazine, Cleveland Scene,* the *Plain Dealer,* the *Heights Observer,* the *West Shore Sun, Wine & Food Travel, Metromix,* and *Cleveland Foodie.*

Growing up in a sleepy little mountain town that boasted only a couple of diners and one McDonald's, Nolan never dreamed he'd someday go on to become one of Cleveland's best chefs. How did this happen? A change of plans, actually.

Nolan was born and raised in the beautiful hamlet of Tupper Lake (population: 6,000), nestled in the Adirondack Mountains area of upstate New York, just a couple of hours' drive south of the Canadian border. It was pure, unadulterated wilderness. The next biggest town, Lake Placid, was a full forty-five minutes away by car.

After graduating from Tupper Lake High School, Nolan left for the big city—Albany, actually—to attend Siena College, where he studied English literature. He had no idea what he wanted to do with this major. He just knew he loved to write . . . and he was good at it.

But as fate would have it, during his sophomore year, in order to help pay for tuition, Nolan started working nights and weekends at a popular local Italian restaurant, Milano. Before he knew it, he was working more and studying less. Not that his grades slipped, mind you, but suddenly his focus and interest started shifting to the

Nolan's secret tip for last-minute entertaining? "Keep things simple but interesting. Have a couple of signature dishes and cocktails in your repertoire that are easy to pull together. That way you can relax, have a good time, and feel confident that people are enjoying themselves."

culinary arts. He became enamored with the possibility of this new career option. He honed his skills in the kitchen and developed a strong work ethic. Three years later, he was able to finally admit to himself what he knew all along: he was hooked on becoming a chef.

After graduation, Nolan geared up for a whole new adventure. His older brother was moving to Cleveland to follow a girl he had met in London. Nolan decided to move with him. During their first night in Cleveland, they ate at Lopez Bar & Grille on the East Side. Nolan liked it so much, he asked to fill out an application and was immediately hired as a line cook. It was there that he met and worked alongside up-and-coming chef Eric Williams. When Eric left to open Momocho, he asked Nolan to follow him. And he did.

Nolan rose quickly through the ranks, from sous chef to chef de cuisine. But after about three years, he hit what he calls "a creative ceiling" and was looking for a new challenge. That's when he joined Tartine Bistro as executive chef. And just three years later, Nolan was able to finally realize his long-held dream of opening his own place. Thus, SOHO Kitchen & Bar in Ohio City was born—and Clevelanders have been enjoying "SOuthern HOspitality" ever since!

When not slaving over a hot stove, Nolan likes to watch films (he's a self-professed movie buff) and run. He'd also like to write a screenplay or a book someday. A fictional story. About a chef, naturally.

Nolan and his life partner, Molly, live in Cleveland Heights with their young daughter, Sophie.

Bacon, Brie, & Peach Toasts

4 servings (2 toasts per person)

Think of this French-inspired appetizer as reminiscent of the types of items you would find on a classic cheese board. Salty cured meats. Rich, buttery cheeses. Sweet and tangy accoutrements. And warm, crusty, delectable bread. But all in one bite. One succulent, mouth-watering bite.

8 slices center-cut bacon
½ cup peach preserves
8 (¼-inch-thick) slices French baguette, cut crosswise
5 ounces mild Brie cheese (such as D'Affinois), cut into 8 thin pieces, rind removed if desired

1. Preheat the oven to 450°.

2. Sauté the bacon in a skillet over medium-high heat until just beginning to crisp. Transfer to paper towels to drain. (Discard the bacon grease or reserve for the Arctic Char recipe that follows.)

3. Spread 1 tablespoon of the preserves over one of the baguette slices. Top with a piece of bacon, add a piece of Brie, and place on a baking sheet. Repeat with the rest of the baguette slices.

4. Bake for about 4 minutes, or until the Brie begins to melt and the bread is just toasted. Serve warm.

Crab-Topped Arctic Char with Wilted Watercress & Tabasco Butter

4 servings

Even though the "poor man's version" of this dish allows for salmon and baby spinach substitutes, the key ingredient of crabmeat still guarantees its sophistication and elevated stature as a gourmet offering. The presentation is quite colorful and impressive as well. Your guests will be convinced you're turning pro.

4 (5-ounce) pieces Arctic char, skin and bones removed (can substitute salmon, preferably wild if available)
¼ cup Dijon mustard
8 ounces crabmeat (either lump, jumbo lump, backfin, or claw meat)
⅓ cup panko bread crumbs
Kosher salt and cracked black pepper
Olive oil
Reserved bacon grease (from the Bacon, Brie, & Peach Toasts recipe above) or additional olive oil
1 large shallot, thinly sliced
2 garlic cloves, thinly sliced
4 bunches watercress (can substitute baby spinach)
¼ cup dry white wine
5 ounces (about ⅔ stick) unsalted butter, at room temperature
2 teaspoons Tabasco sauce

1. Preheat the oven to 450°.

2. Spread the mustard evenly over each char piece. Top with the crabmeat and sprinkle with the bread crumbs. Season with salt and pepper to taste and drizzle with olive oil.

3. Place the char pieces in an ovenproof skillet and bake for 12 to 14 minutes.

4. Meanwhile, heat the bacon grease over medium heat in a second, large skillet. Add the shallot and garlic and cook until just softened. Add the watercress and sauté, tossing repeatedly, until just beginning to wilt. Remove from the heat, season with salt and pepper to taste, and divide evenly among 4 serving plates.

5. Pull the fish from the oven. Using a metal spatula, preferably a fish spatula, carefully remove the fish from the skillet. Place one fish on top of the watercress on each plate.

6. Pour the wine into the skillet that held the fish. Place it over medium-high heat, and when the wine has reduced by about two-thirds, add the butter and whisk continually until the butter has melted. Add the Tabasco sauce and whisk together until just incorporated. Drizzle over the fish and watercress on each plate and serve immediately.

Bourbon-Glazed Bananas with Butter Pecan Ice Cream & Vanilla Wafers

4 servings

This dessert fuses three of Nolan's absolute favorite desserts from the South: Bananas Foster, pecan pie, and banana pudding. Close your eyes, and you'll be able to taste all of them at the same time. In fact, if you didn't know any better, you'd swear you'd been transported to New Orleans!

4 tablespoons (½ stick) unsalted butter
⅓ cup packed dark brown sugar
2 under-ripe bananas, peeled and cut on the bias into
   ½-inch slices
⅓ cup good-quality bourbon
4 scoops butter pecan ice cream
4 to 8 vanilla wafers

1. Combine the butter and brown sugar in a skillet. Cook over medium heat, stirring constantly, until the sugar has dissolved and a caramel has formed, about 2 to 3 minutes.

2. Add the bananas and cook until the bananas just start to soften, about 2 to 3 minutes, gently turning the bananas once or twice. Increase the heat to medium high and slowly add the bourbon (be careful, as the liquor may ignite). Simmer the bananas in the sauce for about another 1 to 2 minutes. Take off the heat.

3. Put one scoop of ice cream into each of 4 bowls or wine glasses. Apportion the bananas and pour the sauce evenly over each serving. Garnish with the wafers and serve immediately.

....

WINE PAIRINGS
....

USA: California, Paso Robles—Viognier
USA: California, Russian River—Pinot Noir
USA: Oregon—Dry Riesling

Zach Ladner

Roasted Rock Cornish Hens
with Brown Butter &
Thirty-year-old
Balsamic Vinegar

Pumpkin-Ricotta Gnocchi
with Hen of the Woods
Mushrooms & Beet Greens

Zach Ladner

Executive Chef, Giovanni's Ristorante

Accolades: Valedictorian of his graduating class at the Culinary Institute of America.

Why would a young man with ambitions to become a college math professor become a chef instead? Passion. Pure, unadulterated passion.

Zach grew up an army brat. As a youngster, he moved quite often with his parents, both military doctors (now retired). Born in San Antonio, Texas, he moved to Denver and then back again to Texas (El Paso and Victoria) before graduating from Memorial High School in Victoria. He decided to attend the University of Texas at Austin as a math major. His plan was to eventually obtain a PhD and teach.

But UT was so large, with over 50,000 students, that Zach found it really difficult to get to know other students very well. So when he became a junior and moved off campus, he decided to throw a few dinner parties in order to bring people together. Before he knew it, his dinners became more and more elaborate—and his circle of friends became larger and larger. That's when it finally hit him. No other profession could make me any happier than this, thought Zach.

In order to test out his new revelation, rather than work another summer in math research, Zach decided to spend the summer between his junior and senior years working at a restaurant. By then, his family had moved to Cape Cod, Massachusetts, so he found a job as a line cook at a small Mediterranean café in Falmouth called Laureen's. He loved it. And his fate was sealed.

Zach's secret tip for last-minute entertaining? "The most important thing when trying to entertain at home in a pinch is to simply use the best seasonal ingredients you can. Tomatoes in the height of summer, or peaches in early fall are things that you need to do very little to in order to make them extraordinary. And that's important when you don't have a lot of time to prepare. Also, from a monetary standpoint, if you use ingredients in the height of their season, they will be the most inexpensive, so it makes home entertaining something that can be done on a more regular basis."

After graduating with a bachelor's degree in mathematics, Zach headed to the Culinary Institute of America in Hyde Park, New York. While there, he also worked a brief stint at Jean-Georges Vongerichten's mega-restaurant, Spice Market, in Manhattan's Meatpacking District.

After Zach graduated at the top of his class, he took a job at the Fishmonger Café back home in Woods Hole, Massachusetts. Almost a year later, anxious to move to Cleveland and join his then fiancée, Zach came across a blind ad online for a line cook at a 5-star restaurant there.

Zach flew in for the interview and was immediately hired by Giovanni's owner, Carl Quagliata. "Zach is probably one of the finest gentlemen I know," says Carl. "He's also everything you could ever want in a chef."

After working as a line cook for about a month and a half, Zach quickly moved up to sous chef. Only two more months after that, he stepped up just as quickly into the top role of executive chef. "More than anything, I love working with Carl," says Zach. "He's the best. So inspiring." The feeling is mutual indeed.

When asked what he likes to do in his spare time, Zach doesn't even hesitate. "Cook!" he says, laughing. His other interests include tennis and ballroom dancing.

Zach and his wife, Alyssa (a pastry chef), live in Highland Heights.

Roasted Rock Cornish Hens with Brown Butter & Thirty-year-old Balsamic Vinegar

4 servings

Rock Cornish hens make quite an impressive and elegant-looking entrée for guests. That's because this plump bird is not only easy to prepare and serve, its small size is suitable for individual servings. Developed in the mid-'50s by a couple in Connecticut, Rock Cornish hens are actually young chickens (no more than 30 days old) with succulent-tasting, all-white meat. Simply prepared, the hens in this recipe are elevated to a whole new level with the addition of the slightest drizzle of thirty-year-old balsamic vinegar. Why thirty years old? Just one sip and you won't have to ask again.

4 (1-pound) Rock Cornish hens
Kosher salt and freshly ground black pepper
4 ounces (1 stick) unsalted butter
Thirty-year-old balsamic vinegar for drizzling (for substitute, see note)

1. Preheat the oven to 375°.

2. Season the hens liberally with salt and pepper, both inside and out, then place on a wire rack that's been positioned inside a rimmed baking sheet so they are not sitting in their own juices as they roast. This allows for very even heat distribution, as well as wonderful crispy skin all the way around. (Be sure not to crowd the hens.)

3. Roast the hens in the oven until a digital thermometer reads 160° internal temperature, about 45 minutes.

4. Remove the hens from the oven. Tent with foil. Allow to rest like this for 10 minutes, during which time the hens will continue to carry over cooking until they reach the desired internal temperature of 165°.

5. Place the butter in a small sauté pan over medium heat. Allow to melt and cook until a nice amber brown color is achieved. Spoon evenly over the hens.

6. If serving with Pumpkin-Ricotta Gnocchi with Hen of the Woods Mushrooms & Beet Greens (recipe on page 106), place each hen on a separate dish atop a bed of the gnocchi and greens. Drizzle the vinegar sparingly over each hen before serving.

NOTE: If you can't find or afford thirty-year-old balsamic vinegar, here's a trick you can do instead: Take 2 cups of ordinary balsamic vinegar, add ½ cup sugar, and reduce over low heat until syrupy, about 20 to 40 minutes. This will give you more of the taste and consistency you need for this recipe. Yields ¾ cup, which means you will have plenty left over for future uses.

WINE PAIRINGS

France: Burgundy—Beaujolais-
   Villages
Italy: Abruzzo—Montepulciano
   d'Abruzzo
USA: Oregon—Pinot Noir

Pumpkin-Ricotta Gnocchi with Hen of the Woods Mushrooms & Beet Greens

4 servings

There is absolutely no need to feel daunted by this recipe. Once you get the hang of it, gnocchi are really and truly a snap to make. This pumpkin version turns the ordinary into the extraordinary. Toss in hen of the woods mushrooms (also known as maitake mushrooms), which boast a fabulous rich flavor, with beet greens, which feature a somewhat bitter taste, and you've got a very sophisticated combination. Nutritious beet greens can be found in the bagged salad section of your local produce department. However, if you choose to purchase an entire bunch of fresh beets just to get the greens, you can always prepare the beets for another meal. See left for some of Zach's favorite beet recipes.

Pickled Beets

1. Combine 1 quart vinegar, 2 cups sugar, and 1 to 2 bunches beets (peeled and diced). Simmer, covered, over low heat until tender. Allow to cool in the liquid. Will stay fresh in the refrigerator for up to 1 month.

Roasted Beets

1. Toss whole, scrubbed but unpeeled beets with oil. Roast at 400° until the beets are tender. Time depends on the size of the beets. Peel the roasted beets after cooking.

3 tablespoons butter
4 ounces fresh hen of the woods mushrooms, wiped clean and torn into large pieces (can substitute portobello or any other combination of mushrooms)
Kosher salt and freshly ground black pepper
8 ounces beet greens, trimmed, washed, and drained
1 tablespoon minced onion
1 garlic clove, minced
1 pound Pumpkin-Ricotta Gnocchi (recipe on page 107)
1 teaspoon chopped fresh sage (can substitute ½ teaspoon dried sage)
2 tablespoons freshly grated Parmigiano-Reggiano cheese

1. Bring a large pot of salted water to a boil.

2. Meanwhile, heat the butter in a large sauté pan over medium-high heat until browned. Add the mushrooms and cook until lightly browned, about 1 to 2 minutes. Add a pinch of salt and pepper.

3. Add the beet greens, onion, and garlic to the mushrooms. Sauté until the greens have wilted but still have texture, about 2 minutes.

4. At this point, carefully drop the gnocchi into the boiling water. Stir gently and continuously with a wooden spoon. Continue to boil until tender, or for about 1 minute after they rise to the surface.

5. Add the sage, gnocchi (right from the boiling water using a slotted spoon), and cheese to the mixture in the sauté pan. Toss lightly just to incorporate. (Don't overbrown.) Adjust the seasoning with additional salt and pepper to taste, if required. Take off heat.

Pumpkin-Ricotta Gnocchi

Makes 1 pound

These hearty gnocchi, which exude a sweet smoothness and lovely mild flavor, are guaranteed to melt in your mouth. And they're gorgeous, too, what with their deep orange hue. Be sure, however, to use only the full-fat ricotta called for in this recipe. Otherwise, the dough will become too watery, which will throw off the texture and affect the finished dish. As for the preferred 00 flour (the most highly refined of all Italian flours), it can be found in most Italian import stores.

1 cup pumpkin puree, canned or fresh (see note)
8 ounces good-quality, full-fat whole milk ricotta cheese, preferably Miceli's Traditional Ricotta
8 ounces Parmigiano-Reggiano cheese, grated
1 tablespoon pure maple syrup (not pancake syrup)
1 large egg plus 1 large egg yolk
¼ teaspoon ground cinnamon
Pinch of salt
2 cups 00 flour (can substitute bread flour)

1. If using canned pumpkin, stir it up in the can first, then measure. Combine the pumpkin puree, ricotta, Parmigiano-Reggiano, syrup, egg, egg yolk, cinnamon, and salt in a food processor. Puree until smooth.

2. Pour the pumpkin mixture into a mixing bowl. Add the flour and mix gently but thoroughly.

3. Turn the dough out onto a lightly floured surface. Knead only until the dough just begins to hold together. Be careful not to overwork or overknead the dough. It should be moist, but not sticky, and feel almost billowy. (Depending on the size of your eggs, as well as the water content of your ricotta, you may need to add additional flour as required.)

4. Form the gnocchi by carefully rolling out strands of dough into a snakelike log about the same thickness as your thumb. Cut into pieces about ¾ inch long. Dust with a bit more flour.

5. If desired, but certainly not necessary, you can use a fork or a gnocchi board to achieve the characteristic indentations on the gnocchi. If using a fork, hold it in one hand and place a gnocchi pillow against the tines of the fork, cut ends out. With a quick but light touch, use your thumb and press in and down the length of the fork. The gnocchi should curl into a slight "C" shape. If using a gnocchi board, hold it in one hand and rest a gnocchi pillow against the board at an angle with the other hand. Again, quickly but gently roll the gnocchi down the board to imprint with the indentations.

NOTE: To make fresh pumpkin puree, preheat the oven to 450°. Cut a sugar or pie pumpkin in half, scoop out the seeds, and place the pumpkin halves face down in a baking dish. Add ½ inch of water to the pan and bake until you can pierce the skin with a fork, about 45 to 60 minutes. Scoop the flesh out of the shell with a spoon and use a food processor or blender to whip it into a puree. Refrigerate or freeze unused puree for another use.

Vid Lutz

....

Fresh Tomato Tartlets

Wild Mushroom & Clam Risotto

Olive Oil Génoise with
Burnt Pineapple

Vid Lutz

Production & Development Chef, Nestlé Professional

Accolades: Ranked as both a finalist and a semifinalist at Bocuse d'Or USA Concours competitions; winner of the DiRōNA award; three-time James Beard award semifinalist nominee; hosted a James Beard House dinner in New York City; named one of the Top Restaurants in America and Best New Restaurants by *Esquire;* listed in the first edition of *The International Who's Who of Chefs;* multiple top Zagat ratings; numerous Silver Spoon awards by *Cleveland Magazine;* featured in numerous publications and media, including *Restaurant Hospitality, Cleveland Magazine, Cleveland Scene,* the *Edmond Sun,* the *Plain Dealer,* and *Free Times.*

Growing up in Detroit, Vid was exposed to many different cuisines from a very early age. In fact, his parents took him to the finest restaurants throughout the United States, Canada, and Mexico. His French nannies also helped "lay the foundation for the culinary tastes, aromas, and sounds that would become my life," says Vid.

When he was twelve years old, Vid and his family moved to Cleveland. As a teenager, he worked at Don's Fish Market on the West Side, washing dishes. After graduating from Rocky River High School, Vid headed straight to Johnson & Wales University in Providence, Rhode Island. He obtained his associate's degree in culinary arts and his bachelor's degree in food service management.

Back home in Cleveland, Vid landed a job at the well-established but transitioning Johnny's Bar on Fulton Road as their sous chef. One and a half years later, he was promoted to executive chef. "I was fortunate enough to work for a restaurant that expanded its units and concepts at the same time that was beneficial for my career to grow as well," he says.

As Johnny's became more and more well known, it started garnering plenty of awards and a steady clientele,

Vid's secret tip for last-minute entertaining? "Keep the pantry well supplied with the usual as well as the unusual. Simple additions of pickled ginger, wasabi, sweet chili, or hoisin find their ways into many dishes today. They have even bridged the Southwest and the Far East. It is easy to make a common dish seem new and exciting by changing one simple ingredient for another of the same. I also always have some homemade Bolognese sauce in the freezer and some pasta on hand, just in case."

which prompted the owners to consider expanding. They eventually opened Johnny's Downtown in the Warehouse District, which Vid also oversaw.

Vid then took a sabbatical and went to a medieval village in the south of France. There he did a *stage* with legendary, Michelin-starred chef Roger Vergé at Le Moulin de Mougins, situated on the swanky French Riviera.

Upon his return to Cleveland, Vid became responsible for all four of Johnny's restaurants, including their newest—and fourth—place, Johnny's Little Bar, in the Warehouse District.

Then suddenly, after nineteen years of overseeing all of Johnny's eateries, Vid was presented with an opportunity to go in a whole new direction. "The Nestlé Professional Customer Innovation Campus was under new construction then," he explains, "and I thought this would be a great way for me to expand my culinary knowledge, create some new and exciting foods, and at the same time spend more time with my family."

Vid joined Nestlé as executive chef of culinary innovation with Culinary Services and later moved over to Culinary Product Development. "I interact daily with a group of technologists and try to create new foods for both the branded and custom channels," he explains. "We support the brands that are sold in the food service channel, such as Toll House, Stouffer's, Lean Cuisine, Chefmate, and Hot Pockets."

How does this job compare to being in a restaurant? "Actually, there are lots of similarities between the two worlds. But my audience is much larger now," says Vid. "I'm still allowed plenty of creativity, plus I get to work with the science behind the manufacturing of the food."

In his spare time, Vid likes to collect antique Mickey Mouse paraphernalia.

Vid lives in Rocky River with his wife, Ann, and their two children, Vid Jr. and Mary.

Fresh Tomato Tartlets

4 servings

These tartlets, especially delicious in the summer using local tomatoes, can be served as an elegant appetizer (as Vid does here), a side dish, or a brunch item. And although Vid would ordinarily make his own tart shell, in the name of efficiency, he calls for 4-inch prebaked tart shells. (He got his savory version online from Albert Uster Imports.) You can also use a refrigerated pie crust, which would need to be prebaked in a 10- or 11-inch tart pan before adding the filling and then served as wedges after completion.

5 large eggs
¾ cup freshly grated Parmesan cheese
⅓ cup heavy cream
1 tablespoon virgin olive oil
1 teaspoon minced garlic (1 medium clove)
½ teaspoon minced fresh rosemary
¼ teaspoon freshly crushed black pepper
4 (4-inch) prebaked tart shells
1 pound heirloom tomatoes, preferably different colors, sliced

TOPPING

½ cup plain bread crumbs
¼ cup freshly grated Parmesan cheese
2 tablespoons almond flour (can substitute all-purpose flour)
2 tablespoons olive oil
1½ teaspoons chopped fresh basil
½ teaspoon chopped fresh parsley
½ teaspoon chopped fresh thyme
½ teaspoon freshly cracked black pepper

1. Preheat the oven to 350°.

2. Thoroughly whisk together the eggs, Parmesan cheese, cream, oil, garlic, rosemary, and pepper in a bowl. Pour evenly into the prebaked tart shells.

3. Arrange the sliced tomatoes on top, overlapping each one around the perimeter of the tart in circles, starting around the outside edge first and finishing with one last slice in the center.

4. Mix all the ingredients for the topping in a separate bowl. Sprinkle over the sliced tomatoes.

5. Bake for about 25 minutes, or until the tomatoes are soft and the topping is golden brown. (Will need to bake longer if using one large tart pan.) Remove from the oven. Let cool slightly before serving.

Wild Mushroom & Clam Risotto

4 servings

This is a very rich and creamy version of risotto, highlighted by the woodsy flavor of the mushrooms and the sweet, slightly "oceany" flavor of the clams. In the rare chance there's any left over, it's also very good reheated the next day. Just be sure, though, when shopping for the clams, they are completely closed with no cracks in the shells and no foul odor. For a wonderful vegetarian version, just leave out the clams and use vegetable stock instead.

4 cups chicken stock, divided
4 tablespoons olive oil, divided
2 tablespoons unsalted butter
½ cup diced white onion (can substitute yellow onion)
3 garlic cloves, minced, divided
12 ounces fresh wild mushrooms, stemmed, wiped clean and chopped
Kosher salt
½ cup dry white wine
1½ cups Arborio rice
2 pounds fresh littleneck clams, scrubbed (can substitute mussels)
¼ cup chopped fresh parsley
Freshly ground black pepper
¼ cup freshly grated Parmesan cheese
8 fresh parsley sprigs for garnish

1. Bring the stock to a boil in a small pot. Take off the heat and keep warm.

2. Heat 3 tablespoons of the oil and the butter in a heavy-bottomed pot over medium heat. Add the onion and cook until translucent. Add two-thirds of the garlic and all the mushrooms. Season with a pinch of salt and sauté for about 2 to 3 minutes.

3. Add the wine and rice. Stir. Cook until the rice has absorbed the wine and is well coated with the oil and butter, no more than 3 minutes.

4. Add 1 cup of the warm stock, lower the heat, and stir. When all the liquid has been absorbed, add 1 more cup of stock and keep stirring. Continue cooking like this until the rice has completed cooking and the risotto is creamy, about 15 to 20 minutes. Set aside.

5. Inspect all the clams and make sure they are closed. If not, discard. Heat the remaining 1 tablespoon oil with the remaining garlic over medium-high heat in a medium-size saucepan. Add the clams and the chopped parsley and lower the heat to medium. Cover the pan and cook until the clams open up, about 5 minutes.

6. Using a slotted spoon, remove the clams from the saucepan and set aside. Pour the clam liquid from the saucepan through a cheesecloth-lined strainer into a small bowl. Add some of this liquid to the risotto and stir thoroughly. Season with salt and pepper to taste and let sit for 5 minutes.

7. Place the risotto in 4 soup plates or bowls. Garnish with the grated cheese and the parsley sprigs. Divide the cooked clams evenly and place them around the risotto in each soup plate. Serve warm.

WINE PAIRINGS

Italy: Abruzzo—Trebbiano
    d'Abruzzo
Italy: Any region—Recioto dessert
    wine
USA: California, Carneros—Pinot
    Noir

Olive Oil Génoise with Burnt Pineapple

4 servings (6 bars per person)

This light, elegant dessert, which Vid learned to prepare in France, is not only quick and simple, it's not overly sweet either. You can easily whip this up at the last minute and wow your dinner guests. Even if you opt to leave off the pineapple, it would still taste great dusted with just a little powdered sugar. But the versatility of this dessert doesn't stop there. The fun is in the garnish you choose, be it a berry chutney topped with a sliver of crystallized ginger, a citrus compote, crème fraîche, gelato, or sorbet—all great choices!

3 large eggs, at room temperature
½ cup fruit sugar (can substitute granulated sugar)
1 tablespoon freshly grated lemon zest
1 tablespoon freshly grated orange zest
⅓ cup good-quality olive oil
⅓ cup whole milk
¾ cup cake flour, sifted
2 tablespoons almond flour (can substitute cake flour)
1 teaspoon baking powder
1 small pineapple
Fruit sugar as needed (can substitute turbinado sugar, more commonly known as Sugar in the Raw)
Berry Chutney (store-bought or homemade, recipe at right), crystallized ginger, Olive Oil–Poached Citrus Compote (recipe at right), crème fraîche, gelato, or sorbet for garnish, optional

1. Preheat the oven to 400°. Grease a small rimmed baking pan (about 12 x 8½ x 1 inches), line the bottom with parchment paper, grease again on top of the paper, and dust with flour. (If using a nonstick pan, there's no need to grease at all.)

2. Whip the eggs in a bowl. Add the sugar, lemon zest, and orange zest. Continue to whip to a thick, ribbon stage. Slowly stream in the oil and milk while still whipping. Set aside.

3. In another bowl, mix the cake flour, almond flour, and baking powder. Firmly but gently fold the flour mixture into the egg mixture with a rubber spatula until blended. Try to do this quickly and only until combined. Don't take too many strokes or you'll break down the air cells. The batter will be relatively thin.

4. Pour the batter into the prepared pan and bake for about 10 to 15 minutes, or until lightly golden brown and firm to the touch. Remove from the oven and let cool slightly.

5. Once the cake is cool enough to turn out, run a knife around the edges and flip it upside down onto a cutting board. Peel off parchment paper. Cut the cake into 2 x 3-inch pieces; you should have about 16. Set aside.

6. Cut off both the top and bottom of the pineapple. Next, cut the sides close to the skin so that the pineapple is squared off. (No need to cut the core.) Slice the pineapple into ¼-inch-thick planks. Last, cut the slices into as many 2 x 3-inch rectangles as the cake pieces.

7. Place one pineapple rectangle on top of each cake rectangle. Sprinkle with the sugar. Either blowtorch or broil the sugar until it turns golden brown on top (see note).

8. Serve with your choice of garnish, if desired.

NOTE: If using a blowtorch, either a specialty butane kitchen torch or a regular propane blowtorch will do. Just make sure you hold it 2 to 3 inches above the sugar surface, moving it back and forth to ensure even browning. And after torching or broiling, make sure the sugar cools before touching it, as it will get very hot.

Berry Chutney

¼ cup small-diced strawberries or other berries
2 tablespoons agave syrup (can substitute honey)
1 tablespoon chopped crystallized ginger
1 teaspoon chopped fresh basil or mint
1 teaspoon freshly grated orange zest

1. Mix all the ingredients together in a small bowl and refrigerate, covered, until needed.

Olive Oil–Poached Citrus Compote

1 grapefruit
1 seedless orange (such as navel)
1½ cups olive oil

1. Peel and segment the grapefruit and the orange (see note); remove any seeds from the grapefruit. Place the segments in a saucepan. Add the oil. Slowly poach on very low heat until warm, about 10 to 20 minutes. Remove from the heat and slightly drain the fruit before serving at room temperature.

NOTE: Holding each peeled fruit in your hand one at a time, gently slide your knife between the membrane walls toward the center of the fruit to loosen each segment.

James Major

Pork Paillard with
Citrus Glaze

Raisin & Scallion Couscous

Fruit Crisp

James Major

Executive Chef, Cleveland Indians Dining (Delaware North Companies)

Accolades: Invited to the White House to help launch First Lady Michelle Obama's Chefs Move to Schools initiative; collaborator with the *Food Network;* won Best of the Fest award at the Taste of Cleveland event; contributing chef at the 2010 World Series in Texas and the 2010 opening of the New Meadowlands Stadium in New Jersey; host chef of Major League Baseball's 2009 All-Star Game gala and pregame party in St. Louis; contributor to the *Home Plate* cookbook; earned Chef de Cuisine certification by the American Culinary Federation; featured in numerous publications and media, including *USA Today, Food Management, Yosemite Park News,* the *Virginia-Pilot, Ohio Magazine, Cleveland Magazine,* the *Plain Dealer,* the *Morning Journal,* the *Packer, Cleveland Scene, Cookerati, The Street, ClevelandPeople, ClevelandWomen, ClevelandSeniors, Examiner,* WKYC-TV 3, and WAVY-TV 10.

James's secret tip for last-minute entertaining? "Don't panic. Cook what you know. This is not the time to reinvent the wheel. And by all means have fun! When you cook from the heart, a great night will be had by all."

James had the best of both worlds growing up. One day he would be learning how to make homemade pasta and meatballs with his Italian *nonna.* The next day he would be learning how to make cabbage noodles and poticas with his Croatian *baka.* Both grandmothers exposed James to the delicacies of Mediterranean and Eastern European cuisines alike. He was predestined to enjoy all of life's bounty.

James grew up in Willowick, Ohio. When he was only sixteen years old, he got his first job at a Kentucky Fried Chicken. Two years later, he graduated from St. Joseph High School and continued working at KFC. He would spend his free time watching the Food Network and dreaming of becoming a chef. When he reached twenty-one, he realized he wanted to do more with his life. But when he looked into culinary school, the tuition was more than he could afford. So he enlisted in the Navy instead.

His plan was to not only see the world, but to also see if cooking was something he'd like to do for the rest of his life. After taking the required entrance exam, which he aced, James was asked to rank his duty preferences. He listed "cook" as number one. He got his wish. James spent the next three and a half years as a cook aboard the USS *Gunston Hall,* an amphibious dock landing ship based in Norfolk, Virginia.

As a Navy cook, James was responsible for serving more than 2,000 meals a day, managing the officer's dining hall, and overseeing the bake shop. It was hard work, but he finally found his answer. Yes, this was indeed what he wanted to do for the rest of his life.

After he left the Navy, James headed straight to the Culinary Institute of America in Hyde Park, New York. While there, he served an externship at the elegant Café Centro on Park Avenue in midtown Manhattan. He also worked weekends at Mohonk Mountain House, a distinguished Victorian castle resort in the Hudson Valley.

After graduating from the CIA, James returned home and joined The Harp on the West Side. He then went to Johnny's Bar for the next three and a half years, rotating between both their downtown and Fulton Road locations. What followed next turned out to be a great adventure for James. He bought—and revamped—the iconic Club Isabella in University Circle and made it his own: Major's Club Isabella.

After four years, James sold the club and joined global food service leader Delaware North Companies Sportservice, a partner of the Cleveland Indians as well as more than twenty other professional sports teams around the country. James first started as the top chef of the Terrace Club at Progressive Field, overseeing a culinary staff that serves more than 40,000 fans in concessions, clubs, and suites on game days.

Within a year, he was promoted to executive chef. And only a year after that, he was promoted to regional executive chef overseeing all the Sportservice locations in Ohio, Pennsylvania, Tennessee, North Carolina, Maryland, and Florida. He's been having a ball ever since (excuse the pun)!

When not working, James can be found either playing golf or hunting.

James lives in Willowick with his wife, Lori, and their two daughters, Leah and Grace.

Pork Paillard with Citrus Glaze

4 servings

Bottom line: James loves pork *and* he loves to grill. ("I'm a charcoal guy!") So when his wife calls on a game day and tells him friends are coming over, this is the dish he's most likely to make. Just be sure to ask your butcher to french your pork chops for you. It's a whole heck of a lot easier that way.

Freshly squeezed juice of 3 limes, strained
Freshly squeezed juice of 3 oranges, strained
1 cup packed brown sugar or palm sugar
1½ teaspoons red pepper flakes
4 (10-ounce) pork chops, frenched and pounded (can substitute boneless sliced pork loin)
Kosher salt

1. Preheat the grill (preferably charcoal) to medium-high heat.

2. In a bowl, stir together the lime juice, orange juice, brown sugar, and red pepper flakes until the sugar is dissolved. Set aside.

3. Season both sides of each pork chop with salt to taste. Place the chops in a large zippered plastic bag and add the marinade. Squeeze out all the air and seal the bag. Shake the bag well to ensure the chops are coated thoroughly. Place in the refrigerator for 30 to 45 minutes (but the longer, the better).

4. Remove the chops from the bag. Drain the marinade into a small saucepan and cook over medium heat to reduce the quantity to half. It should be the consistency of barbecue sauce and coat the back of a spoon. Set this glaze aside.

5. Grill the chops on the first side for 1 to 2 minutes. Flip and brush with the glaze, then cook for another 1 to 2 minutes. Keep flipping, brushing, and repeating every 1 to 2 minutes until the pork is cooked to your liking and has a nice coat of glaze on it. (The internal temperature should be 150° to 160°.) Take off the grill and serve warm.

....
BEER/WINE PAIRINGS
....

England: Brown ale
Germany: Rhein or Mosel—Riesling QBA
Italy: Friuli or Trentino—Pinot Grigio
New Zealand: Marlborough—Sauvignon Blanc

Raisin & Scallion Couscous

4 servings

This simple yet impressive side dish is very user friendly and makes you look like a real foodie. The bonus is that it also tastes great the next day. Just be sure to buy Moroccan couscous (which looks like cornmeal) versus Israeli couscous (which looks like tiny balls). James was actually taught by a Moroccan-born chef to use his hands when rubbing the oil into the couscous. "Become one with the couscous!" the chef would tease. James used golden raisins, currants, and diced dried apricots. If serving with a beef dish, use beef stock instead of chicken. And for a vegetarian version, use water seasoned with dried herbs and salt instead of the stock.

¾ cup Moroccan couscous
1 tablespoon olive oil
3 tablespoons raisins or other combination of diced dried fruit
1¾ cups chicken stock
Salt and freshly ground black pepper
3 tablespoons sliced scallions (green onions)

1. Place the couscous in a metal or glass bowl. Add the oil. Rub thoroughly with your hands, coating all the grains. Add the raisins and stir together. Set aside.

2. Bring the stock to a boil in a saucepan. Pour the boiling stock over the couscous mixture in the bowl, then cover the bowl with plastic wrap and let stand for 10 minutes on the counter.

3. Fluff the couscous with a fork and add salt and pepper to taste. Stir in the scallions and serve warm.

Fruit Crisp

4 servings

The beauty of this dessert is that you can use any fruit that's in season. Make it all one variety or a combination. Some suggestions? Try peaches and plums, pears and apples, strawberries and rhubarb, or mixed berries. James used peaches, apples, and nectarines in his version (with orange juice). His preference is to always include one apple or pear in the mix, no matter what other fruit is being used. "It adds stability," he explains.

2 pounds fresh fruit in season (peeled and cored if using apples, peaches, plums, or pears)
¼ cup water or fruit juice
2 tablespoons cornstarch
½ cup rolled oats (same as old-fashioned oatmeal)
½ cup all-purpose flour
¼ cup packed brown sugar
½ teaspoon ground cinnamon
Pinch of salt
4 tablespoons (½ stick) unsalted butter, sliced and at room temperature
Vanilla ice cream, optional

1. Preheat the oven to 350°.

2. If using a baking dish, slice the fruit into wedges. If using individual ramekins, dice the fruit. However, if using small berries, skip this step as there is no need to cut.

3. Place the fruit in a bowl. Add the water, and sprinkle with the cornstarch. Toss gently, then place the fruit mixture in either an ungreased 8- or 9-inch square baking dish, individual ramekins (any size), or ovenproof ceramic coffee cups or mugs. Set aside.

4. In a second bowl, mix the rolled oats with the flour, brown sugar, cinnamon, and salt. Using either your hands, a pastry blender, a fork, or two knives (one in each hand), thoroughly cut in the butter until the mixture resembles coarse crumbs. Sprinkle over the fruit.

5. Bake for 35 to 45 minutes, or until the topping starts to brown. Serve warm with a scoop of vanilla ice cream, if desired.

Matt Mathlage

Caramelized Onion
& Chèvre Tart

Lamb Burgers with
Greek Yogurt Sauce

Summer Farro Salad

Apple Fritters

Matt Mathlage

Executive Chef/Owner, Light Bistro

Accolades: Awarded four consecutive AAA 4-diamond designations; first place winner in *Cleveland Scene's* Iron Fork competition; won Best New Restaurant awards by *Cleveland Magazine, Cleveland Scene,* and *Northern Ohio Live;* tied for *Northern Ohio Live's* Best Chef in Cleveland; featured panelist at Cleveland's Emerging Chefs presentation sponsored by The City Club of Cleveland; featured in numerous publications, including *Gourmet, Food & Wine, Wine Savant, Kaleidoscope Magazine, Northern Ohio Live's Dining Guide, Cleveland Magazine,* the *Plain Dealer, Chowhound,* WKYC-TV 3, and WJW-TV 8.

When Matt finally figured out he wanted to become a chef, he told his mom. As a restaurant manager herself, what do you suppose was her first reaction? "She cried and begged me not to do it!" laughs Matt.

Growing up in Akron, Ohio, Matt always helped his hard-working parents, who were both in the restaurant business. In fact, when he was only twelve years old, Matt was already working the kitchens after school and on the weekends. When he turned fifteen, he landed his first "fine dining" job at the Akron City Club.

But Matt also found time to participate in extracurricular activities, such as playing linebacker for North High School. After graduation, he attended Ohio Northern on a football scholarship. But his true calling—a career in food—kept tugging at him. He decided to transfer to the (now defunct) International Culinary Academy in Pittsburgh.

Two years later, Matt completed his degree in specialized culinary arts. He landed a position at Jackie McConnell's Restaurant & Pub in Akron. After a year, he left to join the Old Whedon Grille in Hudson and then the Fairlawn Country Club. Afterward, he joined the critically

Matt's secret tip for last-minute entertaining? "A little common sense goes a long way. Be confident when you're cooking . . . keep it simple . . . and roll with the punches. At the end of the day, everyone is just there to be together. Great food is a huge plus, but it's not the end of the world if something doesn't go 'perfectly'!"

acclaimed Bertram Inn & Conference Center in Aurora as their executive chef, remaining there for nearly seven years.

Yet even with all the success he was enjoying, one nagging thought still remained. "It had always been a dream of mine to open my own restaurant," explains Matt. With an investor, he set out to find a site. One place they looked at was Parker Bosley's newly closed bistro location in Ohio City. "Parker and I hit it off right away," says Matt. "To be able to take over his restaurant was a perfect fit."

Within a couple of weeks, they had a signed deal—a time frame virtually unheard of in the industry. Light Bistro was born and has been a success ever since. "Parker set the groundwork for Cleveland's farm-to-table movement," says Matt, "and I'm now proud to carry on that tradition in the same building where he did it before us."

When not cooking, reading, or playing poker, Matt likes to entertain at home. But one of his most talked-about parties was actually a near disaster.

It was a Sunday. They were expecting company. His wife had the house all ready. But after a busy weekend at the restaurant and having been called out of the house nearly that entire day, he was completely unprepared with the food—which was his end of the bargain. He thought he'd have enough time to just whip something up before the guests arrived. *Wrong!* They were already pulling up. "So I basically put on a cooking demo for the first half of the party," explains Matt. "As the courses were cooked, everyone was able to enjoy them. People still ask me to this day when I'm going to host another 'cooking class party.' If they only knew!" he chuckles.

Matt and his wife, Jaimie, live in Sagamore Hills with their two young sons, Aiden and Gaven.

Caramelized Onion & Chèvre Tart

4 servings

The burst of flavors in this appetizer is quite a nice surprise! In fact, when people ask Matt to bring an appetizer to their party, this is his first choice. Served with a salad, it could also be considered a meal in itself. And the secret to working with puff pastry, which can be found in your grocer's freezer section? Simple. "After thawing, be sure to keep it cold until ready to use," says Matt.

5 to 6 ounces chèvre (goat cheese), at room temperature
2 ounces cream cheese, softened
¾ teaspoon whole-grain mustard
1½ teaspoons fresh basil chiffonade
¼ teaspoon freshly ground black pepper
2 tablespoons unsalted butter
1 medium Vidalia onion or other sweet domestic onion, peeled and cut into
    ¼-inch-thick slices
1 (9 x 9-inch) sheet frozen puff pastry, thawed at room temperature for 40
    minutes or in the refrigerator for 4 hours
1 (8-ounce) can artichoke hearts, drained
Good Spanish olive oil for drizzling

1. Preheat the oven to 400°. Line a baking sheet with a Silpat (nonstick baking mat) or parchment paper.

2. Fold together the chèvre, cream cheese, mustard, basil, and pepper in a bowl. Set aside at room temperature.

3. Melt the butter in a sauté pan over medium heat. Add the onion and cook, stirring occasionally, until dark brown and caramelized, about 15 minutes. Remove from the heat and set aside.

4. Place the puff pastry sheet on the lined baking sheet. If the pastry becomes too soft, chill it in the refrigerator for a few minutes. Handle as little as possible to ensure tenderness.

5. Spread the cheese mixture over the puff pastry, leaving a ½-inch border all the way around. If the filling is too stiff to spread, heat it in a microwave at 15-second spurts until it's soft enough to spread.

6. Top with the onions and artichokes. Bake for about 15 minutes, or until golden brown.

7. Remove from the oven and cut into equal squares or triangles. Drizzle with the oil and serve warm or at room temperature.

WINE PAIRINGS

France: Burgundy—Mâcon-Fuissé or Mâcon Villages
USA: California, Napa—Zinfandel
USA: California, Sonoma—Zinfandel

Lamb Burgers with Greek Yogurt Sauce

4 servings

These burgers are big. REALLY big—in flavor, taste, *and* size! A great departure from your run-of-the-mill hamburgers, they will elevate any casual barbecue. And the sauce, well, it's what makes this dish so extra special. (Hint: Don't skimp on the buns. A burger this great deserves the biggest, best-quality buns you can find.)

Greek Yogurt Sauce

Makes about 2 cups

Not only does this delicious sauce (also called tzatziki sauce) pair wonderfully with Matt's lamb burgers, but it is also versatile enough to serve as a vegetable dip or salad dressing. Heck, why stop there? Other uses include a topping or spread for baked potatoes, sandwiches, pita wraps, you name it!

1 cup plain Greek yogurt
1 tablespoon fresh lemon juice
1 small garlic clove
1 teaspoon salt
1 teaspoon chopped fresh dill
1 cup diced English cucumber or
    seedless cucumber, unpeeled
Freshly ground black pepper

1. Place the yogurt, lemon juice, garlic, salt, and dill in a food processor or blender and pulse until well blended. Fold in the diced cucumber. Season with pepper to taste. Place in the refrigerator to chill before serving.

2 pounds freshly ground lamb (can substitute ground lamb/beef combination or beef)
1 tablespoon minced fresh mint
2 teaspoons chopped fresh thyme (can substitute 1 teaspoon dried thyme)
Salt and freshly ground black pepper
4 ciabatta or sourdough buns
Greek Yogurt Sauce (recipe at left)
Lettuce, optional
Tomato slices, optional
Red onion slices, optional

1. Preheat the grill (gas or charcoal) to high heat.

2. Mix the lamb, mint, and thyme and form into 4 equal 8-ounce patties. Season with salt and pepper to taste.

3. Grill the patties on each side until the internal temperature reaches 145° to 160°, meanwhile toasting the split buns on the top rack of the grill, in a toaster oven, or under the broiler.

4. Remove the burgers from the grill, place on the buns, and serve immediately, topped with the yogurt sauce. If desired, garnish with lettuce, tomato, and/or onion.

Summer Farro Salad

4 servings

Farro (or emmer wheat) is an ancient variety of hard wheat. The grain, which is cultivated in Tuscany, Italy, is rich in fiber, protein, and magnesium. Look for farro in health food stores and specialty food stores. This vividly colorful dish, which is especially popular for summer picnics, has a lot of different tastes going on—yet they complement each other so brilliantly. There's a real depth of flavors going on here.

¾ cup semi-pearled farro (can substitute barley, but follow directions on package)
½ bunch asparagus, preferably local, trimmed and cut into 1-inch lengths
½ cup fresh spring peas (can substitute frozen)
2½ tablespoons chopped fresh dill
1 tablespoon chopped fresh parsley
¾ cup cherry, grape, or teardrop tomatoes, halved
¼ medium red onion, diced small
¼ cup olive oil
2 tablespoons sherry vinegar
1½ teaspoons honey
Freshly ground black pepper
4 to 6 ounces feta cheese, crumbled

1. Bring 3 cups of water to a boil in a medium-size saucepan. Add the farro. Cook until tender, about 12 to 15 minutes. Drain and reserve in a large bowl.

2. Meanwhile, bring another pot of salted water to a boil. Add the asparagus and fresh peas. (If using frozen peas, no need to blanch the peas, just thaw.) Blanch for 3 minutes, then drain and chill under cold running water.

3. Add the asparagus and peas to the farro. Stir together. Add the dill, parsley, tomatoes, and onion. Stir again and set aside.

4. In a separate small bowl, whisk together the oil, vinegar, and honey. Season with pepper to taste. (No need for salt since the feta will give you the saltiness you need.)

5. Fold the dressing and feta into the farro and vegetables and serve at room temperature or chilled.

Apple Fritters

4 servings

These sweet, delicious fritters are a very simple dish to make for a quick snack or dessert. Simple is truly the key word here. And if desired, go ahead and serve them with a little pure maple syrup. Just remember, try to buy local apples; they're the best. And even though apples are available year-round, peak season is really only from September through November.

1 cup all-purpose flour
¼ cup granulated sugar
1½ teaspoons baking powder
1 teaspoon salt
⅓ cup milk
1 large egg
1 cup finely chopped, peeled Granny Smith apple (can substitute any other tart apple)
Vegetable oil
Powdered sugar, sifted

1. Sift together the flour, sugar, baking powder, and salt into a bowl. Add the milk and egg and beat until the batter is smooth. Fold in the apple.

2. Pour enough oil into a deep fryer or large heavy saucepan to reach a depth of 2½ to 3 inches. Heat over medium heat until a deep-fry thermometer reads 350° to 375°. (Be sure to follow standard safety procedures when frying.)

3. Drop the batter by teaspoonfuls into the hot oil in batches. Fry until nicely golden brown and cooked through, turning occasionally and adjusting heat to maintain oil temperature. Do not overcrowd.

4. Remove the fritters as they are done with a slotted spoon or wire skimmer and drain well on paper towels. While still warm, dust with the powdered sugar. Serve immediately.

Loretta Paganini

Penne Pasta di Verdura

Italian Mixed Green Salad

Cranberry & Pistachio
Biscotti

Loretta Paganini

Executive Chef/Owner, The Loretta Paganini School of Cooking, Sapore Restaurant; Director, International Culinary Arts & Sciences Institute

Accolades: Earned the American Culinary Chef Federation's Educator of the Year award; winner of the Tri-State Premier Chef Competition; multiyear recipient of the Top 10 Women Business Owners of Northeast Ohio award from the Cleveland Chapter of the National Association of Women Business Owners; multiple awards from *Cleveland Magazine,* including Cleveland's Most Interesting People and Best Cooking School in Cleveland; multiple awards from *Cleveland Scene;* cover story subject for *Avenues;* featured in numerous publications and media, including *Wine Savant, Ohio Magazine, Ohio Authority, Cleveland Magazine,* the *Plain Dealer,* the *Lakewood Observer,* the *Newark Advocate,* the *Star Beacon,* the *News-Herald,* the *Courier Journal, TLC, Epicurious, ClevelandWomen, Examiner, Metromix,* WKYC-TV 3, and WDOK 102.1.

Born and raised in Bologna, Italy, Loretta was literally surrounded by culinary greats since birth. Her mother was a highly respected pastry chef who not only owned her own fine bakery shop but also starred in a TV cooking show and served as the president of the Bakers Association. Both grandmothers were also exceptional cooks who taught Loretta her early ways around the kitchen.

Loretta originally had no intention of following her predestined culinary path. Instead, she earned a degree in elementary education and started to teach in Italy. But then her husband, a doctor, was offered a residency in New York City, so they moved to the States. Some time later he accepted a position at the Cleveland Clinic. Loretta and their young daughters followed—and decided to permanently make Cleveland home.

It was in Cleveland's Little Italy neighborhood that

Loretta's secret tip for last-minute entertaining? "Keep it simple . . . plan ahead . . . be prepared and organized . . . and make sure to have a glass of wine before the guests arrive."

Loretta began to teach cooking classes in her native Italian language, making good use of her culinary experience at the famed Cordon Bleu in Paris, where she took classes after moving to the U.S. As her English improved, her classes grew. That's when Loretta decided to open her own cooking school. Today, the Loretta Paganini School of Cooking in Chesterland offers dozens of classes each month to the nonprofessional home cook.

Not one to rest on her laurels, Loretta eventually decided to open yet another culinary school, this time for individuals who wanted to be professionally trained as chefs. The International Culinary Arts & Sciences Institute (ICASI) now offers four state-registered programs in a brand-new, state-of-the-art facility down the road from her first school. It has an affiliation with both Ursuline College and Lakeland Community College. Plus, she also opened a fine dining restaurant in the area, called Sapore (the Italian word for "flavor").

Loretta makes time to teach classes at Fisher Foods in North Canton, regularly appears on both TV and radio talk shows (just like her mom did years before), coproduces special programs, stars on commercials, creates cooking videos, writes both print and online food columns, authors cookbooks (three so far), leads gastronomic tours throughout Italy and France, and flies. Yes, Loretta is a certified pilot who loves to take to the skies as often as she gets a chance.

Loretta and her husband, Emil, have three grown daughters: Elizabeth, Stefanie (a pastry instructor and director of student services at ICASI), and Julia. They split their time between homes in Chesterland and Chiavari, Italy. Their two dogs, Molly and Sam, tend to stay in Chesterland.

Penne Pasta di Verdura

4 servings

A pasta dish this loaded with so many vegetables is not only good for you, it's so darned colorful, too! (FYI: *Verdura* is the Italian word for "vegetables.") Try using whole-wheat pasta if you wish. But the true beauty of this recipe is that you can substitute any similar vegetables that are growing in your garden or are in season. Serve as an entrée (as done here), or make half a recipe and serve as a side dish with another entrée. Either way, this recipe will probably yield way more than enough, which means you'll inevitably have leftovers, although frankly, that's not a bad thing come tomorrow.

1 teaspoon chopped fresh rosemary
1 teaspoon chopped fresh basil
1 teaspoon chopped fresh parsley
1 teaspoon chopped fresh chives
¼ cup extra-virgin olive oil
1 yellow onion, finely chopped
2 red bell peppers, cored, seeded, and thinly sliced
2 potatoes, peeled and cubed small
2 carrots, peeled and chopped
2 celery stalks, trimmed and chopped
¼ cup sun-dried tomatoes, sliced
1 (15- to 16-ounce) can white cannellini beans, rinsed and drained

½ cup whole snow peas
¼ cup dry white wine
¼ cup chicken broth
Salt and freshly ground black pepper
1 pound penne pasta
¼ cup freshly grated Parmigiano-Reggiano cheese for garnish

1. Bring a large pot of water to a boil.

2. Meanwhile, combine the rosemary, basil, parsley, and chives in a small bowl. Stir well and set aside.

3. Heat the oil in a large skillet over medium heat. Add the onion, peppers, potatoes, carrots, celery, sun-dried tomatoes, and beans and cook for 5 to 10 minutes.

4. Add the snow peas, wine, and broth. Cook for another 5 to 10 minutes to reduce the sauce, then take off the heat. Season with salt and pepper to taste and set aside.

5. When the water in the pot is boiling, add a tablespoon of salt and the pasta. Cook according to package directions until al dente. Drain and place in a bowl, then add the sauce and herb mixture and toss well.

6. Divide the pasta among 4 plates. Garnish with the cheese and serve warm.

Italian Mixed Green Salad

4 servings

There is no better accompaniment to a healthy pasta than a healthy salad. And this one fits the bill exactly. From the perfect balance of flavors in the vinaigrette to the freshness of the baby greens and the complex fruity/nutty taste of the cheese shavings, this salad is sure to become a family favorite in your household.

2 tablespoons balsamic vinegar
½ teaspoon Dijon mustard
½ teaspoon sea salt, plus additional to taste
¼ teaspoon freshly ground black pepper, plus additional to taste
½ teaspoon chopped fresh Italian parsley
¼ cup extra-virgin olive oil

5 ounces mixed baby salad greens
2 ounces Parmigiano-Reggiano cheese, shaved with a vegetable peeler, for garnish

1. Whisk the vinegar and mustard together in a bowl. Add the salt, pepper, and parsley. Slowly whisk the oil into the mixture to create an emulsion. Taste the dressing and season with salt and pepper as needed.

2. Place the greens in a large salad bowl. Add the dressing and toss well.

3. Divide among 4 salad bowls, garnish with the cheese, and serve immediately.

Cranberry & Pistachio Biscotti

4 servings (3 biscotti per person)

Biscotti are an all-time favorite Italian cookie. Serve them for dessert (as in this menu), or save them for an afternoon treat with your *caffè latte*. The soaked cranberries result in a softened texture that contrasts nicely with the crunchy bite of the pistachios. The color combination is beautiful, too. For a more chewy consistency, just undercook the biscotti slightly in the second baking.

¼ cup dried cranberries
2 tablespoons sweet liqueur (such as Amaretto di Saronno, Frangelico, Sambuca,
    or sweet Marsala)
1 cup all-purpose flour
½ teaspoon baking powder
Pinch of salt
1 large egg
½ cup granulated sugar
½ teaspoon pure vanilla extract
Freshly grated zest of ½ orange
¼ cup shelled unsalted pistachios, toasted (see note) and coarsely chopped
Powdered sugar, optional

1. Preheat the oven to 400°. Line a baking sheet with a Silpat (nonstick baking mat) or parchment paper.

2. Soak the cranberries in the liqueur in a small bowl. Set aside.

3. Sift the flour, baking powder, and salt into another small bowl. Set aside.

4. Beat the egg, sugar, and vanilla until creamy. Stir in the orange zest, drained cranberries, and pistachios. Add the flour mixture. If using a mixer with a dough hook, work the mixture with the hook only until it comes together. Or fold in the flour with a spatula just until combined.

5. Divide the dough into three pieces. Roll each one into a log the shape of a sausage (about 1 inch thick). Transfer to the lined cookie sheet, flatten the logs slightly, and place in the oven. Immediately reduce the temperature to 350°. Bake for 20 minutes, or until the logs are golden in color. Remove from the oven and let cool slightly. Leave the oven set at 350°.

6. With a serrated knife, slice the logs crosswise on a diagonal into ½-inch-thick slices. Place the slices back on the cookie sheet, cut side down, in a single layer and return to the oven for an additional 5 minutes.

7. Remove from the oven. If desired, dust with the powdered sugar. Serve warm or at room temperature.

NOTE: To toast pistachios, preheat the oven to 350°. Spread the pistachios in a single layer in a pie plate or on a cookie sheet. Bake until golden, about 3 to 6 minutes. Remove from the oven and let cool.

WINE PAIRINGS

Italy: Piedmont—Arneis
Italy: Piedmont—Dolcetto di Acqui
Italy: Piedmont—Gavi

Jim Perko

Butternut Squash, Carrot,
& Ginger Soup

Herb-Seasoned Wild King
Salmon with Mushrooms
& Grape Tomatoes

Pesto Green Beans

Jim & Debbie's Healthy
No-Bake Dessert Bars

Jim Perko

Executive Chef, Cleveland Clinic Wellness Institute

Accolades: Earned multiple gold medals at the World Culinary Olympics held in Germany as well as at various international competitions held in England and Ireland; awarded a grant by the Marriott Family Foundation for groundbreaking Food Is Knowledge program, which also won the prestigious national Chef & Child and True Spirit awards from the American Culinary Federation (ACF); won multiple top awards from, and was inducted into the honor society of, the ACF's American Academy of Chefs; July 13 officially proclaimed Chef James Perko Day by Lakewood mayor; won the President's Award from the Junior League of Cleveland; earned elite designations as an ACF culinary judge.

Growing up in the Union-Miles Park neighborhood of Cleveland, Jim was always interested in cooking. His parents constantly cooked from scratch, and he enjoyed helping them very much. But it wasn't until he started working as a part-time cook's helper at the swanky Blue Grass Italian restaurant during high school that he realized cooking was something that actually *thrilled* him. Plus, he was good at it, too.

After graduating from Cleveland Central Catholic High School, Jim decided he wanted to learn from the best. So he left for Hyde Park, New York, to attend the elite Culinary Institute of America. While still a student there, he held the distinction of being one of only four apprentices chosen to assist the U.S. team at the 1976 Culinary Olympics held in Germany. The team ended up winning 28 gold medals and a third-place tie with France for overall team standings. The following year, Jim graduated in the top 10 percent of his class.

That fall, Jim accepted his first professional culinary job: a five-month contract to cook for scientists in Antarctica. Yes, at the South Pole. After returning home, he went to work for the Marriott Inn Airport Hotel as their execu-

Jim's secret tip for last-minute entertaining? "Always have fresh produce in the refrigerator . . . canned legumes and whole grains in the pantry . . . and 100% whole-wheat or whole grain bread in the freezer. This way it's easy to make a quick hummus, quinoa tabouli, baba ghanoush, or guacamole that you can serve your guests knowing the food you're providing them is healthy and filled with nutritional benefits."

tive sous chef. He later joined the old Bond Court Hotel as their executive chef.

After seven years in the hotel industry, Jim made a switch to healthcare, joining Lakewood Hospital as their executive chef. He stayed there for thirteen years before being offered a position at the Cleveland Clinic by then CEO Dr. Floyd Loop. Ten years later, Jim was offered yet another incredible opportunity at the Clinic—which is an interesting story in itself.

As Jim tells it, back in 2007 he happened to be passing the renowned Dr. Michael Roizen on the skywalk of the Clinic's main campus. Jim stopped to introduce himself. They spoke for "maybe fifteen seconds, tops," says Jim. Dr. Roizen, who was on his way to Chicago to appear on the *Oprah Winfrey Show,* gave Jim his business card and told him to call him. Jim did. They talked further. And as a result, Jim was offered the opportunity of a lifetime: to become the executive chef of the Clinic's Wellness Institute and to develop the culinary component of what was then their new Lifestyle 180 program. Jim accepted—and has been walking on cloud nine ever since.

In his current position, Jim helps teach patients how to cook healthy. He also works with schools, participates in many community wellness initiatives, is a contributing writer for a wellness website, and has written recipes for a book coauthored by Drs. Roizen and Mehmet Oz.

In his spare time, Jim is working on further developing his award-winning Food Is Knowledge program, which teaches young school children how to make healthy eating choices in a fun and entertaining way.

Jim lives in Brecksville with his wife, Debbie. They have two grown children, Katie and Jim Jr.

Butternut Squash, Carrot, & Ginger Soup

4 servings

Who would have imagined that a soup this rich, this creamy, this incredibly velvety could be both vegetarian and vegan? You'd never even guess that it isn't made with heaps of butter or cream either. As a result, you just taste the sweetness and earthy goodness of the squash that much more. Add as much kick as you'd like with some cayenne pepper. As an added bonus, this soup also freezes particularly well—*if,* that is, you have any left over! (Tip: When choosing your squash, be sure to look for one that has a small bottom and a big top for a greater mass of solid. And for a real time saver, look for precut squash.)

1 tablespoon extra-virgin olive oil
1 cup firmly packed, thinly sliced onion
1 cup peeled and diced carrot (2 to 3 medium carrots)
½ teaspoon minced fresh ginger
4½ cups peeled, seeded, and diced butternut squash (about 2 medium squash; can substitute precut squash from the supermarket)
5 cups water (see note)
3 tablespoons Minor's natural vegetable base (found in the freezer or refrigerated section of better grocery stores; see note)
Pinch of cayenne pepper, optional
Fat-free plain yogurt for garnish, optional

1. Heat the oil in a 4-quart sauce pot over medium-low heat. Add the onion and sauté just until transparent. Add the carrots and sauté, stirring occasionally, for 10 minutes. Add the ginger and sauté for 2 more minutes.

2. Add the butternut squash, water, vegetable base, and cayenne pepper, if using. Increase heat to medium high and bring to a boil. Then turn down the heat to medium low and simmer, partially covered, for 45 minutes.

3. Remove from the heat and puree the soup until smooth, using an immersion or stick hand blender for best results. (You can also use a blender or food processor, but be sure to work in batches.)

4. Divide the soup among 4 bowls. Serve warm, garnished with yogurt, if desired (see note).

NOTE: If desired, you can substitute 5 cups vegetable stock from a carton, preferably Kitchen Basics, for the water and Minor's vegetable base.

NOTE: You can simply add a dollop of yogurt to each bowl. Or dilute some yogurt with a little water and spoon it either into a squirt bottle, a pastry bag with plain tip, or a plastic sandwich bag clipped in the corner. Make a design of your choice on top of the soup. (Jim drew a couple of circles and used a toothpick to drag multiple lines from the outer edges in toward the center.)

Pesto Green Beans

4 servings

The base for this untraditional pesto uses spinach and parsley—both astonishingly high in vitamin K—in addition to basil. The natural oils from the heart-healthy nuts contribute just that much more to the nutritional value of this delicious vegan side dish.

¼ cup firmly packed fresh spinach leaves
¼ cup firmly packed fresh parsley leaves
¼ cup firmly packed fresh basil leaves
¼ cup toasted walnuts (see note), chopped
¼ cup toasted pecans (see note), chopped
¼ teaspoon kosher salt
3 tablespoons extra-virgin olive oil
½ teaspoon finely chopped garlic
5 cups fresh green beans, cut into ½-inch lengths

1. Put the spinach, parsley, basil, walnuts, pecans, and salt in a food processor and pulse until coarsely pureed. Add the oil and garlic and pulse again until well incorporated. Set aside.

2. Boil or steam the green beans until just tender, about 5 minutes. Drain well.

3. Combine the pesto with the green beans and toss well.

NOTE: To toast the walnuts and pecans, preheat the oven to 275°. Spread the nuts on a baking sheet and place in the oven. Check after 10 minutes, then again every 2 minutes until golden. Remove from the oven. Let cool, then coarsely chop.

Herb-Seasoned Wild King Salmon with Mushrooms & Grape Tomatoes

4 servings

Few singular foods bring as many valuable contributions to the table in such significant quantities as the wild king (or chinook) salmon, the largest and rarest of the Alaskan wild salmon species. Not only is it exceptionally high in omega-3 fatty acids—essential for heart and brain health—it is also an excellent source of high-quality protein, niacin, vitamins B_{12} and B_6, and selenium. This choice seafood is full of flavor with a rich color, firm texture, and supreme taste.

¼ cup well-rinsed, drained, and finely diced white part of leek (see note)
2 tablespoons extra-virgin olive oil, divided
1 tablespoon chopped fresh parsley
½ teaspoon finely chopped garlic
¾ teaspoon kosher salt, divided
Coarsely ground black pepper
Freshly grated zest of 1 lemon
4 (4-ounce) wild king salmon fillets, skinned and boned
16 fresh shiitake mushrooms, wiped clean, stems discarded, caps quartered
20 assorted-color grape tomatoes, halved
Leek Garnish (recipe at right), optional

1. Preheat the oven to 375°.

2. Combine the leeks, 1 tablespoon of the oil, the parsley, garlic, ½ teaspoon salt, ¼ teaspoon pepper, and lemon zest in a bowl. Add the salmon fillets and toss until well coated.

3. Fit a wire rack into a rimmed baking sheet. Place the salmon on the rack and bake for about 12 to 15 minutes, or until lightly opaque inside.

4. Meanwhile, heat the remaining 1 tablespoon oil in a sauté pan over medium to medium-high heat. Add the mushrooms and season with the remaining ¼ teaspoon salt and about ⅛ teaspoon pepper. Sauté until lightly caramelized to bring out what Jim describes as "the *umami* flavor" (or savoriness). Remove the pan from the heat.

5. If desired, for each serving, place a salmon fillet on top of a portion of Pesto Green Beans (recipe on page 128) in the center of the plate. Spoon the tomatoes and mushrooms around the beans. If desired, arrange a few strands of Leek Garnish on top of each salmon fillet. Serve warm.

NOTE: To clean a leek, cut off and discard the dark green leaves just at the place where the light green starts, about an inch above the white part. Trim off the roots, then make a lengthwise cut from the top down almost through the bottom. Rinse the leek thoroughly under cold water, separating the leaves to make sure to get any dirt that may be hiding between them. Drain well and prepare as instructed.

Leek Garnish

1. Simmer ¼ cup finely julienned white part of leek in a saucepan with ½ cup vegetable stock until tender, about 5 minutes. Drain.

WINE PAIRINGS

Italy: Veneto—Amarone
Italy: Veneto—Recioto della Valpolicella
USA: California—Conundrum or other white blend

Jim & Debbie's Healthy No-Bake Dessert Bars

4 servings (6 bars per person)

You would never have imagined just how nutritious these luscious vegan bars really are unless someone told you. So we're here to tell you: The healthy attributes of all the combined ingredients in these bars are pretty amazing. There's no added sugar in this recipe either. And the bars freeze beautifully, too! For a creative garnish, Jim used recycled X-ray film to cut out the free-form stencil, which he then dusted with cocoa powder.

1 cup toasted walnuts (see note)
¾ cup golden raisins
¾ cup sugar-free dried cranberries
5 brown rice cakes or 12 ultra-thin 100% whole-wheat rice cake squares, preferably Paskesz brand
½ cup fresh orange juice, divided
2 tablespoons agave nectar (can substitute honey)
1 tablespoon pure vanilla extract
¼ teaspoon ground cinnamon
6 ounces 70% dark bittersweet chocolate
1 tablespoon instant espresso powder
Cocoa powder or ground cinnamon for garnish, optional
Raspberries for garnish, optional

1. Place the walnuts in a food processor. Pulse until fine. Add the raisins and cranberries. Pulse until the mixture becomes sticky.

2. Add the rice cakes. Continue to pulse until the mixture becomes fine and loose. Add 2 tablespoons of the orange juice plus the agave nectar, vanilla, and cinnamon. Pulse one last time until the mixture becomes sticky and gummy.

NOTE: To toast walnuts, preheat the oven to 275°. Place the nuts on a baking sheet and bake, checking after 10 minutes, then again every 2 minutes, until golden.

3. Place the mixture in an ungreased 8 x 8-inch glass baking dish, spreading evenly across the pan. Cover with plastic wrap, pressing the mixture into the bottom of the pan with a flat-bottomed object to evenly distribute it. Remove the plastic wrap and set the dish aside.

4. Combine the chocolate, remaining orange juice, and espresso powder in the top of a double boiler that's been placed over barely simmering water on low heat. Stir just until the chocolate is melted and the mixture is smooth.

5. Remove from the heat quickly and immediately pour the melted chocolate mixture evenly over the top of the pressed walnut mixture. Cover and refrigerate at least 30 minutes. Cut into desired shapes.

6. If desired, dust cocoa powder, cinnamon, or a mixture of both onto your plates before placing the dessert bars. (Using a stencil is optional.) Add a few raspberries, if desired.

Regan Reik

Grilled Mahi Mahi
with Mango Salsa

Brown Rice & Almond Pilaf

Grilled Romaine Salad
with Black Garlic
& Niçoise Olives

Chocolate Fondue for Four

Regan Reik

Executive Chef, Pier W

Accolades: Received AAA 5-diamond award; crowned Top Chef 2010 at the St. John Medical Center's Top Chef competition; awarded Best Sunday Brunch, Best View, and Most Romantic Restaurant by *Cleveland Magazine;* featured in numerous publications and media, including *Travel + Leisure,* the *New York Times,* the *Washington Post,* the *Baltimore Sun, Crain's New York Business, Crain's Detroit Business, Crain's Cleveland Business, Northern Ohio Live, Cleveland Magazine, Cleveland Scene,* the *Plain Dealer,* the *Sun News,* the *Lakewood Observer, Metromix, Examiner,* and WJW-TV 8.

Regan grew up in North Royalton, Ohio, part of a close-knit German family. "My dad and I spent a lot of time together in the kitchen," remembers Regan. "We really appreciated food, and I thought every kid lived that way."

To continue his love of food and cooking, during high school Regan took a job at Carrie Cerino's Ristorante. After he graduated from North Royalton High School, he headed to Cuyahoga Community College to study culinary arts and hospitality. He also served a culinary apprenticeship at Carrie Cerino's.

After graduating, Regan stayed on at Carrie Cerino's a few more years before heading to Johnson & Wales University in Providence, Rhode Island. While a student there, he externed at the Ritz-Carlton in McLean, Virginia. He was so impressed with the Ritz organization and their European-style kitchen that he made it his goal to one day become an executive chef of a Ritz-Carlton hotel restaurant.

After graduating number one in his class at J&W, Regan was offered a full-time position at the McLean Ritz he was working at. He went on to eventually work at various Ritz locations across the country before being offered the position of executive sous chef/chef de cuisine at the Cleveland location. Two years later, Regan was tempted by—and decided to accept—a very attractive offer to become the executive chef of Opus Twenty One, the on-site restaurant of an LPGA golf course in Warren, Ohio.

The owner encouraged Regan to do a two-month *stage*

Regan's secret tip for last-minute entertaining? "Freeze leftovers that you have from other dinners. Those few cups of soup or broth, cookie dough, or meat trim can be the ingredient you need to make something else, instead of running out to the store and starting from scratch."

at the famed, 4-star New York restaurant Alain Ducasse at the Essex House, under one of the most decorated French master chefs of all time: Didier Elena.

"There were about thirty people working in his kitchen, all at the same time," recalls Regan. "But it was like a symphony, and that was the level of perfection I wanted to achieve." He adds, "Learning from Didier was a dream come true. I was taught to hear the music and feel the food, not just follow the recipes. I was told one knows they've become a real chef only when everything they touch turns to gold."

After two years, Regan decided to return to the Ritz organization, this time at their hotel in New York's Battery Park. After a few years, he was transferred to their location in Dearborn, Michigan. Then, out of the blue, Regan got an unexpected call from a good friend back in Cleveland who told him that Pier W was looking for a sous chef. Regan decided to interview for the job and got the offer, but . . . there was just one small catch.

At the exact same time he was offered the sous chef position at Pier W, the Ritz also offered Regan his ultimate dream job, that of executive chef, in Dearborn. "There it was, right in front of me," he says. "This had been my whole goal since culinary school. But then I starting thinking of all the things I would miss being away from my daughters in Cleveland if I stayed in Dearborn. Things like coaching basketball and soccer, band concerts, and spelling bees. In the end, I chose the girls—and it was the smartest thing I ever did."

As serendipity would have it, several months after taking the position at Pier W, he was promoted to executive chef. "I've never looked back since," says Regan. "My dad used to cook with me, and now I'm cooking with my own daughters. There's nothing better than that."

In his spare time, Regan, who recently earned a business degree from Florida Metropolitan University, likes to run competitively. In fact, he just completed his sixth marathon and hopes to qualify for the Boston race soon.

Regan lives in Strongsville with his wife, Tamara, and their four children, Morgan, Sydney, Robby, and Audrey.

Grilled Mahi Mahi with Mango Salsa

4 servings

Full of flavor and eye appeal, this dish is also very light and healthy. You'll find the Asian influence of the sesame oil to be quite an unexpected surprise. The Hawaiian name *mahi mahi* is being used more and more nowadays for this ray-finned, firm-fleshed fish that is also sometimes referred to as dolphinfish or dorado.

½ cup small-diced ripe mango
½ cup small-diced ripe tomato
2 tablespoons minced shallot
2 tablespoons fresh lime juice
1 tablespoon chopped fresh cilantro
1 tablespoon toasted sesame oil
1 tablespoon honey
2 teaspoons fine sea salt, divided
1¼ teaspoons freshly ground black pepper, divided
4 (5- to 6-ounce) portions mahi mahi fillet, skinned
1 tablespoon olive oil

1. Preheat the grill (gas or charcoal) to high heat.

2. Place the mango, tomato, shallot, lime juice, cilantro, sesame oil, honey, 1 teaspoon of the sea salt, and ¼ teaspoon of the pepper in a bowl. Mix well and set aside.

3. Brush the mahi mahi with the olive oil. Season both sides with the remaining 1 teaspoon each salt and pepper.

4. Place the mahi mahi pieces on the hot grill. Cook on one side for approximately 4 minutes. Flip carefully with a spatula and continue to cook for about another 2 to 3 minutes. (Note: The total cooking time for fish fillets is generally 7 minutes per inch of thickness.)

5. When the flesh has completely turned from gray to white, the mahi mahi is done. Remove immediately from the grill.

6. Remix the salsa mixture. If desired, for each serving, place a mahi mahi portion on top of ½ cup of Brown Rice & Almond Pilaf (recipe at right) in the center of the plate. Top each mahi mahi portion with 2 heaping tablespoons of the mango salsa. Serve warm.

WINE PAIRINGS

Chile or California: Any region—Viognier
Portugal: Oporto—10-year-old Tawny Port
USA: California, Napa—Sauvignon Blanc

Brown Rice & Almond Pilaf

4 servings

When it comes to making the most flavorful rice pilaf, which originated in the Near East, there's no better method than oven roasting. Almonds give it just that much more flavor and crunch. This is an extremely easy, no-nonsense side dish.

1 tablespoon olive oil
¼ cup minced shallot
1 cup long-grain brown rice (can substitute white, wild, basmati, or jasmine rice)
¼ cup toasted sliced almonds (see note)
1 bay leaf
Fine sea salt
1½ cups water

1. Preheat the oven to 350°. Place the oil and shallot in a medium-size ovenproof saucepan over medium heat. Sauté briefly, about 2 minutes.

2. Add the rice, almonds, and bay leaf. Season with salt to taste. Mix well. Add the water. Cover the pan with foil. Place in the oven for 25 to 30 minutes, or until the rice is tender.

3. Remove from the oven. Fluff the rice with a fork, then remove the bay leaf. Serve warm.

NOTE: To toast sliced almonds, preheat the oven to 350°. Spread the sliced almonds on a baking sheet and place in the oven for 5 to 7 minutes, or until golden. Remove from the oven and let cool.

Grilled Romaine Salad with Black Garlic & Niçoise Olives

4 servings

You might be skeptical of grilling lettuce, but rest assured, romaine lettuce has the body to stand up to the heat of a grill. Look for bagged hearts of romaine, which are actually the cores of romaine heads and contain the crispiest, most tender leaves, in the packaged salad section of your grocery store. And if you can't find black garlic—a fermented garlic that has a sweet, syrupy taste—just leave it out altogether. The recipe will still work without it. Just don't try substituting ordinary garlic, which would simply make this salad way too strong.

3 black garlic cloves, peeled (don't substitute regular garlic), optional
2 hearts of romaine
4 tablespoons olive oil
Kosher salt and freshly ground black pepper
¼ cup Creamy Lemon Parmesan Dressing (recipe at right)
16 to 20 Niçoise olives, pitted (can substitute kalamata olives from the deli section, not canned)
4 slices French bread, toasted (see note)
2 ounces (¼ cup) shaved Reggiano-Parmigiano cheese for garnish

1. Preheat the grill (gas or charcoal).

2. If using black garlic, bring a small saucepan of water to a boil. Add the garlic cloves and poach for about 7 minutes. Drain. Mash slightly on a cutting board. (Note: This will tenderize as well as minimize the "bite" of the garlic.) Set aside.

3. Cut each heart of romaine in half lengthwise, keeping the core ends intact so the halves stay together. Place in a mixing bowl. Add the oil and salt and pepper to taste and toss gently.

4. Remove the hearts of romaine from the bowl. Gently spread each heart open slightly, keeping the cores still intact. Place the hearts, cut side down, on the grill. They will wilt quickly, so don't walk away from the grill.

5. After 2 minutes, flip the lettuce over. Cook for another 2 minutes. Remove from the grill.

6. Now you can cut the cores off the hearts and discard, but try to still keep the leaves together as much as possible. Carefully place the leaves back into the mixing bowl. Add the poached garlic, if using, and dressing. Toss gently until evenly coated.

7. Divide the grilled romaine among 4 plates. Place the olives and French bread alongside the leaves. Garnish with the cheese and serve immediately.

NOTE: To toast French bread, preheat the oven to 350°. Place the bread slices on an oiled cookie sheet and bake for about 5 minutes, or until lightly golden brown. No need to turn.

Creamy Lemon Parmesan Dressing

Yields about 2 cups

You'll be amazed at how little you'll need of this dressing to make your salad flavorful. Just remember, when applying, less is more. Although the Grilled Romaine Salad calls for only ¼ cup of this dressing, the rest will keep in the refrigerator for a week.

3 tablespoons red wine vinegar
2 tablespoons fresh lemon juice
1 tablespoon freshly grated Parmesan cheese
1 teaspoon minced garlic (1 medium-size clove)
1 teaspoon kosher salt
½ teaspoon freshly ground black pepper
½ teaspoon granulated sugar
½ teaspoon Dijon mustard
2 anchovy fillets
¼ cup pasteurized liquid egg (such as Egg Beaters; see note)
1 cup vegetable oil
½ cup extra-virgin olive oil

1. Combine the vinegar, lemon juice, cheese, garlic, salt, pepper, sugar, mustard, anchovy fillets, and pasteurized liquid egg in a blender. Blend on medium speed until well mixed.

2. Turn the speed up to high. With the motor still running, slowly add the vegetable oil and extra-virgin olive oil until emulsified. Pour into a clean container and refrigerate until ready to use.

NOTE: Pasteurized liquid egg is used in this recipe instead of a regular egg because of the probability of long storage time for the unused portion of the dressing. However, if you plan to use this entire recipe immediately, can substitute 1 whole egg.

Chocolate Fondue for Four

4 servings

Fondue (French for "melt") is a fun and communal way to entertain. Put away your fine linen tablecloth, bring out the skewers, and get ready for this dessert to be an instant hit with your guests! Any number of different items can be used to dip. Mix, match, or change what's listed below as you like. Some other suggestions include fig halves, kiwi slices, clementine segments, apple slices, banana slices, dried apricots, candied grapefuit peels, glacéed orange slices, pretzels, graham crackers (regular and chocolate), shortbread cookies, madeleines, angel food cake cubes, cheesecake cubes, mini Rice Krispies Treats squares, and Regan's personal favorite: vanilla Oreos.

DIPPERS

2 pineapple wedges, cut into chunks
4 strawberries with stems intact, halved
8 blackberries
8 raspberries
16 blueberries
1 small bunch seedless grapes, red or green
2 chocolate brownies, cut into chunks
4 chocolate chip cookies
4 peanut butter cookies
4 marshmallows, plain or toasted
4 slices pound cake, cut into 1-inch cubes

FONDUE

3 (4-ounce) packages semisweet baking chocolate, chopped, or 1 (12-ounce) package semisweet chocolate chips, about 2 cups
1 cup heavy cream
2 tablespoons corn syrup
¼ cup Grand Marnier (for nonalcoholic version, omit)

1. Arrange the pineapple, strawberries, blackberries, raspberries, blueberries, grapes, brownies, cookies, marshmallows, and pound cake on a large serving platter. Be sure to leave room in the center for the pot or bowl of chocolate. Set aside.

2. Place the chocolate in the top of a double boiler, or in a heatproof glass or ceramic bowl, and set over a pot of barely simmering water, stirring constantly until completely melted. (Alternative method: Microwave in spurts of 30-second intervals. Be sure to stir in between the spurts until the chocolate is completely melted.)

3. Add the cream, corn syrup, and Grand Marnier, if using, and stir together well until the chocolate has a smooth and velvety texture. Pour into a fondue pot (as shown) or a serving bowl.

4. Place the fondue pot or bowl of chocolate in the center of the serving platter. Serve immediately with skewers or cocktail forks.

Jonathon Sawyer

Devils on Horseback
(Chocolate, Almond,
& Chili-Stuffed Dates)

Foie Gras Steamed Clams

Spicy Spaghetti Squash

Ohio Edamame
(Whole Grilled Spring Pea Pods)

Jonathon Sawyer

Chef/Owner, The Greenhouse Tavern, Noodlecat

Accolades: Awarded Best New Chef by both *Food & Wine* and the *Gayot Guide;* named one of the Top 10 Best New Restaurants in America by *Bon Appétit;* several James Beard award nominations; named a Rising Star by *Restaurant Hospitality;* singled out as one of America's Top 50 Restaurant Game Changers by *Nation's Restaurant News;* multiple superlative ratings from *Time Out New York* and the *New York Times;* chosen as a Slow Food International Delegate; elected to the Maple Leaf Farms Advisory Board; named Best Restaurant by *Cleveland Magazine;* appeared on the Food Network's *Iron Chef America* and *Dinner Impossible* shows, as well as on the Cooking Channel's *Unique Eats* show; featured in numerous publications and media, including *Nation's Restaurant News, Restaurant Hospitality, American Farm to Table Restaurant Guide, People Magazine, Delta Sky Magazine, EcoWatch Ohio, Crain's Cleveland Business, Cleveland Magazine, Cleveland Scene,* the *Plain Dealer,* the *Independent,* the *Aspen Times, Tasting Table, Metromix,* WKYC-TV 3, WJW-TV 8, and WCPN 90.3.

What did it take for one of the best chefs in Cleveland to figure out his life's destiny? For Jonathon Sawyer, it was a week of torture.

"I was going to school for industrial engineering," he explains, "and I had to shadow an engineer. It was the worst week of my life. At that moment, I knew I had to follow my passion for cooking. I just wouldn't be happy sitting behind a desk all day."

Jonathon grew up in Strongsville, Ohio. He was only a young teen when he got his first job at The Mad Cactus, frying tortilla chips. He also worked at Houlihan's. After graduating from Strongsville High School, he left for the University of Dayton. But two years later—shortly after the shadowing experience mentioned above—he decided to follow his heart instead and enrolled in the Pennsylvania Culinary Institute in Pittsburgh (currently known as Le Cordon Bleu Institute of Culinary Arts). He earned a

Jonathon's secret tip for last-minute entertaining? "Stay in your comfort zone. Only cook foods that you can handle, and don't take on too much. Be sure to always have one ingredient at your house that can make different apps, like Arborio rice. If you have this rice on hand, you can make arancini, risotto, crispy rice balls with tartar, etc."

degree in culinary arts and then landed in Miami at the legendary Biltmore Hotel.

With one year of professional experience under his belt, he decided to head to New York City where he worked alongside—and learned from—one of the industry's greatest: Charlie Palmer. His pivotal stints there were with Charlie's Kitchen 22 in the Flatiron District, as well as Aureole, Astra, and Kitchen 82.

Jonathon was eventually lured back to Cleveland to help Michael Symon open Lolita, only to head back to New York after four years to head up Michael's then newest venture, Parea. He eventually made it back home to Cleveland once again, where he threw himself into realizing his dream: opening a restaurant of his own. Which he did. And he called it Bar Cento. And it rocked.

Following on the heels of this success, Jonathon eventually left Bar Cento and turned his efforts to pursuing yet another venture. But this time it was something never before attempted in the Cleveland area: an "all-green" restaurant dedicated to using recycled building materials, alternative energy sources, modern conservation techniques, local sustainable ingredients, and advanced composting methods. He named it, appropriately enough, The Greenhouse Tavern (complete with a working greenhouse on the rooftop, of course). It became the first nationally certified green restaurant in Ohio. And on the heels of this highly successful venture, Jonathon also opened a second green restaurant called Noodlecat—a Japanese noodle house right around the corner from The Greenhouse Tavern.

On a personal note, he loves to farm, forage, and take on a game or two of racquetball once in a while.

Jonathon and his wife, Amelia, have a son, Catcher, and a daughter, Louisiana, as well as a pit bull named Potato and a pug named Vito. They all call Cleveland Heights home.

Devils on Horseback (Chocolate, Almond, & Chili-Stuffed Dates)

4 servings (2 pieces per person)

This appetizer, which may have a funny name (in fact, a variation called Angels on Horseback uses oysters instead of dates), is actually one of the most-ordered starters on The Greenhouse Tavern's menu. No surprise there, since Jonathon's interpretation of the classic British pub snack creates a thrilling sweet-salty-spicy taste in every bite. We dare you to eat just one.

4 cups canola oil
4 slices bacon, thick or thin, halved crosswise
8 dates, pitted
2 pieces (1 x 1-inch) Manjari chocolate, preferably Valrhona, quartered (can substitute your favorite dark bittersweet or unsweetened chocolate, preferably 72%)
2 pinches of fleur de sel (can substitute coarse sea salt), divided
1 Fresno chile, seeded and thinly sliced into ¼-inch pieces (can substitute ⅛ teaspoon cayenne pepper)
8 Marcona almonds, coarsely chopped separately (can substitute regular almonds)

1. Preheat the broiler.

2. Heat the oil in a medium-size saucepan until it reaches 300°. Carefully drop in the bacon and blanch for 15 seconds. Remove from the oil and drain on paper towels. Set aside.

3. Stuff each date with one quartered piece of the chocolate, 2 grains of fleur de sel, one piece of pepper, and one chopped almond.

4. Wrap each stuffed date with one strip of bacon. Secure with a wooden skewer or toothpick, if desired. Place on a baking sheet (seam side down) and broil for 3 to 4 minutes, or until the bacon is golden brown. Serve warm.

WINE PAIRINGS

France: Burgundy—Premier Cru or any village wine
France: Champagne—sparkling brut
France: Rhône—Saint-Joseph

Foie Gras Steamed Clams

4 servings

Don't let the name fool you. Although this recipe, a very popular signature dish at The Greenhouse Tavern, may sound fancy, it truly is a super easy one-pot luxury. The only trick is procuring the key ingredient: *foie gras* (French for "fat liver" and pronounced "fwah grah"). Foie gras, a popular delicacy in French cuisine, is the fattened liver of a waterfowl (either duck or goose) produced by a special feeding process. The result is a luxurious ingredient that is at once velvety and meaty. Your butcher can order it for you, or look for it in the freezer or canned section of a higher-end grocery/specialty store. If you're really determined, you can also order it online from D'Artagnan.

1 unpeeled red onion, cut in half

1 cup extra-virgin olive oil, plus additional for grilling bread

Kosher salt

2 tablespoons raw Grade A foie gras (can substitute pâté made with duck or goose liver)

24 mahogany or cherrystone clams, scrubbed

1 cup water

1 tablespoon Sauternes vinegar (can substitute Reisling, viognier, or ice wine vinegar, or a high-end, late-harvest cider vinegar)

3 tablespoons unsalted butter, cut in pieces

4 slices round crusty rustic bread, halved

Freshly ground black pepper

1. If using a grill (gas or charcoal) to grill the bread, preheat to medium-high heat. If using a broiler instead, preheat after step 2. Preheat the oven to 500°.

2. Place the onion halves, cut side down, in a small baking dish. Add 1 cup of the oil. Season aggressively with salt. Cover with foil. Roast in the oven until tender, about 40 minutes, creating caramelized onion. Drain, reserving the oil for another use. Peel and coarsely chop the onion into small, bite-size bits. (Time permitting, it is highly preferable to roast the onion much slower at 350° for 4 hours instead, creating red onion brûlée.)

3. Place the caramelized onion, foie gras, and clams in a 4-quart sauce pot. Cover with a lid. Turn the heat to medium, and "let them get to know each other," as Jonathon quips. After 2 minutes, add the water and vinegar. Re-cover the pot. Continue to cook until the clams open up, about 10 minutes. Remove the clams and set aside. Add the butter pieces to the pot and stir to emulsify. Taste for seasoning, but it should not need any more salt.

4. Brush some oil, plus salt and pepper to taste, on both sides of the bread slices. Grill on both sides until nicely browned but not so long that they burn, about 2 minutes on each side.

5. Divide the clams (and cooking juice) among 4 serving bowls. Serve warm with the grilled bread slices.

Spicy Spaghetti Squash

4 servings

This is a healthy and unique dish that makes either a wonderful accompaniment to any number of entrées or a simple meal in itself. Be sure to look for a hard squash that is heavy for its size, with a pale, even color. It can be safely stored at room temperature for about a month. The crab paste can be found in Asian stores. And here's a helpful, do-ahead tip: Roast the squash the night before and refrigerate until ready to use. It also freezes well. If frozen, partially thaw before ready to use. Then, steam until tender but still firm, about 5 minutes.

1 medium-size spaghetti squash
Extra-virgin olive oil
Salt
2 to 4 Fresno chiles (can substitute red jalapeños), depending on how spicy you like it
4 tablespoons (½ stick) unsalted butter
6 ounces peppery pancetta, diced (can substitute bacon patted with pepper)
8 garlic cloves, sliced
2 tablespoons fresh thyme leaves, divided
2 tablespoons raisins, plumped (see note)
2 teaspoons capers, coarsely chopped
Freshly grated zest and juice of 1 lemon, reserved separately
2 teaspoons crab or shrimp paste (can substitute a dash of fish sauce)
2 teaspoons red pepper flakes
Freshly ground black pepper
Toasted bread crumbs for garnish (see note)

1. If using a grill (gas or charcoal) to char the chiles, preheat to medium-high heat. If using a broiler instead, preheat after step 2. Preheat the oven to 400°.

2. Line a baking sheet with parchment paper. Cut the spaghetti squash in half lengthwise. Using a spoon, scrape away the seeds and stringy bits. Drizzle the inside of the squash with oil and season with salt to taste. Place, cut side down, on the lined baking sheet. Roast in the oven until the flesh pulls away from the skin with a spoon, about 45 minutes. Scoop out 2 cups of the roasted squash and set aside for use in the recipe. Reserve any remaining pulp for another use.

3. Meanwhile, thoroughly brush the Fresno chiles with the oil. Place on the grill (or under the broiler) and cook, using tongs to turn as needed, until blistered, blackened, and charred on all sides. Remove the chiles and place in a brown paper bag. Fold the bag shut. (Alternatively, place in a container covered with plastic wrap.) After 5 minutes, remove the chiles. Peel off the skin and discard. Remove the stems, seeds, and veins. Dice the chiles and set aside. (See note.)

4. Heat the butter in a large sauté pan on medium-high heat until smoking hot and brown. Working quickly, add the pancetta and sauté for only 30 seconds. Immediately reduce the heat to medium. Add the garlic and lightly brown, then add half of the thyme and toss thoroughly. Add the charred chiles, drained raisins, capers, and lemon zest. Stir well, then add the lemon juice, crab paste, and roasted squash to the pan. Stir. Season with the red pepper flakes and salt and pepper to taste. Heat through. Take off the heat.

5. Place on a serving platter. Garnish with the toasted bread crumbs and remaining thyme. Serve warm.

NOTE: To plump raisins, soak in a mixture of 1 cup hot water plus 1 to 3 teaspoons vinegar, depending on how tart you like them, for about 10 minutes. Once plump, drain and use as directed.

NOTE: To make toasted bread crumbs, toast a few slices of bread. Crush or pulse in a food processor.

NOTE: To significantly cut back on the heat of the Fresno chiles, cut in half lengthwise and remove the stems, seeds, and veins before charring.

Ohio Edamame (Whole Grilled Spring Pea Pods)

4 servings

Jonathon likes to call this dish, playfully, Ohio Edamame. Although not an edamame, the English pea used in this recipe is eaten just like one—thus, the good-humored name. Also of interest: A little-known ingredient included here is Real Salt, an all-natural unrefined sea salt that's free of any additives, chemicals, or heat processing of any kind. It has a unique pinkish appearance and flecks of color resulting from more than 60 naturally occurring trace minerals. You'll discover it also has a delicate "sweet salt" flavor that elevates this dish from ordinary to extraordinary. Look for it at your local grocery store, or ask the manager to order it. It'll be worth the effort, believe me.

40 fresh English peas in the pod (also called green peas, garden peas, or shell peas)

3 tablespoons extra-virgin olive oil, divided

Coarse Real Salt (can substitute kosher salt)

¼ cup water

Freshly grated zest and juice of ½ lemon, reserved separately

3 small radishes, trimmed and thinly sliced, for garnish

1 to 2 tablespoons finely grated horseradish root for garnish

This recipe can be prepared in two different ways. Take your pick.

METHOD #1: "POT STICKER" STYLE

1. Toss the peas in 2 tablespoons of the oil and the salt to coat.

2. Heat a flat griddle or cast-iron pan over medium-high heat. Add the peas, then the water, and cover. Steam for about 4 minutes. The peas should be a bright vibrant color with a pliable shell. Remove from the heat.

3. Transfer the peas to a bowl. Toss with the lemon juice and the remaining 1 tablespoon oil to coat.

4. Place on a serving platter. Garnish with the radish, horseradish, and lemon zest. Serve warm.

METHOD #2: GRILLING STYLE

1. Preheat the grill (gas or charcoal). Bring an 8-quart pot of salted water to a boil on the stove.

2. Have ready a bowl of ice water. When the water boils, add the peas to the boiling water and blanch for about 2 minutes. Remove from the water and shock in ice water. The peas should be a bright vibrant color with a pliable shell.

3. Transfer the peas to a bowl. Toss with 2 tablespoons of the oil, salt, and lemon juice to coat. Place in a vegetable grill basket.

4. Place the basket on the grill. Cook until the pea skin is browned, about 5 minutes, or until heated through. Remove from the grill.

5. Place the peas on a serving platter. Garnish with the radish, horseradish, and lemon zest, and drizzle with the remaining 1 tablespoon of oil. Serve warm.

Steve Schimoler

Mushroom Tarte Tatin
with Truffled Parmesan
Anglaise

Capellini Caprese

Stevie & Kirsten's Caramelized
Apple French Toast

Steve Schimoler

Chef/Owner, Crop Bistro & Bar, Crop Bistro & Brewery (Stowe, Vermont); Founder, Localcrop.com

Accolades: Earned an Award of Excellence from *Wine Spectator;* awarded top Zagat rating; featured on both the Cooking Channel's *FoodNation with Bobby Flay* show and the PBS *Master Chef* series; named one of the Top 10 Cleveland Restaurants by *Gayot Guide;* two-time winner of *Cleveland Scene's* Best Restaurant award; regular contributor to *Flavor & The Menu;* two-time past president of the Research Chefs Association; featured in numerous publications and media, including *Newsday, Santé, Restaurants & Institutions, Food Arts, Continental Magazine, Balanced Living, Cleveland Magazine,* the *Plain Dealer,* WKYC-TV 3, and WJW-TV 8.

Steve grew up on Long Island, New York, in a large, tight-knit family. When he was in the second grade, he spent two weeks at home convalescing from a hernia operation. The whole time, he watched *The Galloping Gourmet* on TV. If he liked a dish, he'd make it for the family dinner that night.

When Steve was seventeen, he was working at an after-school job as a prep cook at a local restaurant. It started to rain. Business died down. And the chef left early. Suddenly, a busload of forty-five people showed up and ordered everything on the menu. Steve was completely on his own—and loving every minute. "It was the rush of being slammed and doing a good job that got me hooked," he says.

After graduating from Jericho High School on Long Island, Steve attended Paul Smith's College in the Adirondacks, where he earned a degree in hotel and business management. His college internship at Marriott enabled him to join the hospitality company full time after graduation, first in Chicago, then in Washington, D.C., and New York. He finally decided to buy his first restaurant—Terrace on the Plaza in Locust Valley—at the tender age of twenty-three. Within the next three years, he also started a catering business, Terrace Too; bought Loafers

Steve's secret tip for last-minute entertaining? "Keep it simple and don't overcommit yourself to complicated dishes. Do one or two things really well and focus on your guests. Don't be so immersed in the work that they are left standing around waiting for some elaborate preparation."

Bakery & Gourmet; and built The Black Walnut, which went on to garner glowing national attention.

About eight years later, restless and eager for a new challenge, Steve sold everything and moved to Vermont, where he joined Cabot Creamery as their vice president of product development. Subsequent ventures included a consulting business called Right Stuff; a prepared foods company called Chef Stuff; an Internet web market solely for chefs called Chef Express; and an award-winning restaurant called Mist Grill, which he remodeled from an abandoned gristmill dating back to the early 1800s. Oh, and he also wrote a cookbook.

Sysco (the world's largest food distributor) eventually bought Steve's Chef Express business and offered him the position of general manger of culinary business development, which took him to Houston for the next three years. Finally, northeast Ohio beckoned with a position as director of innovation and development for Nestlé North America. Steve maintained that position for almost two years, after which he opened his own place again and named it Crop, an acronym for Customized Restaurant Operations Platform.

While running Crop in Cleveland and its namesake in Stowe, Vermont, Steve also started a few more ventures, including a consulting and food development company called Rolling Fire Enterprises; an online farmers' market serving Cleveland, Columbus, and Cincinnati called Localcrop.com; and a nonprofit, grass-roots collaboration of local restaurants called Cleveland Food Rocks.

When not working, Steve likes to perform on the drums with his band, playfully called Cream of the Crop, or join in on a good game of lacrosse.

Steve lives in Cleveland's Ohio City neighborhood. He has two grown children, son Steve and daughter Kirsten (after whom his dessert is named), both living in Vermont.

Mushroom Tarte Tatin with Truffled Parmesan Anglaise

4 servings

Steve first created this dish as a vegetarian option for his restaurant in Vermont. Yet it became so popular he began featuring it as a regular menu staple. Not only is it easy and fast, it's also perfect for that "wow factor" when entertaining at home. No one, and we mean no one, will be able to resist its woodsy mushroom and truffle flavors.

SAUCE

1 cup heavy cream
1 large egg yolk
½ cup freshly grated Asiago or Parmesan cheese
Salt and freshly ground black pepper
1 tablespoon white truffle oil, optional

1. Bring the cream to a simmer in a small saucepan over low heat. Continue to simmer until it thickly coats the back of a spoon, reduced in volume by about 40 percent. Remove from the heat. Let cool for 10 minutes.

2. Add the egg yolk and cheese and whisk well. Place back over low heat and continue to stir until the sauce just begins to simmer again. Season with salt and pepper to taste. If desired, add the white truffle oil. Immediately remove from the heat. Pour into a clean container and set aside, covered. (This will keep in the refrigerator for 2 to 3 days.)

TARTE

1 sheet frozen puff pastry dough, thawed but kept chilled
1 tablespoon unsalted butter
2 tablespoons minced shallot
1 teaspoon minced garlic (1 medium-size clove)
3 cups sliced assorted fresh mushrooms (such as shiitake, portobello, oyster, chanterelle)
1 teaspoon minced fresh herb blend of choice (such as parsley, sage, rosemary, thyme)
Salt and freshly ground black pepper
Truffle oil for garnish, optional
Freshly cracked black pepper for garnish, optional
Fresh microgreens or herb sprig for garnish, optional

1. Preheat the oven to 400°. Using a 10-inch nonstick ovenproof sauté pan (not cast-iron and not with a plastic, rubber, or wood handle) as a template, cut a circle out of the pastry sheet to match the top dimension of the pan. Refrigerate the pastry disc.

2. Heat the butter in the sauté pan on medium-high heat. When melted, add the shallot and garlic. Cook for about 30 seconds, stirring constantly. Add the mushrooms and herbs, season with salt and pepper to taste, and continue to cook and stir for about 2 minutes. Turn off the heat.

3. Place the refrigerated pastry disc on top of the mushroom mix, tucking the edges inside the outer lip of the pan. Place the pan in the oven and bake for approximately 10 minutes, or until the pastry has ballooned and is a rich golden brown.

4. Carefully remove the pan from the oven and use a knife to loosen the pastry around the edge of the pan. Hold a large plate at a 45-degree angle up to the edge of the pan, then, with the plate directly underneath it, turn the tarte upside down onto the plate. The pastry crust will now be on the bottom and the mushrooms will be facing up. Set aside and keep warm.

5. Return the empty pan to the stovetop. Pour about ¼ to ½ cup of the sauce mix (per your liking) into the pan. Heat on high until it comes to a boil, about 1 minute. Immediately take off the heat. Drizzle over the top and around the perimeter of the tarte.

6. If desired, garnish with a little truffle oil, pepper, and microgreens. Cut like a pie into 4 equal slices. Serve warm.

Capellini Caprese

4 servings

Not only does this make a colorful side dish, but it's also Steve's go-to recipe for a super-fast light meal, especially during tomato season when, he says, "I could eat this pasta every day!" It makes an ideal summer picnic dish, too.

8 ounces capellini or angel hair pasta
Olive oil
2 large ripe tomatoes or 3 to 4 ripe plum tomatoes (ideally a selection of various heirlooms), diced into ¼-inch pieces
¼ cup finely diced red onion
2 tablespoons julienned sundried tomatoes
2 tablespoons minced fresh basil
1 teaspoon salt
½ teaspoon freshly ground black pepper
Balsamic Vinaigrette (recipe at right)
1 pound fresh mozzarella, cut into 12 (¼-inch-thick) slices, for garnish, optional
Freshly grated Parmesan cheese for garnish
Fresh basil chiffonade for garnish

1. Bring 2 to 3 quarts of water to a boil in a large saucepot. Add the pasta and cook according to package directions until al dente, or about 5 to 6 minutes. Drain the pasta in a colander and run cold water over it to chill quickly.

2. Transfer the pasta to a bowl and lightly toss with a little oil to coat the pasta slightly. Set aside at room temperature.

3. Combine the tomatoes, onion, sun-dried tomatoes, basil, salt, and pepper in a bowl. Toss well, then add ¼ cup of the vinaigrette and toss again. Let sit at room temperature for at least 30 minutes. (If making the day before, refrigerate overnight, but be sure to remove at least 30 minutes before serving. The flavors are more bold and luscious when not chilled.)

4. When ready to serve, place about 1 cup of the pasta into each of 4 individual serving bowls. Re-toss the tomato mixture to ensure that all the ingredients are well coated with the vinaigrette, then into each bowl spoon ¼ cup of the tomato mixture. If desired, top with 3 mozzarella slices and drizzle with 2 tablespoons of the remaining vinaigrette. Garnish with the cheese and basil.

Balsamic Vinaigrette

Makes about ¾ cup

½ cup olive oil
2 tablespoons plus 2 teaspoons balsamic vinegar
4½ teaspoons Dijon mustard
1½ teaspoons finely minced fresh basil
¼ teaspoon salt
¼ teaspoon freshly ground black pepper

1. Combine the oil, vinegar, mustard, basil, salt, and pepper in a small bowl. Whisk vigorously until the dressing is completely blended and deep mahogany in color. Refrigerate until needed.

WINE PAIRINGS

France: Rhône—Côtes du Rhône
Italy: Friuli or Trentino—Pinot Grigio
Italy: Veneto—Prosecco with a splash of apple cider
New Zealand: Marlborough—Sauvignon Blanc

Stevie & Kirsten's Caramelized Apple French Toast

4 servings

One of the first dishes Steve's children made together as youngsters was this special treat, created for a Sunday brunch when house guests were visiting. The kids improvised and ended up with this version of good old-fashioned French toast, which quickly became a family favorite. It's so versatile, you can make it for breakfast, brunch, or dessert, as Steve does here.

2 tablespoons unsalted butter
4 apples, unpeeled and thinly sliced (preferably McIntosh or Cortland, but any kind will do)
1 cup granulated sugar
½ cup pure maple syrup (not pancake syrup)
1 teaspoon ground cinnamon
1 tablespoon pure vanilla extract
1 cup milk
3 large eggs
8 slices 1-inch-thick day-old bread of your choice (such as French baguette, sourdough, or raisin bread)
Powdered sugar or whipped cream for garnish, optional

1. Melt the butter in a large sauté pan over medium heat. Add the apples and sauté, stirring occasionally, for about 8 to 10 minutes, or until they start to soften. Using a slotted spoon, remove the apples to a platter or bowl and set aside.

2. Add the sugar and maple syrup to the same pan over medium heat and mix well. Cook until the sugar is fully dissolved, begins to boil, and turns deep brown, stirring occasionally to keep the mixture cooking evenly.

3. Return the apples to the pan, then stir in the cinnamon and vanilla. Continue to cook and stir for 1 minute. Reduce the heat to very low and hold until ready to use. (If the mixture is allowed to cool too much, it will become thick and sticky. In that case, you will need to turn up the heat and stir until the desired consistency is achieved again.)

4. Whisk the milk and eggs together in a bowl to blend well. Dip the bread, one slice at a time, into this mixture. Place on a hot buttered skillet or griddle. Cook until golden on both sides, about 3 minutes per side. Serve immediately, topped with a healthy spoonful of the warm apples and sauce. Garnish with powdered sugar or whipped cream if desired.

Karen Small

Individual Herb Omelets
with Goat Cheese
& French Ham

Organic Field Greens with
Sherry Dijon Vinaigrette

Fig Scones

Karen Small

Executive Chef/Owner, The Flying Fig, Market at The Fig

Accolades: Named one of the Top 100 Farm-to-Table Restaurants in the Country by *Gourmet*; two-time Diner's Choice award from OpenTable; top Zagat rating; restaurant award from the World Society for the Protection of Animals; earned a Recommended Restaurant award from TripAdvisor; named Best Outdoor Dining by Citysearch; won an A-List Restaurant award from the *Plain Dealer*; earned multiple awards from *Northern Ohio Live* and *Cleveland Scene*; featured in numerous publications and media, including *Food & Wine, Esquire, Continental Magazine,* the *New York Times, Chef Magazine, Arts in Ohio, Cleveland Magazine,* the *Plain Dealer, Chowhound, Metromix,* and *Cool Cleveland.*

Karen's Italian grandfather was probably the first influential figure in her culinary pursuits. "My grandmother was a very, very good cook," explains Karen, "but it was my grandfather who truly inspired me." She fondly remembers his postage-size garden brimming with fresh fruits and vegetables, salamis hanging to dry in the basement, and a wide variety of home-canned goods just waiting to be opened and shared.

Born in Warrensville Heights, Ohio, but raised in Shaker Heights, Karen attended Beaumont High School, then Ohio University. It was while working as a part-time student cook at OU's deli that she first started to develop a new-found interest—and talent—in the culinary arts. Coming up with new food combinations became her specialty. She jump-started her new career by joining the hugely popular and quirky Chicalini's Pasta Palace, before eventually opening up a beverage and deli store of her own.

Karen's secret tip for last-minute entertaining? "Always keep a well-stocked pantry. If you've got olives, tinned fish (like olive oil–packed tuna or sardines), olive oil, eggs, and cheese, then you're good to go. Canned beans can also be used in a pinch. Add some high-quality pasta and greens, and you've got yourself a very simple, nice meal. Time permitting, you can even run to a local bakery for some fresh bread."

While raising her children, Karen would take every chance she could to attend cooking classes. She especially enjoyed learning from French-born Madeleine Kamman, a guest instructor at the famed Zona Spray Cooking School, and Parker Bosley's professional program.

Little by little, Karen perfected her craft at a number of well-known Cleveland eateries, including The Baricelli Inn, Ninth Street Grill, and Fulton Bar & Grill. She finally got the chance to open her very own bakery café in Chagrin Falls, which she named Jezebel's and ran for three years.

Eventually, with her children grown, Karen began to itch to leave the suburbs for the city. When the opportunity presented itself to open up her own restaurant in the very urban Ohio City neighborhood of Cleveland, she jumped at the chance.

"What are you going to call your new restaurant?" everyone kept prodding. *"I don't give a flying fig about the name right now!"* retorted an exasperated Karen as she tried to juggle all the details of opening a new establishment. The name stuck, and thus The Flying Fig was born.

Building on the success of her restaurant, Karen has also ventured to open a directly adjoining "urban pantry" (as she calls it), appropriately named Market at the Fig. It features light menu options, charcuterie, artisanal cheeses, craft beers, and wines. In fact, wines are a special personal interest of hers. She also likes to garden and travel as much as she gets a chance.

Karen lives happily in Cleveland's Tremont neighborhood with her dogs, Duncan and Barkley. She has two grown sons, Dustin and Lucas.

Individual Herb Omelets with Goat Cheese & French Ham

4 servings

Whether you're serving these for breakfast, lunch, brunch, or dinner, there's no arguing the fact that omelets make a wonderful meal. And Karen's individual-portions version is particularly fun because everyone gets their very own personal one. Time permitting, let your guests choose their own herb mixture for a truly customized offering.

¼ pound good-quality deli ham, preferably French, sliced ¼-inch thick
8 to 10 large eggs, preferably farm fresh and free range, at room temperature
2 tablespoons heavy cream
Salt and freshly ground black pepper
2 tablespoons unsalted butter
Olive oil
2 to 2½ ounces goat cheese, crumbled
4 teaspoons mixed fresh herbs (such as chives, parsley, and tarragon)

1. Dice the ham. Set aside.

2. Thoroughly whisk the eggs, cream, and salt and pepper to taste in a bowl until well combined. Set aside.

3. Heat ½ tablespoon of the butter and a dash of oil in an 8- or 9-inch omelet pan over medium-high heat until hot but not smoking. Pour ¼ of the egg mixture into the pan. Let set a little, gently pushing the mixture from the edge to the center with a spatula.

4. When the center is almost set, sprinkle one-fourth each of the goat cheese, ham, and herb mixture in a line across the middle. Fold one side of the omelet over onto itself toward the middle and slide onto a serving plate. Keep warm.

5. Continue to make the remaining three omelets by repeating steps 3 and 4 above.

Organic Field Greens with Sherry Dijon Vinaigrette

4 servings

The lovely mixture of ingredients in the dressing makes this salad exceptionally light, healthy, and delicious! A perfect choice for an everyday quick salad. (Tip: If you want to get things ready for the salad ahead of time, simply refrigerate the dressing and greens separately and toss together in the garlic-seasoned bowl at the last minute.)

1 large garlic clove, halved
¼ cup olive oil
1½ teaspoons sherry vinegar (can substitute red wine vinegar)
1 teaspoon Dijon mustard
Salt and freshly ground black pepper
4 to 6 cups mixed organic field greens

1. Rub the inside of a large salad bowl with the garlic, cut sides down.

2. Whisk the oil, vinegar, mustard, and salt and pepper to taste in a separate bowl until well blended, then pour into the salad bowl.

3. Add the field greens and toss with the dressing, then divide among individual plates to serve.

....
WINE PAIRINGS
....

France: Burgundy—Bourgogne Rouge (Pinot Noir)
France: Languedoc—any white blend
France: Rhône—Côtes du Rhône

Fig Scones

4 servings

A tribute to The Flying Fig, these namesake scones make a wonderful accompaniment to this particular meal. But don't discount the fact that they are also a perfect choice for a breakfast or afternoon treat with your favorite cup of coffee or tea. The beauty of this recipe is that, although Karen is obviously partial to figs, you can always substitute any other dried fruit you like or have on hand (such as raisins, currants, sultanas, apricots, cherries, cranberries, blueberries, dates, or prunes). The choices are many, but the result is always the same: simply delicious.

2 cups all-purpose flour
1½ teaspoons baking powder
¼ teaspoon salt
3 tablespoons granulated sugar
6 ounces (1½ sticks) unsalted butter, chilled and chopped
⅓ cup chopped dried figs (can substitute other dried fruit)
¼ to ½ cup heavy cream
1 large egg
Turbinado sugar (sold as Sugar in the Raw), for sprinkling (can substitute granulated sugar)

1. Preheat the oven to 375°. Line a baking sheet with a Silpat (nonstick baking mat) or parchment paper.

2. Combine the flour, baking powder, salt, and sugar in a food processor; pulse just to mix. Add the butter and pulse until the mixture looks sandy. Transfer to a large bowl, then add the figs and mix well.

3. In a separate bowl, beat ¼ cup cream and the egg. Add the egg mixture to the flour mixture. Using your hands, mix quickly and briefly just until evenly moistened. The dough should feel sticky. If not, continue to add more cream, one tablespoon at a time, until it does feel sticky. Do not overwork!

4. Turn the dough onto a floured surface and knead a few times. Flatten with your hands to about a ½-inch-thick circle. Cut into your desired shape (round or triangular), using either a 3-inch round biscuit cutter or a sharp knife to cut wedges.

5. Place the scones on the lined baking sheet. Sprinkle with turbinado sugar and bake for about 15 to 20 minutes, or until the bottoms are golden brown; check to see if the scones are done by lifting with a spatula. Serve warm or at room temperature.

Rachael Spieth

Molasses-Nutmeg—Marinated
Pork Chops

Apple Cider—Braised Cabbage

Homemade Savory Biscuits

Rachael Spieth

Executive Chef, Georgetown (formerly Three Birds)

Accolades: Named one of the 20 Best New Restaurants in America by *Esquire;* won Best New Restaurant award from, and named one of Cleveland's Most Interesting People by *Cleveland Magazine;* recognized by *Cleveland Scene;* invited participant in the Top Chef cook-off at St. John West Shore Hospital, Taste of the NFL for the Cleveland Foodbank, Food & Wine Celebration at the Chef's Garden for Veggie U, Signature Chefs Auction for the March of Dimes, and Market Under Glass for Harvest for Hunger; featured in numerous publications and media, including *Wine Savant, Balanced Living, Ohio Authority, Cleveland Magazine, Cleveland Scene,* the *Plain Dealer,* the *Morning Journal,* the *Lakewood Observer, Chowhound,* and *Examiner.*

Rachael's secret tip for last-minute entertaining? "Relax and have fun! Anyone can follow a simple recipe at home. And equally as important to me: don't overcook vegetables! Plus, there's no such thing as fresh frozen vegetables."

As a young girl growing up in Macedonia, Ohio, Rachael was absolutely sure of just one thing: she wanted to do something exciting with her life. She just couldn't bear the thought of waking up to an alarm each and every single day, dragging herself to a job she simply dreaded. So when the teachers from her cooking classes in high school—first at Nordonia High and then at Hudson High—started noticing and commenting that she had a natural talent for cooking, she began to seriously think about it as a career choice. To give it a try, she took part-time jobs after school at such fast-food places as Mr. Chicken, Subway, and Zeppe's Pizzeria. She found she really did like it!

Eight days after her high school graduation, Rachael was already sitting in her first class at the famed Le Cordon Bleu Institute of Culinary Arts in Pittsburgh. She loved every minute of it. And when not in class or studying, she was working in the kitchen of the elegant St. Clair Country Club, located just outside Pittsburgh in tony Upper St. Clair. After earning her degree in specialized technology, she worked briefly at an upscale, now defunct seafood restaurant.

Rachael eventually found her way back to Cleveland and immediately took a position at The Cabin, a posh restaurant located on the property of Mario's International Spas and Hotels in Aurora. But when an opportunity to join Three Birds restaurant in Lakewood presented itself, she seized it. (The restaurant's name was subsequently changed to Georgetown.)

Rachael first started as a line cook. She worked hard. Relentlessly hard. And she never stopped asking questions . . . and learning . . . and growing. So much so that after three years she was offered the position of executive chef. She accepted and continues to helm this award-winning kitchen. Her use of local ingredients and sources ensures that customers are constantly thrilled with each season-changing menu.

Speaking of seasons, Rachael's favorite is winter, which is when she takes every free chance she gets to go snowboarding, whether it's in Ohio or Colorado. She's actually very good. A pro, you might say. And when not on the slopes, this avid football fan can be found watching her favorite team, the Browns!

Rachael calls North Royalton home, where she shares an apartment with her dog, Dyson.

Molasses-Nutmeg–Marinated Pork Chops

4 servings (2 chops per person)

When shopping, be sure to choose chops that are pale pink with a small amount of marbling and white (not yellow) fat. The loin is, in fact, the leanest and most tender cut of pork—which also means it's the easiest to dry out if it's overcooked. Just remember, pork is safe to eat once it's reached an interior temperature of 145° for medium. If you prefer yours well done, the temperature should reach 160°, but no more. And, of course, the sublime molasses-nutmeg marinade will double ensure your chops are not only moist but also richly flavorful, distinguishing them from ordinary, everyday chops.

8 (4-ounce) boneless pork loin chops
½ cup molasses
2 tablespoons cider vinegar
1 teaspoon freshly grated nutmeg (can substitute 1 teaspoon ground nutmeg)
Salt and freshly ground black pepper

1. Preheat the grill (gas or charcoal) to medium heat. Be careful the grill does not become too hot or else the molasses will burn very quickly and the meat will char.

2. Place the pork chops in either a large zippered plastic bag or a nonmetal pan with cover. Mix the molasses, vinegar, and nutmeg together in a small bowl. Pour over the pork chops and let marinate for about 30 minutes.

3. Remove the chops from the marinade, discarding the marinade or saving it to use for optionally basting the chops as they cook. Season the chops with salt and pepper to taste, then place on the grill and cook on each side for about 4 minutes. Remove when the internal temperature reaches 145°. Allow to rest for at least 3 minutes before serving.

4. If you prefer your pork to be well done, finish cooking in a preheated 400° oven until the internal temperature reaches 160°. Serve warm.

Apple Cider–Braised Cabbage

4 servings

The perfect accompaniment to pork, cabbage is also an excellent source of manganese, calcium, and potassium. And it's pretty inexpensive, too. Just remember to remove the core before slicing. You'll find that this recipe, which has earned high praise, turns out a particularly tender dish that is steeped with just the right amount of natural sweetness. And if you'd like, feel free to garnish with some crumbled crispy bacon for extra crunch.

¼ cup rendered duck fat (can substitute bacon fat or lard)
1 small onion, julienned
2 garlic cloves, minced
1 extra-small head green cabbage (the smallest you can find), cored and thinly sliced (about 4 packed cups)
1 Granny Smith apple, peeled, cored, and grated
1 cup apple juice
1 bay leaf
Salt and freshly ground black pepper

1. Melt the duck fat in a large skillet over medium heat. Add the onion and garlic and sauté for about 4 to 5 minutes. Add the cabbage and apple and cook, stirring occasionally, for another 10 minutes, just until they start to become translucent. You do not want to color the vegetables.

2. Add the apple juice and bay leaf. Continue to cook until the liquid is reduced by half, about 5 minutes.

3. Add just enough water to come halfway up the cabbage. Cook on medium heat, covered, until tender, about 35 to 45 minutes, stirring occasionally. Once done, all of the water should be cooked out of the cabbage.

4. Remove the bay leaf and season with salt and pepper to taste. Serve warm.

WINE PAIRINGS

France: Bordeaux—Bordeaux Rouge
USA: California, Sonoma Coast—Pinot Noir
USA: Oregon—Pinot Noir

Homemade Savory Biscuits

4 servings

These are not your ordinary biscuits. That's because not only are they lusciously savory, they're also interspersed with a secret ingredient: *fines herbes*. Often used in Mediterranean cuisine, fines herbes is a classic French herb seasoning mix made up of equal amounts of finely chopped chervil, chives, parsley, and tarragon. (Fines herbes is not to be confused with bouquet garni, which is made up of more pungent, resinous herbs used in long cooking.) Fines herbes can also be used in omelets and soups, or on fish and poultry. Make your own like Rachael does (see note) or simply use chives only, which is perfectly fine, too.

2 cups all-purpose flour
4 teaspoons baking powder
¼ teaspoon baking soda
¾ teaspoon kosher salt
2 tablespoons fines herbes (can substitute finely chopped fresh chives; see note)
2 tablespoons unsalted butter, chilled and cubed
2 tablespoons rendered bacon fat, solidified (can substitute lard; see note)
1 cup buttermilk, chilled

1. Preheat the oven to 400°. Line a baking sheet with a Silpat (nonstick baking mat) or parchment paper.

2. Combine the flour, baking powder, baking soda, salt, and fines herbes in a large mixing bowl.

3. Using your fingertips, rub the butter and fat into the dry ingredients as quickly as possible (you don't want the fat to melt) until the mixture looks like crumbs. Do not overhandle!

4. Make a well in the center of the mixture. Pour in the buttermilk. Stir with a wooden spoon just until the dough comes together. Again, don't overmix! The dough will be very sticky.

5. Turn the dough onto a floured surface. Dust with flour, then gently fold the dough over on itself 5 to 6 times only.

6. Press the dough into a round shape about 1 inch thick. Cut out biscuits with a round 2½- or 3-inch cookie cutter. You can reform the dough scraps just once to get a few more biscuits.

7. Place the biscuits on the lined baking sheet so that they just touch. Bake until golden brown, about 12 minutes. Serve warm.

NOTE: To make Rachael's own blend of fines herbes, mix together 1 tablespoon chopped fresh parsley with 1½ teaspoons each of chopped fresh chives and tarragon.

NOTE: To render bacon fat, cook bacon strips in a skillet over low heat, turning occasionally. When nicely browned and crispy, remove the strips to a paper towel–lined plate. Strain the remaining melted fat through a paper filter or fine cheesecloth to remove any residue. After it has cooled, pour into a glass jar and store, covered, in the refrigerator.

Michael Symon

Roasted Rack of Pork with
Pumpkin Puree &
Cilantro Salad

Michael Symon

Chef/Partner/Owner, Lola, Lolita, B Spot (multiple locations); Chef/Partner, Roast (Detroit)

Accolades: James Beard award winner for Best Chef: Great Lakes Region; four-time James Beard award nominee; winner of the Food Network's *The Next Iron Chef: Season 1*; host/co-host of and participant in numerous television shows, including the Cooking Channel's *Cook Like an Iron Chef* and *Symon's Suppers*, ABC's *The Chew*, and the Food Network's *Next Iron Chef, Food Feuds, Dinner: Impossible, The Best Thing I Ever Ate, Ready...Set... Cook!, Food Nation with Bobby Flay,* and *Sara's Secrets with Sara Moulton;* many guest appearances on both network and syndicated programs, including *Anthony Bourdain: No Reservations, The View,* and the *Rachael Ray Show;* first chef to ever host the annual Farm Aid benefit concert; named one of the Best New Chefs by *Food & Wine;* named one of America's Best Restaurants by *Gourmet;* named one of Top 10 Best New Burger Joints by *Bon Appétit;* multiple winner of Best Burger in America award at the Food Network South Beach Wine & Food Festival; coauthor of *Michael Symon's Live to Cook;* contributor to *Bon Appétit, Esquire, Food Arts, Gourmet, Saveur,* and *O, The Oprah Magazine;* featured in numerous publications and media.

Photo by Donna Ruhlman

Michael's secret tip for last-minute entertaining? "Everyone loves bacon!"

The precise moment of destiny that would define Michael's illustrious path in life happened in one split second during wrestling practice in the eleventh grade. It was the very instant his right arm snapped like a twig.

Then and there, Michael knew that his wrestling career—as well as a possible scholarship and his dream of becoming a wrestling coach—had come to an abrupt end. So, after convalescing and figuring out another way to pay for college, Michael got an after-school job. As a broiler cook. At a local pizzeria called Gepetto's.

Michael was finally earning money. But what he didn't count on was falling in love with "the biz," as he calls it. He loved the rush. He loved the instant gratification. He loved it all!

After graduating from St. Edward High School in Lakewood, Michael attended Cleveland State University, majoring in architecture. But after a year, his passion for cooking led him to leave his hometown of North Olmsted for the Culinary Institute of America in Hyde Park, New York, instead.

He thrived there, and he got a taste of the Big Apple with impressive externships in the heart of Manhattan. But after graduating, he was antsy to get back home and make his mark.

Michael apprenticed at Sammy's in the Flats, then landed his first "real" job with Player's in Lakewood as a sous chef, followed by Piccolo Mondo in Cleveland's Warehouse District as a chef. It was there that he started to attract a small but devoted following. That following got even larger when he joined Giovanni's, and larger still when he joined Caxton Café as executive chef.

Then, borrowing money from family and friends, Michael decided to finally make his dreams a reality by opening up his own place in Tremont. He named it Lola, after a favorite aunt. And from the day it opened it has been nothing but a huge success. Seven years later, Michael renamed it Lolita and opened another brand-new Lola downtown on East 4th Street.

One year after that, Michael opened Parea in New York to critical acclaim. He then ventured to Detroit and opened Roast in the Westin Book Cadillac Hotel. Bar Symon in Avon Lake and B Spot in Woodmere followed. New menu items for Cavaliers basketball fans at the Quicken Loans Arena also ensued. Then, more B Spots followed—and even more to come!

When not working (which isn't often), Michael can be found either zipping down Cleveland's back roads on one of his two vintage Harleys, playing golf, or contemplating another tattoo.

Michael lives in Shaker Heights with his wife, Liz, and stepson, Kyle. Ruby, a bullmastiff, and Ozzy, an Old English bulldog, are part of the family, too.

Roasted Rack of Pork with Pumpkin Puree & Cilantro Salad

4 servings

"Pork's versatility makes it my first choice for holiday dinners," says Michael. But no matter what time of year it is, this dish is a winner, hands down. The secret may very well be in the choice of mildly fragrant, aromatic spices: coriander and cumin seeds. Then again, it may be in the amount of time the rubbed pork spends in the refrigerator. In fact, the longer it sits, the more flavor it will infuse, resulting in a radically tasteful, juicy, and tender pork roast. The final stacked, multi-layered creation is a trifecta of culinary bliss: creamy pumpkin puree, succulent pork, and a lively cilantro salad. You'll never taste a better combination.

1 tablespoon cumin seeds
1 tablespoon coriander seeds
1 tablespoon kosher salt
1 teaspoon chipotle chile powder
1 teaspoon granulated sugar
1 (4 rib) rack of pork, center cut, frenched and chined (backbone removed)
Pumpkin Puree (recipe on page 158)
Cilantro Salad (recipe on page 158)

1. Preheat the oven to 375°.

2. Combine the cumin, coriander, salt, chipotle chile powder, and sugar in a small bowl. Rub the rack of pork with this seasoning mixture. Transfer to a shallow pan and cover with plastic wrap, then place in the refrigerator for at least 15 minutes. (Time permitting, it is best to refrigerate overnight. In that case, preheat the oven 15 minutes before you are ready to roast.)

3. Place the pork on a rack in a shallow roasting pan. Bake until an internal temperature of 145° to 150° has been reached. Remove from the oven, tent the roast with foil, and let rest for 10 minutes (or until it reaches an internal temperature of 160°) before carving.

4. To serve, spoon some Pumpkin Puree on each plate. Top with a carved chop and then some Cilantro Salad. Serve immediately.

WINE PAIRINGS

Australia: Victoria—Chardonnay
Germany: Rheingau—Dry Riesling QBA
USA: Oregon, Willamette—Pinot Noir

Pumpkin Puree

4 servings

No ordinary pumpkin puree, this version gets a wonderful makeover with the addition of five-spice powder, which is a heady mixture of five ground spices (naturally!) that imparts all the flavors: sweet, sour, bitter, pungent, and salty. You can easily find it in most supermarkets. Or if you're feeling extra adventurous, try grinding your own with equal parts cinnamon, cloves, fennel seed, star anise, and Szechuan peppercorns. Just remember, though, a little goes a long way.

1 ripe medium-size baking pumpkin, preferably New England Pie, Sugar Pie, Cinderella, Connecticut Field, or Tricky Jack
3 tablespoons unsalted butter, at room temperature
1 tablespoon packed brown sugar
1 teaspoon five-spice powder
Large pinch of kosher salt
1 cup chicken stock

1. Preheat the oven to 300°.

2. Split the pumpkin in half and scoop out the seeds. (Reserve the seeds, if desired, for use in the Cilantro Salad recipe at right.) Rub the flesh side of each pumpkin half with ½ the butter and all the sugar and five-spice powder. Place in an ovenproof casserole dish, add the stock, cover with foil, and bake until tender, about 1 hour.

3. Scoop out the flesh into a mixing bowl and add the salt. Mash until smooth, adding the rest of the butter and any remaining stock a little at a time until you reach the desired texture. Serve warm.

Cilantro Salad

4 servings

This zesty salad is so tasty and yet so simple, you'll think we left out something. But it's the *quality* of the ingredients that really matters here. Find the freshest cilantro (also known as Chinese parsley or coriander) you can. It's actually easy to grow yourself, either in a garden or on a windowsill. Jalapeños are easy to grow, too. And try to get a lime in season (June to August). But the real bonus is in using, if you possibly can, fresh seeds right from a pumpkin. It's definitely worth the extra effort, trust me.

Reserved pumpkin seeds from the Pumpkin Puree recipe at left (can substitute purchased raw pumpkin seeds or pepitas)
3 tablespoons olive oil, divided
Kosher salt
Freshly squeezed juice of 1 lime
1 jalapeño chile, seeded and finely minced
1 bunch cilantro, picked over, stemmed, and cleaned

1. If using fresh pumpkin seeds, wash under warm running water. A colander works nicely here. Dry well with paper towels.

2. Heat 1 tablespoon of the oil in a large skillet over medium heat. When hot, add the seeds and toss. Continue to stir until the seeds begin to pop and turn golden, about 6 to 8 minutes, holding a lid over but not directly on the skillet to prevent the seeds from popping out of the skillet. Season lightly with salt and immediately remove from the skillet. Let cool.

3. Combine the remaining 2 tablespoons oil, lime juice, and jalapeño chile in a separate bowl and whisk to blend. When ready to serve, gently toss the cilantro with the dressing until well combined. Garnish with ⅓ cup of the cooled pumpkin seeds, evenly divided among the servings. (Reserve any remaining seeds for another use.)

Eric Williams

Guacamole Tradicional

Sofrito Green Beans

Grilled Steak with
Honey-Chipotle Mojo

Eric Williams

Executive Chef/Owner, Momocho; Executive Chef/Partner, Happy Dog

Accolades: Named one of Top 10 Best Restaurants by *Food & Wine*; earned spot on *Bon Appétit*'s Hot 10 List; two-time James Beard award nominee for Best Chef in America: Great Lakes Region; featured on both the Food Network's *Diners, Drive-ins and Dives* show and the Cooking Channel's *Unique Eats* show; #1 restaurant in Cleveland as rated by TripAdvisor; earned Best Mexican and Best Margarita awards from *Cleveland Magazine*; named Best Modern Mex Restaurant and Best New Restaurant by *Cleveland Scene*; celebrity participant at the Fabulous Food Show; featured in numerous publications and media, including *Food & Wine, Wine Savant, Fodor's, Crain's Cleveland Business, Ohio's Authority, Cleveland Magazine, Cleveland Scene*, the *Plain Dealer, Cleveland Foodie*, and WKYC-TV 3.

As he tells it, Eric Williams never quite had an "aha!" moment when he simply knew he wanted to be a chef. With Eric, it happened slowly . . . methodically . . . and quite accidentally.

"The restaurant business has a way of grabbing hold of you and never letting go," laughs Eric. "I love what I do for many reasons."

Born in Erie, Pennsylvania, but raised in Garfield Heights, Ohio, Eric was only fifteen when he took a job as a cook at a local mom-and-pop pizzeria just to earn some extra spending money. But after graduating from Chanel High School, he took on a second job as a cook at a local sports bar. From there, he just kept on learning, advancing, and rising as far as he could at a myriad of successful Cleveland eateries, among them Cleveland

Eric's secret tip for last-minute entertaining? "Always keep some good cheese and wine around. There's nothing better or easier than drinking wine and eating good cheese."

PM, Maria's Roman Room, Pete & Dewey's Planet, Keka, Johnny Mango, Napa Valley Grille, and Moxie.

"All my training came from on-the-job experience," explains Eric. "I developed my own style of cooking by combining techniques with flavor combinations I myself enjoy eating."

While helping to open and run Lopez Bar & Grill, where he developed his particular fondness for Mexican fare, Eric simultaneously turned to consulting for nearly five years. That's when the bug finally bit him. He *had* to open up his own restaurant . . . and it *had* to feature his own interpretations of Mexican cuisine . . . and it *had* to be in Ohio City. Thus, with great serendipity, his restaurant Momocho was born. And it has been a booming success ever since.

Eric specializes in what he likes to call "Mod Mex" cuisine. He loves Latin flavors and is committed to using local seasonal ingredients to create his signature dishes.

Certainly not one to be bored out of his mind with running "only" one thriving, award-winning restaurant, Eric decided to also open up a second eatery: a lively hipster joint called Happy Dog. This time, hot dogs are the main attraction—along with any choice of fifty (yes, fifty!) toppings.

When not running between his restaurants or coming up with new menus, he likes to build low-rider bikes and paint.

Eric lives in Cleveland with his wife, Heather, and their son, Jaxson (after whom Momocho—slang for "hellion little boy"—is named).

Guacamole Tradicional

4 servings

The pebbly textured, almost black Hass avocado, developed in 1926 by Los Angeles mail carrier Rudolph Hass and now available year-round, represents 95 percent of all the avocados grown in the U.S.—which is a lot, considering that Americans eat a billion pounds of avocados each year. And for good reason. Avocados, considered to be an almost complete food, are cholesterol and sodium free; they're nutrient dense in dietary fiber and vitamins B_6, C, and E; they contain monounsaturated fatty acids; and they're loaded with phytonutrients, which help fight chronic illnesses. Tasty *and* healthy? Now that's a great combination!

4 Hass avocados, preferably Calavo brand
1 teaspoon kosher salt
2 teaspoons chopped garlic (4 medium-size cloves)
1 tablespoon fresh lime juice
2 to 4 tablespoons finely minced Spanish onion, depending on your taste
2 to 4 tablespoons stemmed and finely minced fresh cilantro, depending on your taste
¼ small jalapeño chile, minced (see note; can substitute canned as a last resort)
Corn tortilla chips, grilled bread, or fresh vegetables for serving

1. Peel, pit, and scoop the avocados into a mixing bowl. Add the salt, garlic, and lime juice. (Tip: Adding the salt and garlic at this point creates an abrasive texture for the next step and also infuses flavor.)

2. Using a potato masher, begin to mash the avocado mixture. Once you achieve the consistency of your liking (chunky, smooth, or anything in between), add the onion, cilantro, and jalapeño chile. Stir to fold in the flavors, then serve with the tortilla chips.

NOTE: Removing the seeds and veins from the jalapeño chile before mincing will reduce the heat level.

COCKTAIL/WINE PAIRINGS

Margarita
Chile: Any region—Sauvignon Blanc
Spain: Any region—red Sangria

Sofrito Green Beans

4 servings

Sofrito is a Spanish word referring to a savory and flavorful sauce that is essentially the marriage of various aromatic seasonings and vegetables. In fact, it's used as a base for many dishes. Here, it serves to heighten the taste of otherwise pretty ordinary but healthy fresh green beans.

SOFRITO
1 bunch fresh cilantro, stemmed
1 bunch scallions (green onions), root ends trimmed off, both green and white parts roughly sliced
3 tablespoons fresh lime juice
2 garlic cloves
1 shallot
¼ cup water
½ jalapeño chile, seeded
2 tablespoons fresh oregano leaves
2 tablespoons fresh thyme leaves
2½ teaspoons kosher salt

GREEN BEANS
1 to 1½ pounds fresh green beans, trimmed
2 to 3 tablespoons vegetable or canola oil
½ cup cooked corn kernels (can substitute frozen corn kernels, thawed)
1 small shallot, diced
1 garlic clove, finely minced

1. To make the sofrito, put the cilantro, scallions, lime juice, garlic, shallot, water, jalapeño chile, oregano, thyme, and salt in a blender. Puree until smooth, then transfer to a bowl and set aside.

2. Bring a pot of salted water to a boil. Have ready a bowl of ice-cold water. Add the green beans to the boiling water and blanch, uncovered, for 3 minutes. Drain in a colander, then immediately shock the beans by dropping them into the bowl of ice-cold water to stop the cooking. Drain well again and set aside.

3. Heat a large sauté pan over medium-high heat. When a few drops of water splashed over the surface evaporate instantly on contact, add the oil, then the corn, shallot, and garlic to the pan. Stir to mix, then add the green beans. Sauté, stirring continuously, until just tender, about 2 to 3 minutes. Take off the heat and toss with the reserved sofrito to finish. Serve warm.

Grilled Steak with Honey-Chipotle Mojo

4 servings

Two secrets to grilling the perfect steak: grade of meat and grill heat. Be sure to buy the best grade you can afford. A prime steak will have lots of marbling (white streaks of fat), while a select cut will have very little. Generally, the more marbling, the more tender the cut will be. (Tip: For a poor man's version of this recipe, try London broil.) And make sure to get your grill as hot as you can before cooking. If using a gas grill, wait at least 15 minutes (if you're starving) or up to 30 minutes (if you've got the patience) before cooking. Either way, don't rush it. Then watch what a difference it makes. (The mojo—consider it a sauce, dressing, glaze, or marinade—is also sure to elevate your steaks to a whole new level. Guaranteed.)

1 to 3 chipotle peppers in adobo sauce (canned, not drained), depending on how spicy you like it
¼ cup fresh lime juice
3 tablespoons honey
3 tablespoons balsamic vinegar
3 tablespoons yellow mustard
2 tablespoons vegetable oil
¼ bunch fresh cilantro, stemmed
¾ teaspoon chopped garlic (¾ medium-size clove)
¼ teaspoon ground cumin
4 (6- to 8-ounce) cuts of your favorite steak (hanger, filet mignon, or Eric's favorite: rib-eye)
Salt and freshly ground black pepper
Herbed Compound Butter (recipe at right), optional
Sliced habañero chiles for garnish, optional

1. Heat the grill (gas or charcoal) to high heat for at least 15 minutes. Put the chipotle peppers, lime juice, honey, vinegar, mustard, oil, cilantro, garlic, and cumin into a blender. Puree until smooth. Pour into individual ramekins and set aside.

2. Season each side of the steaks with salt and pepper to taste. Place them on the hot grill for about 3 to 5 minutes. Flip and continue to cook for another 3 to 5 minutes. Check the internal temperature with a digital meat thermometer. Remove when they reach your preferred doneness. Rare: 120° to 125°; medium rare: 130° to 135°; medium: 140° to 145°; medium well: 150° to 155°; well: 160°.

3. After taking the steaks off the grill, tent with foil for 5 to 10 minutes. If desired, garnish each steak with a pat of Herbed Compound Butter and sliced habañero chiles. Serve warm alongside the mojo.

Herbed Compound Butter

Yields 8 tablespoons

4 ounces (1 stick) unsalted butter, at room temperature
3 to 4 tablespoons chopped fresh herbs of choice
Salt and freshly ground black pepper

1. In a small bowl, mash together the butter, herbs, and salt and pepper to taste using a fork or spoon. Spoon onto a piece of waxed paper in the shape of a log. Fold the waxed paper over the butter and roll into a tight cylinder. Twist the ends of the waxed paper to seal, then refrigerate or freeze to chill until needed. (Frozen butter should sit at room temperature for 15 to 20 minutes before serving.)

MIX-AND-MATCH MENU PLANNER

Although each chef has crafted his or her own unique menu for this book, we'd like to give you a chance to mix it up and create your own. Take a recipe from one chef and combine it with that of one or more others. The possibilities are virtually endless! To make things easier, below we've listed every recipe in this book under one of six categories: Starters, Entrées, Sides, Desserts, Savory Fare, and Sweet Toppings. Pick and choose as you wish!

SPECIAL TECHNIQUES & PROCESSES

TECHNIQUES

Blanch: To partially cook vegetables in boiling water.

Boil: To heat a liquid until bubbles break the surface (compare to *Rolling Boil; Simmer*).

Caramelize: To cook until the sugar in the food has browned.

Chiffonade: To cut into thin strips or shreds.

Chop: To cut into bite-size (or smaller) pieces using quick, heavy blows of a knife or cleaver. Chopped food is more coarsely cut than minced food (compare to *Chop Fine*).

Chop Fine: To cut into very small cubes, about ¼- to ½-inch pieces (compare to *Chop*).

Dice: To cut into cubes, about ⅛- to ¼-inch pieces (compare to *Dice Fine; Mince*).

Dice Fine: To cut into cubes, about ⅛-inch pieces (compare to *Dice; Mince*).

Julienne: To cut into thin, matchstick strips, about ⅛-inch-thick slices. The slices are stacked and then cut into ⅛-inch-thick strips. The strips may then be cut into whatever length is desired. If the object is round, cut a thin slice from the bottom so it will sit firmly and not roll on the work surface.

Mince: To cut into very fine pieces, generally ⅛ inch or smaller. This is the finest of all cuts (compare to *Dice; Dice Fine*).

Pan fry: To cook in a frying pan with a small amount of fat.

Poach: To simmer in liquid at just below the boiling point.

Puree: To mash into a thick, smooth consistency.

Rolling Boil: A boil that cannot be dissipated by stirring or by dropping ingredients into the water (compare to *Boil; Simmer*).

Sauté: To fry in a small amount of fat (less fat than pan-frying, which isn't as fast as sautéing).

Sear: To cook the surface quickly with intense heat.

Simmer: To cook gently in liquid at a temperature low enough that tiny bubbles just begin to break the surface (compare to *Boil; Rolling Boil*).

Sweat: A technique by which ingredients are cooked in a small amount of fat over low heat until they are soft but still hold their shape. The ingredients are covered directly with a piece of foil or parchment paper and then the pot is tightly covered. With this method, the ingredients soften without browning and cook in their own juices.

PROCESSES

To Brine

A Chicken: In a container big enough to hold both a 3- to 4-pound chicken and the brine without spilling over, stir together 3 quarts cold water, 1 cup salt, and ¼ cup sugar to dissolve. Remove the giblets from the chicken and slip the bird into the brine. Cover and refrigerate for 4 to 6 hours.

To Clarify

Butter: Melt 4 ounces (1 stick) butter slowly in a pan over low heat. Do not stir! Also, do not cook too much longer after it has all melted; you don't want it to burn. Let it sit for a bit to separate. With a tablespoon, skim off and discard the white foam on the top. Then either slowly pour the butter out, being careful to leave the remaining solids at the bottom of your pan, or strain the butter through a fine sieve or cheesecloth-lined strainer. (Any unused clarified butter can be refrigerated, covered, almost indefinitely.)

To Clean

A Leek: Cut off and discard the dark green leaves just at the place where the light green starts, about an inch above the white part. Trim off the roots, then make a lengthwise cut from the top down almost through the bottom. Rinse the leek thoroughly under cold water, separating the leaves to make sure to get any dirt that may be hiding between them. Drain well and prepare as instructed.

To Cook

Fish: The cooking time for fish fillets is generally 7 minutes per inch of thickness.

To Grind

Walnuts, Shelled: Use a food processor, clean coffee grinder, nut mill, or blender. Pulse the nuts in small batches, continuously scraping down the sides of the container, until the the desired consistency is reached. Don't overgrind or the nuts will turn to butter. (It helps to freeze the nuts before grinding.)

To Make

Balsamic Vinegar: If you can't find or afford thirty-year-old balsamic vinegar, you can make a substitute. Take 2 cups of ordinary balsamic vinegar, add ½ cup sugar, and reduce over low heat until syrupy, about 20 to 40 minutes. Yields ¾ cup, which means you will have plenty left over for future uses.

Bread Crumbs: Toast a few slices of bread. Crush or pulse in a food processor.

Fresh Pumpkin Puree: Preheat the oven to 450°. Cut a sugar or pie pumpkin in half, scoop out the seeds, and place the pumpkin halves face down in a baking dish. Add ½ inch of water to the pan and bake until you can pierce the skin with a fork, about 45 to 60 minutes. Scoop the flesh out of the shell with a spoon and use a food processor or blender to whip it into a puree. Refrigerate or freeze unused puree for another use.

A Quenelle: Warm two tablespoons in hot water, leaving them wet to provide some "slip" when transferring the mixture. Take one tablespoon and scoop out a spoonful of mixture. Take your second spoon and scoop the chèvre out from the first one in a smooth motion, following the contour of the bottom spoon as much as possible. Continue to alternate from spoon to spoon until you have a smooth result. (Hint: It may help to dip each spoon in hot water again between scoops.)

To Plump

Raisins: Soak raisins in a mixture of 1 cup hot water plus 1 to 3 teaspoons vinegar, depending on how tart you like them, for about 10 minutes. Once plump, drain and use as directed.

To Render

Bacon Fat: Cook bacon strips in a skillet over low heat, turning occasionally. When nicely browned and crispy, remove the strips to a paper towel–lined plate. Strain the remaining melted fat through a paper filter or fine cheesecloth to remove any residue. After it has cooled, pour into a glass jar and store, covered, in the refrigerator.

To Roast

A Bell Pepper: Rub a large bell pepper with olive oil. Place the pepper over a flame on your grill or directly over a lit burner on your stovetop and turn often until the outside is blackened, 3 to 4 minutes. Once it's blackened, remove to a small bowl and cover with plastic wrap for 5 minutes. Remove the skin and seeds.

To Toast

Almonds, Sliced: Heat the oven to 350°. Spread the sliced almonds on a baking sheet and place in the oven for 5 to 7 minutes, or until golden. Remove from the oven and let cool.

Almonds, Slivered: Place almonds in an ungreased heavy skillet over medium heat. Stir or shake often until golden brown, about 1 to 3 minutes.

Bread Cubes: Heat the oven to 300°. Stack 4 slices of white bread on top of each other. Using a serrated knife, cut into large cubes; removing the crust is optional. Arrange the cubes in a single layer on a baking sheet and bake for 10 to 15 minutes, shaking once or twice, until lightly browned and crisp. Let cool.

French Bread: Heat the oven to 350°. Place the bread slices on an oiled cookie sheet and bake for about 5 minutes or until lightly golden brown. No need to turn.

Pecans: Heat the oven to 275°. Spread the nuts on a baking sheet and place in the oven. Check after 10 minutes, then again every 2 minutes until golden. Remove from the oven and let cool.

Pistachios: Heat the oven to 350°. Spread the pistachios in a single layer in a pie plate or on a cookie sheet. Bake until golden, about 3 to 6 minutes. Remove from the oven and let cool.

Walnuts: Heat the oven to 325°. Spread the walnuts in a single layer on a cookie sheet and bake until golden brown, about 10 to 12 minutes, checking and stirring frequently. Or cook walnuts in a skillet on medium-high heat for 3 to 5 minutes, stirring frequently.

To Use

A Blowtorch: If using a blowtorch, either a specialty butane kitchen torch or a regular propane blowtorch will do. Just make sure you hold it 2 to 3 inches above the sugar surface, moving it back and forth to ensure even browning. And after torching or broiling, make sure the sugar cools before touching it, as it will get very hot.

CHEF LOCATIONS

You can find all the chefs featured in this book at the following locations (current as of publication date):

AMP 150—4277 W. 150th St., Cleveland, OH 44135, (216) 706-8787, amp150.com

B Spot Crocker Park—20 Main St., Westlake, OH 44145, (440) 471-8270, bspotburgers.com

B Spot Eton—28699 Chagrin Blvd., Woodmere, OH 44122, (216) 292-5567, bspotburgers.com

B Spot Strongsville—18066 Royalton Rd., Strongsville, OH 44146, (440) 572-9600, bspotburgers.com

Blue Canyon Kitchen & Tavern Kalispell—1840 US-93 South, Kalispell, MT 59901, (406) 758-2583, bluecanyonrestaurant.com

Blue Canyon Kitchen & Tavern Missoula—3720 N. Reserve St., Missoula, MT 59808, (406) 541-2583, bluecanyonrestaurant.com

Blue Canyon Kitchen & Tavern Twinsburg—8960 Wilcox Dr., Twinsburg, OH 44087, (330) 486-2583, bluecanyonrestaurant.com

Blue Point Grille—700 W. St. Clair Ave., Cleveland, OH 44113, (216) 875-7827, hrclcvcland.com

The Cabin Club—30651 Detroit Rd., Westlake, OH 44145, (440) 899-7111, hrcleveland.com

Chez François—555 Main St., Vermilion, OH 44089, (440) 967-0630, chezfrancois.com

Chinato—2079 E. 4th St., Cleveland, OH 44115, (216) 298-9080, chinatocleveland.com

Cleveland Clinic Wellness Institute—1950 Richmond Rd./TR2-203, Lyndhurst, OH 44124, (216) 448-8502, my.clevelandclinic.org/wellness

Cleveland Indians Dining (Delaware North Companies)—Progressive Field, 2401 Ontario St., Cleveland, OH, 44115, (216) 420-HITS, http://cleveland.indians.mlb.com/cle/ballpark/dining

Cowell & Hubbard—1305 Euclid Ave., Cleveland, OH 44115, (216) 479-0555, cowellandhubbard.com

Crop Bistro & Bar—2537 Lorain Ave., Cleveland, OH 44113, (216) 696-2767, cropbistro.com

Crop Bistro & Brewery—1859 Mountain Rd., Stowe, VT 05672, (802) 253-9311, cropvt.com

DANTE Restaurant—2247 Professor Ave., Cleveland, OH 44113, (216) 274-1200, danteboccuzzi.com

DBA—21 Furnace Street, Akron, OH 44308, (330) 375-5050, danteboccuzzi.com

The D.C. Pasta Company—12214 Pearl Rd., Strongsville, OH 44135, (440) 238-8500, danteboccuzzi.com

Delmonico's Steakhouse—6001 Quarry Ln., Independence, OH 44131, (216) 573-1991, hrcleveland.com

Flying Fig—2523 Market Ave., Cleveland, OH 44113, (216) 241-4243, theflyingfig.com

Georgetown—18515 Detroit Ave., Lakewood, OH 44107, (216) 221-3500, georgetownrestaurant.net

Ginko—2247 Professor Ave., Cleveland, OH 44113, (216) 274-1202, danteboccuzzi.com

Giovanni's Ristorante—25550 Chagrin Blvd., Beachwood, OH 44122, (216) 831-8625, giovanniscleveland.com

The Greenhouse Tavern—2038 E. 4th St., Cleveland, OH 44115, (216) 443-0511, thegreenhousetavern.com

Happy Dog—5801 Detroit Ave., Cleveland, OH 44102, (216) 651-9474, happydogcleveland.com

International Culinary Arts & Sciences Institute—8700 Mayfield Rd., Chesterland, OH 44026, (440) 729-7340, icasi.net

Johnny's Bar—3164 Fulton Rd., Cleveland, OH 44109, (216) 281-0055, johnnyscleveland.com

L'Albatros—11401 Bellflower Rd., Cleveland, OH 44106, (216) 791-7880, albatrosbrasserie.com

La Campagna—27337 Detroit Rd., Westlake, OH 44145, (440) 871-1771, lacampagnaonline.net

Leutner Café at Case Western Reserve University (c/o Bon Appétit Management Co.)—11424½ Bellflower Rd., Cleveland, OH 44106, (216) 368-8810, cafebonappetit.com/case

Levy Restaurants at Cleveland Browns Stadium—100 Alfred Lerner Way, Cleveland, OH 44114, (440) 824-3504

Light Bistro—2801 Bridge Ave., Cleveland, OH 44113, (216) 771-7130, lightbistro.com

Lola—2058 E. 4th St., Cleveland, OH 44115, (216) 621-5652, lolabistro.com

Lolita—900 Literary Rd., Cleveland, OH 44113, (216) 771-5652, lolitarestaurant.com

Loretta Paganini School of Cooking—8613 Mayfield Rd., Chesterland, OH 44026, (440) 729-1110, lpscinc.com

Lucky's Café—777 Starkweather Ave., Cleveland, OH 44113, (216) 622-7773, luckyscafe.com

Luxe Kitchen & Lounge—6605 Detroit Ave., Cleveland, OH 44102, (216) 920-0600, luxecleveland.com

Market at The Fig—2523 Market Ave., Cleveland, OH 44113, (216) 241-4243, theflyingfig.com/market.html

Melt Bar & Grilled South—6700 Rockside Rd., Independence, OH 44131, (216) 520-1415, meltbarandgrilled.com

Melt Bar & Grilled East—13463 Cedar Rd., Cleveland Heights, Ohio 44118, (216) 965-0988, meltbarandgrilled.com

Melt Bar & Grilled West—14718 Detroit Ave., Lakewood, OH 44107, (216) 226-3699, meltbarandgrilled.com

Michaelangelo's—2198 Murray Hill Rd., Cleveland, OH 44106, (216) 721-0300, mangelos.com

Molinari's—8900 Mentor Ave., Mentor, OH 44060, (440) 974-2750, molinaris.com

Momocho—1835 Fulton Rd., Cleveland, OH 44113, (216) 694-2122, momocho.com

Moxie the Restaurant—3355 Richmond Rd., Beachwood, OH 44122, (216) 831-5599, moxietherestaurant.com

Nestlé Professional—Customer Innovation Campus, 30003 Bainbridge Rd., Solon, OH 44139, (440) 264-6600, nestleprofessional.com

Noodlecat—234 Euclid Ave., Cleveland, OH 44114, (216) 589-0007, noodlecat.com

Parallax—2179 W. 11th St., Cleveland, OH 44113, (216) 583-9999, parallaxtremont.com

Pier W—12700 Lake Ave., Winton Place, Lakewood, OH 44107, (216) 228-2250, pierw.com

Pura Vida by Brandt—Public Square, 170 Euclid Ave., Cleveland, OH 44114, (216) 987-0100, puravidabybrandt.com

Red the Steakhouse Boca Raton—1901 N. Military Trail, Boca Raton, FL 44341, (561) 353-9139, redthesteakhouse.com

Red the Steakhouse Cleveland—3355 Richmond Rd., Beachwood, OH 44122, (216) 831-2252, redthesteakhouse.com

Red the Steakhouse South Beach—119 Washington Ave., Miami Beach, FL 33139, (305) 534-3688, redthesteakhouse.com

Riverfront Café—555 Main St., Vermilion, OH 44089, (440) 967-0630, chezfrancois.com

Roast—1128 Washington Blvd., Detroit, MI 48226, (313) 961-2500, roastdetroit.com

Rosewood Grill Hudson—36 E. Streetsboro St., Hudson, OH 44236, (330) 656-2100, hrcleveland.com

Rosewood Grill Strongsville—16740 Royalton Rd., Strongsville, OH 44136, hrcleveland.com

Rosso Italia Boca Raton—1901 N. Military Trail, Boca Raton, FL 44341, (561) 353-9819, rosso-italia.com

Salmon Dave's Pacific Grill—19015 Old Lake Rd., Rocky River, OH 44116, (440) 331-2739, hrcleveland.com

Sapore Restaurant—8623 Mayfield Rd., Chesterland, OH 44026, (440) 729-1110, saporerestaurant.net

Shoreby Club—40 Shoreby Dr., Bratenahl, OH 44108, (216) 851-2582, clubcorp.com/clubs/shoreby-club

SOHO Kitchen & Bar—1889 W. 25th St., Cleveland, OH 44113, (216) 298-9090, sohocleveland.com

Spice of Life Catering Co.—3901 Lakeside Ave., Cleveland, OH 44114, (216) 432-9090, spiceoflifecaters.com

Spice Kitchen+Bar—5800 Detroit Ave., Cleveland, OH 44102, (216) 961-9641, spicekitchenandbar.com

Sweet Mosaic—777 Starkweather Ave., Cleveland, OH 44113, (216) 374-9030, sweetmosaic.com

Table 45 at The InterContinental Cleveland—9801 Carnegie Ave., Cleveland, OH 44106, (216) 707-4045, tbl45.com

Thyme²—113 W. Smith Rd., Medina, OH 44256, (330) 764-4114, thymetherestaurant.com

Touché—555 Main St., Vermilion, OH 44089, (440) 967-0630, chezfrancois.com

SOURCES FOR INGREDIENTS & EQUIPMENT

There may be some ingredients or cooking equipment mentioned in this book that you are unfamiliar with, do not own, or don't know where to find. Here are a few suggestions on where to look. And although this list is certainly not exhaustive, it should be somewhat helpful in your search.

WEST SIDE MARKET—all stands

LOCAL FARMERS' MARKETS—such as:

Downtown—Cleveland State University Market, Downtown Farmers' Market at Public Square, and North Coast Harbor Farmers' Market

East—Blue Pike Farm Market, Chagrin Falls Market, Cleveland Clinic Market, Coit Road Farmers' Market, Euclid Community Farmers' Market, Geauga Fresh Farmers' Market, Indoor Winter Market at Shaker Square, Lake Metroparks Farm Park Farmers' Market, Shaker Square Market, Warszawa Farmers' Market, and Willoughby Farmers' Market

South—Canton Farmers' Market, Countryside Farmers' Market at Howe Meadow, Countryside Farmers' Market at Stan Hywet, Hudson Farmers' Market, Parma Market, Strongsville Farmers' Market, and Twinsburg Farmers' Market

West—Crocker Park Market, Gordon Square Farmers' Market, Kamm's Corners Farmers' Market, Lakewood Market, Oberlin Farmers' Market, and Tremont Farmers' Market

LOCAL GROCERY STORES—such as Acme, Aldi, Bi-Rite, Buehler's, Chuppa's Market Place, Dave's Supermarket, Giant Eagle, Heinen's, IGA, Miles Farmers' Market, and Save-A-Lot

SPECIALTY FOOD STORES—such as Catanese Classic Seafood, Cinagro's Natural Foods Market, Cleveland Food Co-op, GFS Marketplace, J Pistone Market and Gathering Place, Lake Erie Creamery, Mustard Seed Market, Nature's Bin, The Olive and The Grape, Penzey's Spices, Trader Joe's, West Point Market, Whole Foods Market, and Zagara's Marketplace

LOCAL ETHNIC IMPORT STORES—such as Alesci's, Asia Food Co., Athens Imported Foods, Euro Food Mart, Ferrara's, Good Harvest Food Market, Gust Gallucci's, Hansa Import Haus, Jasmine's, La Borincana, La Campagna, Mayfield Italian Imports, Mediterranean Imported Foods, Park to Shop, Sidari's Italian Foods, Super Mercado Rico, and Tink Holl

LOCAL BREAD BAKERIES—such as Blackbird Baking Co., Breadsmith, Mazzone, On the Rise Artisan Breads, Panera, Presti's, The Stone Oven, and Zoss the Swiss Baker

COOKWARE STORES—such as Bed Bath & Beyond, The Chagrin Cook, Crate & Barrel, Dean Supply, Sur la Table, and Williams-Sonoma

ONLINE SOURCES FOR FOOD—such as Albert Uster Imports, Amazon, Bob's Red Mill, D'Artagnan, Dean & DeLuca, igourmet, King Arthur Flour, La Tienda, L'Epicerie, Market Hall Foods, Purcell Mountain Farms, Sparrow Lane, Zabar's, and Zingerman's

ONLINE SOURCES FOR EQUIPMENT—such as Amazon, Broadway Panhandler, CHEFS Catalog, Chef's Resource, Cooking, Cuisipro, Cutlery and More, Emile Henry, and JB Prince

INDEX